Protocol in Srimad Bhagwat

Other Books by the Author

1. India Ever Independent : Why Only 50 Years
2. Protocol in Sri Ramcharitmanas
3. मानस में शिष्टाचार
4. श्रीमदभागवत में शिष्टाचार

Protocol in Srimad Bhagwat

Devi Dayal Aggarwal

Foreword by

Dr. L.M. Singhvi

1999

Kaveri Books

New Delhi–110002

First Published in 1999

ISBN : 81-7479-022-5

Published by : **Rakesh Goel**
Kaveri Books
4697/5-21A, Ansari Road,
New Delhi–110002 (India).
Tel. : 3288140 Fax : 011-7198902
e.mail : kaveri @del3.vsnl.net.in

Laser Typesetting by : **Delite Printers, Delhi–110035**

PRINTED IN INDIA

Dr. L.M. Singhvi,
LL.B., LL.M., S.J.D.;
Honoris Causa LL.D., D.litt
Honoris Causa :
Sahityavacaspati,
Vidyavacaspati,
Nyayavacaspati
Member of Parliament;
Formerly High Commissioner for India in U.K.

सत्यमेव जयते

**4F-White House,
Bhagwan Das Road,
New Delhi.-110001.**

Foreword

Protocol has come to acquire in contemporary life a special connotation as a term of art and signifies in its generic sense official, and more particularly diplomatic, formality and etiquette observed on State occasions.

In a general sense, protocol is a code of propriety and good manners secured by reciprocity and the common understanding and approval of the community which regulates behaviour patterns at different levels.

In ancient times too, protocol had a wider as well as a narrower ambit. In its wider applications, protocol had social, legal, cultural, political and diplomatic applications. It reflected the social hierarchies and ethos of the society and was translated into legal, political and diplomatic norms and their culture. Protocol was thus rooted in the sense of social and cultural proprieties and the sense of who owed what to whom, where and when. It was the hall mark of considerable sophistication and refinement.

Mr. D.D. Aggarwal, the author of this remarkable work on protocol in Srimad Bhagwat, has in an earlier work delved deep into various aspects of protocol in Sri Ramcharitmanas. It was an interesting and engaging analysis of the elements of protocol in the saga of the life and time of Lord Rama as seen in Ramcharitmanas. The present book is a veritable intellectual, literary and spiritual excursion into one of the most popular and revered sacred texts of the Pauranic era.

The present book is not merely a book on protocol in Srimad Bhagwat. It is a book which mirrors the life and times of an ancient era. On that larger than life canvas, the author tells us, with protocol as his principal focus, of what he finds in Srimad Bhagwat regarding the mobility of the caste system, the status of the Grihastha Ashram, social, political, diplomatic and spiritual precedence, seating arrangements, personal and family laws, crime and punishment, the status of women, the role and status of seers, sages and preceptors and their relationship with their pupils and disciples, the protocol of meetings and diplomatic representation, royal duties, and behavior, inheritance, contracts, international understandings and treaties, laws of war and peace, relationships between sovereign, suzerain and vassal states, espionage and intelligence-gathering, ambassadorial immunity, peace negotiatious, and most importantly, protocol in the heaven and among the Olympian gods of Indian mythology.

Through the entire narrative, there runs the golden thread of the philosophy of Dharma and the sense of the sacred enlivened by episodes which are embedded in the Hindu heritage and which have been the warp and woof of the ethos of that heritage.

I congratulate Mr. D.D. Aggarwal for providing in the present work a glimpse of the life of men, women and gods and the elements of protocol in their relationships in the Pauranic era through a book which is one of the most popular Pauranic sacred Bhakti texts.

Dr. L.M. Singhvi

Preface

Hinduism is a way of life designed to be led following the dharma as per varnashram and vedic tenets. This dharma is based on the advent of various incarnations of God. Such incarnations have taken place for the protection of dharma and to annihilate the asuras whenever there was increase in their number, and who tried to eliminate dharma. God incarnate, therefore, took place to annihilate the asuras and in turn provide protection and pleasure to the sadhus.

Srimad Bhagwat is a comprehensive granth propounding the advent of Vishnu in various incarnations. In this book, I have tried to trace the protocol in the life of people—political, administrative, international, social and spiritual—in our pauranic era comparing it with the modern concept of protocol. Since this book is by and large based on the relation of the creator (ब्रह्म) and creature (जीव), the spiritual protocol could be traced to a greater extent distinct from the many faceted life, narrated in Ramcharitmanas, where all aspects of the life, including international relation, are available in plenty. I have, therefore, attempted to project the same, which, it is claimed, is of advantage to the people of this era viz. Kalyug.

For the sake of maintaining flow and continuity, some portions have been written in this book not pertaining particularly to the protocol aspect. In this way, this book has taken the shape of a precised form of Srimad Bhagwat itself.

In the end, I hasten to mention that but for the cooperation and inspiration by my wife and son and constant instigation by my brother Jagan Nath, I may not have been able to accomplish this job.

H-13 Ashok Vihar, Delhi — D.D. Aggarwal
Tele : 7428669

Contents

Introduction

As per Indian mythology, Indian culture dates back to lacs of years. It started with the start of mankind. The first phase is named as Satyayug. As its name indicates, it was all truth. Vedas had come up at that time. These are said to be God's voice. Rightly so, as so far nothing untoward has been noticed in vedas. They throw light on the human behaviour, human living, management rules, social behaviour, political administration etc. The functions of all God's creations—mortal and immortal, the science—chemical and physical—astrology, hemisphere, space, astronomy, philology, spiritual attainment etc. *i.e.* it covers all sciences, humanity, art, spirituality, transmigration of soul etc. In Satyayug, Hindu society was divided into four varnas—Brahmin, Kshatriya, Vaish and Shudra. Each had the notified function. If the persons of all varnas did their jobs religiously as per laid tanets, there would be no ailment, disease, famines etc. The raja and praja would live cordially—The raja was prepared to do everything possible for the welfare and proper living of his people. The praja too were always prepared to sacrifice their lives for the sake of raja and the rajya. All people worked as per vedic sermons. Raja Harishchandra is said to be belonging to that era, otherwise not much of history is available for that period.

Then came the Tretayug. In this yug, the asuras like Ravan started destroying the vedic tenets resulting in chaos and anarchy. To do away with this, Lord Vishnu came as incarnate in Ram. Ram killed all rakshashas, responsible for creation of chaos and irreligious mentality and established Ram Rajya. This is the fulfilment of known motto of God incarnate to human beings whenever there was breach of religious concepts.

"यदा यदा हि धर्मस्य ग्लानिर्भवति भारत"
अभ्युत्थानमधर्मस्य तदात्मानं सृजाम्यहम्। (गीता 4-7)

In Ram Rajya, people had been living and discharging their duties as laid down for various varnas. It is a historical fact that in India there had been prosperity and peace, whenever people of all varnas had been discharging their duties, religiously and, whenever there had been a breach of the same, there had been chaos and anarchy. The division of mankind in 4 varnas and each person passing through the ashramas had been the fundamental of Hindu way of life and Hindu cult. With the establishment of Ram Rajya, where each person was conducting himself as per tenets of varnas and ashramas, there was complete peace and prosperity. The Satyayug had again turned up in India during the Ram Rajya Kal.

Then came the Duapur. Rakshasas had again cropped up after the Ram Rajya, like Kansa, Shishupal, Jarasandha, etc., who had been caring for themselves, treating themselves as God and were responsible for all kinds of cruelty and criminality on public. As per Hindus' belief, God Vishnu again came as incarnate in Krishna, who eliminated all rakshasas culminating in Mahabharat. With Mahabharat came the end of Duapur too yielding place to Kalyug. In fact Kalyug had started in the life time of Pandava Raja Parikshit itself. With the passage of time in Kalyug, the religious concepts started declining. The rajas had become selfish and leisurely and did not care for the uplift and welfare of public. The public in turn also started behaving with the rajas differently resulting in foreign invasions like that of Alexander. Now and then some good Rajas did come up like Chandragupta Maurya and Ashoka in Maurya dynasty, Vikramajit Chandra Gupta in Gupta dynasty. At that time itself, India had been divided in small kingdoms,—In East there were so many kingdoms, in South there were separate kingdoms and even there were many kingdoms in North and West. In North India too there were rulers having small kingdoms. With small kingdoms, each Raja had become ambitious of conquering more and this resulted in never lasting fight. Taking advantage of such an era in Indian sub-continent, the Muslims, who had by then come up as a strong religious race, with the advent of Hazrat Mohammed Sahib, and all kingdoms in Middle East having accepted that religion; started a Jehad war for the spread of Islam. Wherever there had been a religious revolution, the people united and marched to spread their religion in adjoining countries. India could not escape from that aggression. At first Mohammed Gazni came for the purpose of looting India as in those days, there was starvation and poverty in Middle East but there was a unity of purpose amongst the people. So taking advantage of disunity in Indian subcontinent and existence of wealth, Mohammed Gazni invaded India in eleventh century (within about 4 centuries of the advent of Islam) and went unchecked by our so called brave Indian Rajput rajas from Hindukush to Somnath temple in Gujrat and looted Somnath temple which was said to be a store house of all riches. He went back with the booty to Iran. But this did not end here. Further invasions started having known the riches of India and the disunity in the people of this land so much so that the invaders were at times invited by Hindu rajas to defeat their rivals. Jaichand is the example. He invited Mohammed Ghori to invade Prithvi Raj and for this he even extended his help. Although by that time Prithvi Raj had gathered some force and unity in his people but after continuous raids, he got defeated and this time Mohammed Ghori, in addition to looting and going back, also left his slave Sardar Kutab-ud-din to rule the conquered portion of India. This was the start of Muslim rule in India. There was no opposition from the public or other rajas and consequently the Muslim rulers consolidated their position, expanding their kingdom and creating confidence in the public by thrust and thrashing. It is from here that the Indian public had forgotten their self and had learnt to bow and surrender to the ruler. Taking advantage of the situation, other invaders too came from Middle East conquering Muslim or Hindu Rajas, as the case may be. In the sequence, Slave kings ruled for many years. Then` came Khiljis, Tuglaks, Suris, Lodhis and in the end the Mughals. Mughals, because of their policy of cordiality between the Hindus and Muslims—by that time Hindus had also started becoming conscious of their position and started uniting—divided Hindus and won and annexed a few of the Rajput Rajas on their side by giving them chieftainships, marrying their daughters etc. Mughal rule continued for about three centuries. During Mughals itself because of Aurangzeb's anti Hindu Policies—contrary to what Akbar had established a pro Hindu Policy—gave rise to Hindu chiefs in Marathas, Rajputs etc. resulting in downfall of Mughal empire and again India getting subdivided into small kingdoms. By this time, Europeans had started establishing themselves and again taking advantage of disunity and rivalry amongst the various Indian rulers, they created further division by helping one against the other, purchasing their commanders etc. and in this way established the English Rule in India. Despite Indians' rising in 1857—the first war of independence—the English were able to subdue Indians and ruled upto 1947. Then came the Indian independence dividing the subcontinent into India and Pakistan (subsequently India, Pakistan and Bangladesh).

The above historical background has been given with a view to indicate that whenever there had been the following of religious tenets of varnas/ashramas and in Raja-Praja relations, there was harmony and peace and whenever there was breach, there was disunity, anarchy and chaos. Further, whenever the anarchy and chaos had reached the culmination, there came the turn of God incarnate to annihilate the irreligious element and again establishing the rule of religion. Let us expect the Kali Avtar anytime now in view of the already spread selfishness, reversion from religious tenets, non-following of varna/ashram etc. Leaving aside the irreligious part of it, there has been the development in the universe in its own way. This has led to the development in the era of science, space technology, leisure and pleasure. Also there are the modern ethics of protocol, international relations and understanding, detailed laws of war and peace and economic development. In other words the modern concept of development is restricted only to the development of worldly materialistic life and the religion is not in the preview of the modern ethics of governance.

Let us now revert back to the tenets of Shrimad Bhagwat, which has confirmed the God's incarnation from time to time whenever rakshasas had started holding the public at large to ransom to have their selfish ends fulfilled. Also we have to see how far the modern concepts of protocol and governance could be traced during the various periods of evolution of Hindu culture and Indian History. In other words like the mythological concept of "सम्भवामि युगे युगे", in the evolution of state too, whenever there is chaos and anarchy in the governance of the state, a stronger king comes up, who unites the disintegrating forces to give a strong government and this strong government continues for a few decades or a century or two and then again the downfall starts. This cycle goes on.

Along with the political stability also goes the spiritual stability and bhakti. This generally is available only during peace periods from the point of view of political stability. Leaving aside the ancient times, when there was rule of dharma, many Shastras, Vedas, Puranas had been written in India in Satyayug, Treta, Duapur etc., Shrimad Bhagwat was written by Rishi Ved Vyas after Mahabharat war was over, and there was complete peace during the rule of Pandavas. Such granths are also written when there is need for the same. First time Bhagwat was read to Parikshit on his having been cursed by a Muni that he would die after seven days due to biting of a snake. Parikshit attained salvation after listening to Bhagwat through Muni Shukdeva.

In Kalyug also, the literature has prospered according to the pace of rule. In Gupta period poets like Kalidas were born and then in Rajput period, there were wars and wars amongst various Rajput rajas and others. Invasions from Muslim countries also took place, and with the establishment of Muslim rule in India, there was constant war between the Muslim rulers on the one hand and Indian rulers on the other. This gave birth to the poets coming up, who wrote about the bravery of the Rajput kings like Prithvi Raj Raso by Chandra Bardai etc. This continued for about 400 years when the Mughals came up on the scene. Through cordial approach between Hindus and Muslims by Akbar, there was enough of peace. This gave birth to many bhakta poets coming on the scene. At that time there were many cults in Hindus and each one considered his cult as superior and distinct from others, such as Nirgun Bhakti by Kabir, Ram Bhakti by Tulsidas, Krishna Bhakti by Surdas, Nand Das etc. and Shiva Bhakti by Shaivites. There was no cordiality between any two. So much so that when Tulsidas went to meet his brother, who was a Krishna Bhakta, and he took Tulsidas to a Krishna temple, Tulsidas did not bow and at that time the Krishna bhakta had to request his deity.

तुलसी मस्तक तब नवे धनुष बाण लो हाथ

It is said the Krishna idol was thereupon seen with Dhanusban in his hand and Tulsidas thereafter became Krishna Bhakta along with his being Ram Bhakta. Tulsidas thereafter wrote Krishna Geetavali too in praise of Lord Krishna. Similarly, in Ramcharit Manas too, Tulsidas made a mention of Vishnu's incarnation as Krishna in Duapur, besides mentioning that Ram was the bhakta of Shiva and Shiva used to worship Ram. At the time of Shiva-sthapna at Rameshwaram before proceeding to indulge in the battle with Ravan, Ram had said—

"शिव द्रोही मम दास न होई"

meaning thereby that Shiva and Ram are sort of complementary to each other. Also to bring about cordiality between the Nirguna and Saguna bhaktas, Tulsidas brought about the dialogue of Garud and Kagbhusand in Ramcharit Manas, Uttarkand, specifically for this purpose and told—

सगुनहिं अगुनहिं नहीं कछु भेदा।

and— अगुन अरूप अलख अज जोई,
भगत प्रेमवश सगुन सो होई।

This was the need of bringing about a unity in Hindus in 16th century when Manas was written and the poet saw alround disunity amongst Hindus. Manas had a great hand in bringing about the unity in various cults of Hindus. Also Tulsidas has brought out that for the purpose of attaining bhakti, one has to have viswas in the almighty. This was also the need of hour as Muslims, who did not believe in idol worship, had been raising questions on the bonafides of Ram and Krishna and Hindus were finding themselves helpless. At that time Tulsidas came up with manas saying—

बिनु विश्वास भक्ति नहीं तेहि बिनु द्रवहिं न राम
राम कृपा बिनु सपनेहुँ जीव न लह विश्राम।

Here Tulsidas indicated that for Bhakti—whether Saguna or Nirguna—the incumbent needed to have full belief (विश्वास). This was needed as at that time people had become more prone to criticism than having viswas in the God.

Srimad Bhagwat Mahatmya

In the beginning of each Grantha, the mahatmya of that granth is indicated with a view to inculcate viswas (belief) in the people about what was contained in the book. Rishi Vyas too understood this need while writing Srimad Bhagwat, as even at that time a lot of criticism on Krishna policy resulting in Mahabharat was coming up from various quarters. With a view, therefore, to restore belief and bhakti in the people toward Krishna as incarnate of God, Muni Vyas had brought about the incarnation of God in various forms like Narsingha, Vraha, Krishna, Ram etc. establishing that Krishna was not an ordinary person but the incarnate of God Vishnu only. Therefore, in the beginning of the book, one chapter on Bhagwat Mahatmya has been written. This has proved a necessity in modern concept of religion, where people want reasoning for everything they are made to believe. Ram Mahatmya has been indicated in Uttarkand in Manas in detail as stated in the beginning of the book also. Also Tulsidas in Manas had kept it in mind to say through Ram himself on the top, the Ishwar-Jeeva relation, Rambhakti, Shiva Bhakti, definition of Saint and non-Saint etc. so that these could be believed by the people. Similarly spiritual fundamentals have been narrated through the medium of learned gurus, rishis etc. such as at the time of Dasratha's death, to console Bharat, Vashistha Muni said—

सुनहु भरत भावी प्रबल बिलखि कहेउ मुनिनाथ,

हानि लाभु जीवनु मरनु जसु अपजसु विधि हाथ। (मानस)

Such policy statements were told through the learned Gurus only or even Shiva had said based on the experience that "Ram name was the fact, rest all was maya".

उमा कहउँ मैं अनुभव अपना,
सत हरि भजनु जगत सब सपना। (मानस)

So we were talking about the need of mahatmya of the Lord on whom the book had been written.

Then as per protocol, one has to remember the God before starting any project. Book writing being a project within itself, the poet has in the beginning written—

सच्चिदानंद रूपाय विश्वोत्पत्त्यादिहेतवे,
ताप त्रय विनाशाय श्री कृष्णाय वयं नमः। (मा. 1-1)

We bow to Shri Krishna, who is responsible for the creation, bringing up and annihilation of mankind and who only can absolve the man from worldly evils. Srimad Bhagwat, as it is, has come up in the shape of what transpired between Shukdeva and Raja Parikshit, who got all his doubts cleared (obviously for the well-being of the humanity) about the God's incarnation and the relations between God and the human beings. Vyas Muni had written it, when after birth, Shukdeva (his son) left Muni's Ashram, with a view to attract Shukdeva to the universal fold of Krishna Bhakti and this did work when Shukdeva heard the slokas of Bhagwat in cave and got inspiration to read the entire granth and to see that granth. Apart from mending his son, Vyas Muni had given this granth as a media of Krishna Bhakti, which had become necessary after killing of lakhs of people in Mahabharat and when people had started thinking that the war was uncalled for. To remove their doubts and inculcate bhakti in the people, Vyas Muni wrote this book and has been narrated through the medium of Sootji, Shukdeva Muni etc.. Saunik Muni had desired this narration for the salvation of people in Kalyug. Therefore, it can be said that the book narrates the philosophy in such a way that it inculcates in the mind of the people in this era of Kalyug, the way to their attaining salvation. Saunik Muni had made Sootji as his guru, who only could educate the pupil to enable him to attain salvation. Here again the protocol of guru and pupil comes in and a coaching by guru is considered necessary in Hindus.

Even in the modern concept of seeking knowledge one has to have a guru in the form of an instructor in the institution or otherwise. The guru also used to coach the pupil when he found the belief in the mind of the pupil to have that coaching. This is nothing but the aptitude test conducted now to admit a pupil to a certain discipline of education. Sootji had considered Saunik as eligible for the same. In this context even the worldly concept of 'give and take' does not augur well and the eligibility for listening the katha is determined by the guru only. That is why when Shukdeva started narrating Bhagwat to Raja Parikshit, gods had come with Amrit pitcher in consideration of being permitted to listen the katha but seeing the gods not full of bhakti but wanting in exchange of Amrit, Shukdeva did not consider them eligible to listen the katha and declined to accept their request. It was then considered that Bhagwat is the only granth to provide salvation to the people in Kalyug, by listening it and by reading it—

पठनाच्छ्रवणात्सद्यो वैकुंठं फलदायकम्। (मा.-1-20)

The poet has through the medium of Narad, who had frequently been visiting this universe, told that during Kalyug the environ would be—

(1) There would be no piety—inner or outside—no truth or tap (तप); pity or alms (दान).

(2) Everyone would somehow try to live and think of nothing else.

(3) People would be liars, lethargic, unintelligent, unfortunate.

(4) Only the hypocrites shall assume to be sadhus. They would in appearance seem to be sadhus but would be womanisers and thieves.

(5) Ladies would rule the houses and the brothers-in-law (साले) would be the advisors in the household.

(6) People would sell off their daughters out of greed and there would be constant quarrel between men and women.

(7) The ashramas of mahatmas would be inhabited by irreligious persons.

(8) There would be no yogi, sidhha, or well-doers.

(9) Brahmins would be imparting education on consideration of wealth.

(10) Women shall resort to prostitution to earn money.

This is what had been explained of the Kalyug, thousands of years back and today this all exists. To redress the grievances of people involved in this sort of environ, Narad suggested the reading of Srimad Bhagwat. The Kalyug had entered the universe during the period of Raja Parikshit itself. He had forbidden Kalyug from entering during his regime but then he was told that there were some good points of Kalyug too and one such point was that the salvation, which could be attained in Satya yug, Treta, and Duapur by jap, tap, yog and samadhi, could be attained in Kalyug by simply praising God (कीर्तन).

यत्फलं नास्ति तपस्यान योगेन समाधिना
तत्फलं लभते सम्यक्कलौ केशव कीर्तिनात। (मा.-1-68)

On this consideration, Parikshit allowed Kalyug to enter the universe. In the previous yugas, gyan and vairagya were necessary to attain salvation but in Kalyug only bhakti was needed for this purpose. So Krishna, while leaving the universe had directed only bhakti to help enliven his bhaktas, who would not be able to attain gyan and vairagya. Even otherwise, gyan and vairagya lead to be in Swarga but not the achievement of God, which is possible only through bhakti and bhakti in turn can be had by reading/listening to Srimad Bhagwat. Although the main content in Bhagwat is the vedas and puranas, but the Bhagwat provides the same in a condensed form and in an easily digestible way and is a combination of gyan, vairagya and bhakti. Modern age does not want to go through the tedious language and deep thought of vedas and shastras. They want the extract in a simpler language and in brief. That purpose is served by Bhagwat. This is the aim of the writer to project this as a comprehensive book still in a precised form suiting the requirement of the people in Kalyug. It redresses all doubts that arise in the minds of the people regarding the behaviour and social and political conduct of people, along with the spiritual brushing. But for attaining the maximum out of the Bhagwat—

(1) one has to find proper environ as environ has great effect on the understanding and efficiency of a person. When one goes to a temple one feels like bowing in reverence to the almighty. Similarly, if one goes to the house of a prostitute, he would just be down with passion. Proper environ for Bhagwat can be, say on the bank of river Ganga, where there are trees, flowers, good water, fresh air etc. In such a place, if one puts one's thinking in reading and digesting the contents of Bhagwat, it would be easier. Similar environ is described in Manas at the place where Kagbhusand used to narrate Ramkatha.

(2) Apart from natural environ, there should be the collection of learned persons, whose presence would make the people believe the importance of Bhagwat. So when Shukdeva narrated Bhagwat, at the bank of Ganga, all big rishis, and munis like Vashistha, Viswamitra, Gautam, Kapil, Vyas etc. were present along with their pupils and wives and sons.

(3) There should be a learned Kathawachak (Narrator). His word should be admitted by all as the word from God and acted upon. Inspite of the best environ and presence of all great rishis etc., if the narrator of the Bhagwat is not an apt person, people would just laugh it away. Therefore, for narrating Bhagwat to Parikshit, Lord Shukdeva was available. Here to tell what Shukdeva had narrated, Sankadik Rishi is also on the stage.

(4) In the gathering the people sat in a particular fashion. This shows there was some thing like order of precedence of present day.

वैष्णवाश्च विरक्ताश्चन्यासिनो ब्रह्मचारिण:,

मुखभागे स्थितास्ते च तदग्रे नारद: स्थित:। (मा.-3-19)

In the audience, vaishnav, sanayasis, detached people sat in front and before them sat Narad. Behind them sat other pupils, rishis' wives, sons and then the general public. People sat not as per their caste like brahmin, kshatriya, vaish, sudra etc. but on the basis of there capability. Accordingly Vishwamitra, though an kshatriya by birth sat with the rishis, munis etc. The wives sat together and the pupils at one place. The gods sat on one side and the ladies and children on the other. They all sat in a systematic way.

(5) At first as per protocol, the Pooja of the almighty was performed, shared by all present.

(6) Belief is the primary thing in the minds of the listeners. If they have no belief in what is narrated, then their presence would be of no avail. Therefore, the narrater has at first to state the importance of the Katha. Here Shukdeva or Sankadik Rishi had first narrated the sanctity and importance of Bhagwat to imbibe interest in the audience. As already indicated, Bhagwat is aimed at the well-being of the people of Kalyug. These people did not want to go through the elaborate and detailed vedas, shastras etc. Therefore, the essence of all those had been produced in Bhagwat. Even if Bhagwat is considered elaborate, then the narrator has indicated that even one sloka "Om Nama Bhagwate Vasudevaya" (ॐ नमः भगवते वासुदेवाय"।) is enough, if uttered daily, with adequate belief and environ. So much so that in vedas, particular days have been stated to be good for certain purposes but in Bhagwat it is indicated that it can be heard/read anytime, any day and in any condition so that it is easily done by the leisurely people of Kalyug. Shukdeva has indicated that rather than in a particular period, Bhagwat can be completely heard/read in a week's time in any month.

श्रद्धातः श्रवणे नित्यं माघे तावद्धि यत्फलम्,

तत्फलम् शुकदेवेन सप्ताह श्रवणँ कृतम्। (मा.-3-48)

A week's duration has been prescribed keeping in view the duration for which one could live with control on self (संयम), free from ailments, short life and many other limitation of Kalyug. As per Shukdeva, the achievement from one week's study/hearing of Bhagwat is much more than the continuous tap, yog and samadhi, tirathyatra, yagyas, vrats etc. Also Lord Krishna had put his entire strength in Bhagwat at the time of leaving this universe as Krishna had come as incarnate of God for the well-being of his bhaktas and in his absence, the bhaktas had to be provided with some patronage and Krishna projected Bhagwat for this purpose. Such is also the dictum in Muslims, who see prophet in Kuran and Christians in Bible. So provision of a patronage for the people in the absence of the almighty, is the general practice available in all religions. The belief in the bhaktas is possible when they have bhakti in their mind and listening of Bhagwat provides bhakti in the minds of listeners.

(7) Once such Bhagwat katha is narrated and listened, Bhagwan Krishna appears on the scene to bless his bhaktas.

(8) This is possible where Bhagwat is listened with concentration, without having any doubts and without permitting the mind to go estray. Then only would there be any use of listening the Bhagwat and also if it is listened with full belief and concentration, then one gets his ambitions fulfilled.

अद्दढ़ं च हतं ज्ञानं प्रमादेन हतं श्रुतम,
संदिग्धो हि हतो मंत्रो व्यग्रचित्तो हतो जपः। (मा.-5-73)

(9) In old Hindu belief, shudras were not considered eligible to listen to Harikatha. But Bhagwat had been written specially for the downtrodden people of Kalyug, including shudras, who had been isolated. As per modern concept of equality, Bhagwat provides for and makes everyone eligible for listening the Bhagwat katha.

दूरे हरि कथाः केचिद्दूरेचाच्युत कीर्तनाः
स्त्रियः शुद्रादयो ये च तेषां बोधो यतो भवेत्। (मा.-6-6)

Similarly, women were also debarred from Bhagwad bhakti but Bhagwat makes them too eligible for listening the katha and having their ambition fulfilled. In Ramcharit Manas too, Tulsidas had in 16th century (when Manas was written) found women and shudras as excluded, and so had indicated that not only human beings, irrespective of race or caste, even the other creatures like birds and animals etc., were also eligible to listen to Ramkatha. That is why Ram befriended Nishadraj and granted mukti to Jatayu who lost his life for the cause of Shri Ram and Kagbhusanda, who narrated Ramkatha. The misnomer existing even now that shudras and women are excluded from Bhagwad bhakti is, therefore, without any base.

(10) In Ramcharit Manas, creature is indulged in the universe because of the Ram 'Maya' but in Bhagwat one is considered to have been involved in the worldly ambitions because of one's own karmas. Therefore, one gets absolved of bad karmas and accordingly gets rid of Bhagwat 'maya', once he engages himself in Bhagwat Katha.

"कर्म मोह गृहीताङ्गं मामुद्धर भवार्णवात्" (मा.-6-27)

Further, in Duapur, the person got riddance from the 'mohmaya' created by one's 'karmas' only by 'karmas' in that direction. In Tretayug, one could get rid of Ram's 'maya' either by over-powering 'maya' by gyan and vairagya or by bhakti. In Duapur too, the riddance by karma was also through gyan or vairagya or bhakti-karma. Arjun was coached by Krishna in Mahabharat by pronouncing Gita, stressing only on karma. Therefore, in Duapur 'karma' theory had been evolved. In Kalyug one can get salvation by remembering 'Name' only.

(11) The audience should at first worship and praise the Bhagwat katha narrator as with this, one develops devotion/belief in katha. The narrator too gets encouragement and considers the audience as eligible to listen to the katha. The audience is also expected to listen to the katha with concentration. To enable them to concentrate on katha, they are not expected to go for bath/toilet etc. and for this purpose, a

procedure of less eating/one time eating is prescribed. The audience should be above the worldly passions, rage, pride, greed (काम, क्रोध, मद, लोभ) etc.

(12) Women and shudras, poor, ailing, unfortunate, sinner, issueless etc. all have been considered eligible to listen to Bhagwat provided they live with self control as prescribed above.

(13) After having done all this and having heard katha in the manner above said, one attains the fulfilment of ambitions including salvation.

(14) After the katha is over, the narrator has to be worshipped and praised. Adequate alms are given to poors and others deserving. It is said that with the completion of katha in the above said manner, Shri Krishna appears on the scene and grants fulfilment of each other's desires and salvation to non-desirees.

(15) With a view to inculcate belief in the audience of Bhagwat, the poet has explained how such katha was narrated by Shukdeva to Parikshit, who attained salvation. Wherever this katha is narrated, all rishis, munis, gods, Bramha, Shiva etc. come to listen to it and in the end Vishnu grants all listeners the ultimate. Such description is necessary before Bhagwat is narrated to infuse sincerity, sanctity and belief in audience of Bhagwat.

Skandh – I

After having inculcated necessary belief in audience by describing the importance of Bhagwat, the poet starts narrating the Bhagwat. As per protocol, in the beginning the poet worships the almighty God as is done before starting any job in the modern world too.

Srimad Bhagwat is nothing but narration of all the incarnations of Vishnu. The narration starts as usual with the gathering of many rishis, then development of a desire to listen to Bhagwat and then finding a suitable and capable narrator. Here rishis came across Rishi Sootji. So they invited him to narrate Bhagwat katha. As per protocol, he was requested to sit on a prestigious stage (आसन) above all. Then he was requested to narrate the katha after making all necessary arrangements/pre-requisites for the occasion as described.They requested Sootji, who was well versed with all vedas, shastras etc. to narrate some katha which could be of use to the people of Kalyug as in Kalyug, people would be lethargic, involved in worldly ambitions, short lived, not so intelligent and indulged in all sorts of vices. The vedas and shastras were there, but they were very detailed and deep and were beyond the comprehension of the people of Kalyug. Therefore, something easier, shorter and easily assimilable was required to be narrated. For this purpose it is explained that God adopts to come incarnate in this universe for the purpose of the well-being of his bhaktas and the people at large and for annihilation of evil doers. The God incarnate is independent and He, conducts Himself independently in this universe. The lilas of God in this universe are easy to be remembered and their remembrance lead the person to salvation. Muni Vyas has described the conduct of God in various incarnations at one place in Srimad Bhagwat. This contains all that is available in vedas in the form of questions asked by Parikshit and replies given by Shukdeva. Even the trees had confirmed this aspect when Shukdeva left Vyas's ashram and adopted sanyas and Vyas had been trying for his son to come back. At that time, everyone including the immortals, expressed that Bhagwat would bring him back to the Ashram. This gave consolation to Vyas Muni that one day, when Shukdeva would come to know of Bhagwat and its importance, he would return to Ashram and this did happen. This granth is, therefore, a fit one for the people of Kalyug to remain in universe and even then attain salvation as Shukdeva, even after having become sanyasi could revert back to his father's ashram after hearing a few shalokas of Bhagwat. Now to affirm it to the people at large, Bhagwat had been narrated by Shukdeva to Parikshit and with this narration, he attained salvation. In Satya yug etc. gyan and vairagya were required to achieve mukti but in Kalyug, Bhakti has been described as the sole criterion for achieving the ultimate aim. Bhakti develops by listening the biographies of God's incarnations, particularly the conduct of Krishna, whose bhakti, while living in this universe and leading a normal life, granted salvation to the gopis and gwalas of Brindavana and to the people of Dwarka. Here bhakti grants gyan, vairagya and salvation. So the medium is bhakti and not gyan etc. Shri Krishna in Gita, has envisaged 'Karma' as the main job of the people in this universe. This karma has to be with reference to what and where one has to do.This is as per the dharma of Varnas and Ashramas—A brahmin has to do his karma of attaining the knowledge of vedas, shastra and teaching the same to others. A kshatriya has to fight for his kingdom and protect people from outside invasion and maintaining law and order in his kingdom. A vaish has to perform the karma of production, trade, distribution of the products etc. and for the shudras the karma is serving the people of all the other three varnas. This is coherent unit of society as per Hindu shastras and each person doing his karma leads to a prosperous and peaceful society. Whenever there had been breach in the discharge of these duties, there had been anarchy and chaos. This is evidenced by history. These karmas are conducted by the mankind to live in this universe peacefully but then he has to do something for the ultimate salvation also. Here also this has been made a part of karma only. That karma is through bhakti and the bhakti is also easily practised by reading/listening to the lilas of incarnation of God and getting absolved in the same so that one becomes a part of God himself and that is the ultimate end or achievement of a person. This is an easier course compared to the one prescribed in vedas/ shastras *i.e.* the attaining of gyan, vairagya through jap, tap, dan, vrat etc. which is very tedious and cannot ordinarily be followed and practised by the people in Kalyug because firstly there is no capable pandit to lead the people on that path and then the people do not resort to such a tedious way. So the achievement of gyan and vairagya through bhakti rather than through jap, tap, vrat, yagya etc, has been prescribed in Bhagwat. To make it easily understandable by the people at large, it has been narrated in the form of redressal of all doubts about God's bhakti in the minds of ordinary persons through the medium of Parikshit by Shukdeva, who himself was not less than the incarnation of God himself so that people not only felt satisfied with the redressal of their doubts and having full determination in bhakti but also developed belief in the contents of Bhagwat leading to salvation, if performed as a spiritual karma in getting absorbed in the bhakti of the almighty. This bhakti is through keertan, reading, listening and thinking of the lilas of various incarnations of God. Therefore, one has to first have inclination to read or to listen to Bhagwat; have belief in its contents and then getting absorbed in it leading to salvation. The karma in this process leads to annihilation of all vices in the mind of a person and converts him into a pure person and then the purity leads to one getting lost in Bhagwad-bhakti. In the nature, there are three elements Satva, Rajo and Tamo. These refer to the existence of the universe, creation of universe and annihilation of the universe or conversely controlled by Vishnu, Brahma and Shiva. Since a person is not aware of his having been created nor is he aware of what happens after annihilation, he is concerned with the present form *i.e.,* satva or existence or Vishnu. Therefore, the Bhakti of Vishnu is relevant to the existence of the human being and hence one has to leave rajo and tamo and concentrate on satva or the bhakti of Vishnu.

Vishnu is said to be complete with 16 kalas—ten senses (इन्द्रियाँ), one mind (मन) and five ingredients (पाँच भूत-भूमि, आक़ाश, अग्नि, जल और वायु). He produced one Brahma and entrusted the job of further creation to Brahma. Then there was the need for annihilation of the creation too. For this purpose he created Shiva. Although, therefore, there are three distinct jobs of God—creation, maintenance and annihilation —yet these are all imbibed in one almighty God. This God only has been coming incarnate in various forms in this universe to annihilate the vices and to exhilarate the virtues. There were 18 main incarnations of God although now and then God had been visiting the universe in various forms like that of Manu, Prajapatis, etc. The God incarnates in the universe in different forms for the well-being of the public, when there is increase of irreligious elements. He creates the creatures, maintains and annihilates them but does not involve himself in this universe rather keeps himself independent of its sorrows and happiness. He experiences and exercises, while in the universe, all senses like an ordinary human being but still remains away from the effect of the sensuous activities like Krishna had been playing and dancing with the gopis of Brij but he never indulged in worldly passions or when Ram was ordered by Dasratha to go to forest when he was to be coronated, Ram was neither happy to be coronated nor was sorry to go to forest. Ved Vyas had been engaging himself in well-being of the people. He had written Mahabharat, narrating therein what was contained in vedas, whereby all people including women and shudras could know their dharma and karma.

भारतव्य पदेशेन ह्याम्नायार्थश्च दर्शितः
दृश्यते यत्र धर्मादि स्त्री शुद्रादिभिरप्युत। (1-5-29)

It is here that Vyas Muni had recognised that at that time the society or the Pandits had kept women and shudras ineligible for listening/reading Hari katha or performing Hari bhakti. He, therefore, with the support of quotation from vedas, indicated in Mahabharat that women and shudras were also eligible to perform Hari bhakti. Therefore, after having felt the sorrows of more than half of the population having been deprived of the reading/ listening to Hari katha, took the initiative of making them too eligible for it. Subsequently in Ramcharit Manas, Tulsidas too had honoured Nishadraj being a shudra as Ram bhakta and even the birds like Jatayu, who was granted salvation by Ram himself for having sacrified his life for the cause of Shri Ram. At that time, Narad told him to write a granth which should convincingly redress all doubts standing in the way of Hari bhakti, narrating God's incarnations in various forms, which could inculcate bhakti in the minds of people and forcing them to leave the path of worldly passions. Narad had indicated that even he, in his childhood, born of a maid of the rishi, had by dint of serving rishis and listening to Krishna lila narrated by them, had achieved closeness to God and ultimately could absorb himself in God leading to salvation. Therefore, the way of attaining salvation was to continue doing as per their dharma but to ultimately dedicate their doings and themselves to the attainment of the ultimate aim. After Narad had left, Vyas went to Saraswati river and sitting at its bank, he concentrated on Bhagwat lila and through this concentration he could know the Bhagwat maya through which God controls the entire universe. Human being, even though knowing the maya as worldly involvement, indulges in the effects of maya—one or the other. He, after having indulged in these passions, suffers from one vice or the other. The Bhagwat bhakti can only help getting riddance from these vices. Now the question arises as to how to do Bhagwat bhakti. In fact people at that time were unaware of the method of reaching upto God and this is what had been worrying Vyas Muni as to how to create a process by following which one could get absorbed in Hari himself. Thus came the idea of writing

Bhagwat to his mind. He thought that Bhagwat, if heard or listened or read/followed, could lead the man to ultimate salvation. Salvation can be attained through gyan, vairagya etc. too but this was very tedious way for the people in Kalyug, who wanted an easier and shorter process. Bhakti serves this purpose. One does achieve gyan, vairagya and consequently salvation but achievement of gyan, vairagya through bhakti is easier than through jap, tap, vrat etc. Bhagwat does provide the way for the bhakti through knowing the lilas of the almighty in various forms. Even Shukdeva Muni, who already had been able to absorb himself in God through gyan and vairagya, was attracted to bhakti after listening to a few of the slokas of Bhagwat. Bhagwat is, therefore, the surest way of attainment. Shukdeva had gone through Bhagwat and kept it to himself till he got a chance of narrating the same to Raja Parikshit. The great people (rishis, munis etc.) always make use of any occasion available to do good to the people at large making someone as the medium for the same. So Shukdeva, who had gone through Bhagwat and had known the contents, read it to Raja Parikshit, redressing all his doubts and through him sent the katha to the public at large. To know Bhagwat, therefore, it is essential to know something about Raja Parikshit.

After Mahabharat had come to an end with Duryodhan on his last breath and Aswatthama, having killed 5 sons of Daropadi taking them to be the five Pandvas, felt ashamed when he came to know that they were the sons of Daropadi. Killing the sons when they were sleeping was against the laws of war and law, therefore, condemned it all through. Even Duryodhan was not happy with this action although Pandvaas were his enemies. This shows that some laws of war were there according to which the battles were fought and any breach of the same was widely condemned and the breacher was duly punished. Then Arjun undertook to kill Aswatthama. When Arjun went out to kill him, he ran and Arjun was following him. Aswatthama then threw Brahmastra, which created havoc althrough. Arjun too was perplexed with what had happened. Then Krishna told him that it was the effect of Brahmastra thrown by

Aswatthama and its effect could be finished only by Brahmastra. Arjun had, therefore, thrown Brahmastra too but the effect of two Brahmastras started burning the entire universe. Arjun then withdrew the astras and caught hold of Aswatthama. Krishna told Arjun to kill him as he was not excusable having killed the five children while sleeping. This is a non-pardonable offence.

मत्तं प्रमत्तमुन्मत्तं सुप्तं बालं स्त्रियं जडम्
प्रपन्नं विरथं भीतं न रिपुं हन्ति धर्मवित। (1-7-36)

The learned persons do not kill an inattentive, drunk, sleeping, children, women, refugees, and frightened enemy and if any one does so, he should immediately be killed otherwise he would repeat his action and it would be a continuous crime. But Arjun did not favour killing a Guru's son even though he had done the unpardonable action and also Arjun had undertaken to kill him. He brought him before Yudhisthra. Perhaps this was with a view to fulfil another protocol that the right of punishment lies with the king. If he had been killed in encounter then the matter would have ended but since he was caught and arrested, then the decision lay with the king only. Even according to modern laws, if a criminal is killed during encounter with the police then alright, but if he is arrested then the punishment is awarded by the judiciary and not by the police, judiciary being the representative of the king. Accordingly, Arjun, rather than killing him, brought him before Yudhisthra, the king, and Daropadi the justice seeker. Daropadi took pity on him and requested her husband to excuse him as

(1) He being the son of the guru, was guru's representative after the death of the guru.

(2) He was brahmin and killing of a brahmin was a crime.

(3) As she had been worried due to the death of her five children, so will Aswatthama's mother, who was a pious lady.

(4) It was not advisable to offend the brahmins by killing Aswatthama. Whatever Daropadi had said was as per social protocol and had humanitarian consideration.

Present International Law too condemns inhuman actions by either side in the war that is why no one is allowed to attack on Red Cross vehicles, men in hospitals etc. as these are considered inhuman actions even during war. Daropadi's observation had been seconded by Yudhisthra and others except Bhima. Then it was for Krishna to tell the law. He said that as per vedic tenet even an inhuman brahmin was not to be killed and a tyrant (even though brahmin) should be killed.

ब्रह्मबंधुर्न हन्तव्य आततायी वधार्हण:
मयैवोभय माम्नातं परि पाह्यनुशासनम्। (1-7-53)

He, therefore, told that his both verdicts should be implemented. Arjun understood it and he at once took out the brain and his hairs. Taking out brain means he did not kill the brahmin but made him brainless at the same time even as a tyrant without brain and with shaven head, all would recognise him as such and hence he would not be able to do any tyranny. This was the way justice was granted in old days as per tenets of vedas, which are even today followed. Thereafter as per religious ordain, the Pandvaas cremated the five sons and remembering their good deeds, they had been crying. Then, as usual, the rishis/guru or someone elder comes to pacify/console the bereaved. So this job was done by Krishna himself and some rishis saying that all in universe had to die and no one could save anyone from the clutches of death.

भूतेषु कालस्य गतिं दर्शयन्न प्रति क्रियाम। (1-8-4)

Thereafter Yudhisthra was coronated. He had, during his regime, held three Aswamedha yagyas. Aswamedha yagya was performed by an emperor to test and make others know the extent of the emperor's power in his kingdom. Also all his vassals in the kingdom pay their homage at that time in recognition of his being their overall Lord emperor. This is like the present day system of colonial and vassal system under which the vassals offer presents/ annual fund to the emperor's exchange. This was the system which continued during Muslim rule in India too.

After sometime, Krishna took the permission to go back to Dwarka, his kingdom. He paid respects to Vyas Muni and Vyas also respected him as God. Others also exchanged the requisite respect. But when Krishna was to leave, suddenly, Uttra, the wife of Abhimanyu, started having some pain in her abdomen. She requested Krishna to help her as all others were thinking of killing only. Krishna could know that Aswatthama had again played mischief to kill the foetus in Uttra's abdomen as he would have been the only survivor of the Pandva Dynasty. Also it shows that it is never advisable to spare an avowed enemy. Pandvas took pity on him and spared inspite of Krishna having told Arjun to kill him. Anyway Krishna came to her help and made the Brahmastra ineffective and saved the pregnancy. Although as told by Krishna himself when Aswatthama first used Brahmastra on Arjun that its effect could not be undone except by Brahmastra alone, God was above all these effects and Krishna as God could mar the effect of Brahmastra because he is almighty responsible for creation, maintenance and annihilation of the mankind.

यद्यप्यस्त्रं ब्रह्मशिरस्त्वमोघं चाप्रतिक्रियम्,
वैष्णवं तेज आसाद्य समशाम्यद् भृगूदह। (1-8-15)

After Krishna had saved the pregnancy and was preparing to depart, Pandvas and Kunti praised him, recognising him as the incarnate of God. Kunti said that even the rishis and munis could not know him then how Kunti, a lady, could know him. So the ladies were generally treated as less intelligent and ineligible for Bhagwad bhakti.

तथा परमहंसानां मुनिनाम मलात्मनाम्,
भक्ति योगविधानार्थं कथं पश्येम हि स्त्रियः। (1-8-20)

Kunti even said that Krishna had saved them from Lakshgriha, Daropadi episode, in the forests, in Mahabharat, and now from the Brahmastra of Aswatthama. Shri Krishna accordingly came for help at the time of difficulty. She,therefore, wished difficulties to visit frequently so that Krishna would appear for help. She even recognised that as Krishna, he had been conducting himself as an ordinary human being but nobody knows when, what and where Krishna had been doing for the well-being of his bhaktas. As a matter of spiritual protocol, therefore, God is always there to help the bhaktas once the bhakta had developed full belief and trust in him. God comes as incarnate to the universe in one form or the other (even as animal in Varaha or Matsya Avtar) for helping his bhaktas and finishing the chaos and anarchy created by ṛakshasas. On the one side, Kunti had been praising/narrating the deeds of Krishna, a God, on the other Yudhisthra was upset because of his being responsible for causing death of millions of people, including his brothers, gurus etc. He was not able to console himself inspite of having been consoled by Krishna and others in many ways. This is the law of this universe, that unless one comes out of the Ram 'maya' created by passion, greed, pride etc., one cannot get relief in this universe. Yudhisthra, even though a very religious person, had not been able to come out of these worldly involvements and hence this upsetting. Krishṇa then took Yudhisthra and others to Bhishmapitamaha, who had been counting his days so that they could get consoled after listening to him. After all it is one's own, who could console better and in an effective way than many others in whose case it is considered as only a traditional ritual. As per protocol, while going to Kurukshetra to meet Bhishma, Yudhisthra was in the front followed by his other brothers, Vyas Muni etc. as the king had to lead the others. They all paid respects to Bhishma. At that time, all rajas, rishis and munis had also come there. They had come to listen to Bhishma, who was expert in religion and ruling the kingdom as to what, where and when is to be done. He paid respects to all rishis etc. He also knew Krishna as God. He, therefore, worshipped Krishna from his heart as also outwardly. This was all being done as per protocol. Bhishma asked the Pandvas as to why they were so much upset even after gaining rajya and having all rishis etc. (including Shri Krishna) with them. He told that Pandu had died in young age when they were all too young and had suffered many difficulties. All these difficulties and achievements are ordained by God himself and the man cannot change what is written in his fortune otherwise how the Pandvas, with whom Krishna was always there to help them and the brave and experts in dhanush vidya like Arjun were with them, could be expected to go through all those difficult times. Bhishma, therefore, told Pandvaas to take all that had happened as the wish of almighty God and now rule the kingdom for the well-being of the public at large. He even told that Krishna was the overall Lord and God and it is he, who had been monitoring the entire show in the guise of a human being. He was God incarnate and not mere their cousin brother. He keeps the well-being of everyone in view that is why he had appeared here to bless Bhishma when he was dying. Yudhisthra asked him many questions with a view to redress all his doubts about religion. As is already said, one cannot uphold religion, if one has doubts about its existence and does not have full belief in it. Yudhisthra was upset because he was under the shadow of God's 'Maya' and one cannot get riddance from the clutches of 'maya' till one is completely religious and one cannot be completely religious unless one has full belief without an iota of doubt in it. Bhishma narrated all about the institution of Varnashram, the fundamentals of Hinduism, and people's karma and religiously following the same, in addition to the tenets of vairagya, gyan, religion, rajdharma (duties of a king), attainment of salvation etc. in brief, and in detail as per requirement. He also narrated the man's desires in attaining dharma, richness (Arth), fulfilment of ambition (काम) and in the end salvation (मोक्ष). Then came the end of the life of Bhishma. He made himself fully absorbed in Lord Krishna and allowed his soul to depart from the body, after praising Krishna. After that Krishna and Yudhisthra went to Hastinapur and Yudhisthra started ruling as per religious verdicts.

Yudhisthra was in peace after having listened to the sermons of Bhishma since the Pandvas had no selfish interest and they wanted to rule as per vedic concept.

पित्रा चानुमतो राजा वासुदेवानुमोदितः,
चकार राज्यं धर्मेण, पितृपैतामहं विभुः। (1-10-49)

Concept of 'Dharma-rajya' would confirm that all canons of ruling (rajya) have been indicated in our shastras. These would include all working as per varnas and ashramas. The king would do everything for the well-being of the praja and the praja in turn would do all that is possible for the kingdom. If everything is done as per religion, then rains would be in time; there would be no famine (in case there was one, the king was held responsible for having somewhere ignored the religious discourse); there were no young deaths; no chronic ailments; the brahmins were educated and they taught others too; the kshatriyas protected the kingdom from foreign invasions; any expansion of kingdom was not for the sake of greed but to annihilate the bad ruler and then handing over the kingdom to be ruled as per rules under suzerainty of the overall samrat. The samrat had been conducting Aswamedha yagyas from time to time to establish his sovereignty over smaller rajas; to collect money for the central empire and to keep all gods happy so that they did not cause any harm to the people of the kingdom. All brothers had been working under one leadership of Yudhisthra. There were many cows in the gaushalas and so there was no dearth of milk. So much so that even the rivers, ocean and mountains had been awarding to the kingdom, whatsoever was asked for from them.

After establishment of rajya in Hastinapur, Krishna begged for permission to go to Dwarka. Here Krishna, although was God, but was living in the kingdom of Yudhisthra as an human being. Therefore, for leaving from that place he, as per protocol, had to ask for permission to depart. King also permitted him after performing protocolic requirements, some (of equal age) embraced him, some (younger in age) bowed before him. At that time Krishna was so much popular and was a part of the Rajyavansha that Kunti, Daropadi, Dhritrastra, Subhadra, Gandhari, Kripacharya, Bhima, Nakul, Sehdeva etc. felt unconsciousness due to the separation of Krishna, indicating that a person once under the protection of the Lord, cannot afford to be without that protection ever as he would have dedicated himself and everything to him and would feel orphaned without his protection. The ladies were full of tears on Krishna's departure but they did not allow the tears to come out lest it should cause bad omen at the time of Krishna's departure. This would indicate that for every occasion the good and bad omens had been indicated and the people took care of avoiding the bad omens and welcomed happening of the good omens. In Ramcharitmanas too when Ram left Ayodhya, bad omens started happening in Lanka indicating a bad time in wait for the Lankans. Similarly when Raja Dasratha started for Ram's marriage, all good omens had been happening indicating a peaceful marriage. So, to make the occasion of departure assimilable and pleasant, although a separation of the beloved one was rather shocking, the music was in full play and all people present to witness the departure had only smiles. Arjun held the umbrella in respect; others held chanwar in their hands; flowers were being thrown from all sides; the brahmins had been showering their ashirwad on Krishna. Those, who had dedicated themselves and got absorbed in Lord Krishna as God, had been looking into him in the capacity of Brahama, who comes as incarnate to protect Hari bhaktas and for annihilating the asuras. Raja Yudhisthra had, for escorting Krishna to Dwarka, deputed many sainiks on elephants, horses, chariots and on foot as per protocol. The Pandvas too accompanied Krishna for quite some distance out of affection and protocol. Then Krishna returned them after consoling them. On the other side, the people of Dwarka were upset because of the separation from Krishna for such a long period (entire duration of Mahabharat and subsequently establishment of Yudhisthra's rajya). When Krishna blowed his shankh (shell), all came to know that Krishna had come and all came out of their houses to welcome Shri Krishna. Although Shri Krishna is perfect within himself yet the praja presented him with many things to welcome. Everyone felt fulfilled after seeing Shri Krishna back to Dwarka and narrated their woes in separation, whenever Krishna left Dwarka and went to Hastinapur, etc. Like Hastinapur during Yudhisthra's rajya, Dwarka too (where Lord Krishna himself ruled) was protected from all sides by his brave sons, and other Yadvas. All weathers were fruitful; there was full production from land; rains were in time; the trees, rivers, etc. gave their all to the kingdom. On the way bandanwars (garlands) had been hung in the streets and roads to welcome Shri Krishna. Banners were displayed and music was on the play; people were standing on the way on both sides to receive their raja. Such welcome is done even in present days to welcome the king of other countries etc. Balram and Krishna's sons etc. went forward to receive Krishna by putting on elephant first (representing Ganesh, who is remembered first before starting any job), then the brahmins, mahajanas, musicians, even the ladies too on their chariots came forward to receive Krishna. Here there is a mention of ladies too coming forward to receive Krishna in their chariots, would indicate that in Krishna kingdom, women must have been quite learned, educated and had been granted equal rights together with men folk at that time.

वारमुख्याश्च शतशो यानैस्तद्दर्शनोत्सुकाः
लसत्कुण्डलनिर्भात कपोल वदनश्रियः। (1-11-19)

Whereas the residents of Dwarka were doing their part of job in welcoming Krishna back to Dwarka, Shri Krishna too had some protocol to observe. He conducted himself with all the brother and other people as per their capacity and capability. To some he bowed in respect; some were embraced; with some he shook hands; to some he only verbally conveyed wishes and for some he simply smiled—this all he did as per everybody's wishes. This way he pleased everyone, including the 'shudras'. Here, including 'shudras', has been intentionally mentioned by the poet as in those days shudras were excluded as untouchables. But the poet has clearly stated that all had a role to play in all state functions irrespective of caste, creed etc. In other words, there was equality before law for all people and the concept of equality before law of the present day is nothing new to Hindus/Indians. Similarly women were also not excluded as already indicated and they too marched with the men-folk in all state functions. As at the time of departure from Indraprastha, in Dwarka too, there was umbrella on Krishna's head held by some one and chanwar was held by others; flowers were being showered from all sides as per usual protocol observed on departures and receptions. Further, following social protocol laid down in this regard, Krishna at first went to the mahal of his parents and bowed in the feet of all mothers and the mothers after blessing him, made him sit in their laps. They were very happy. Then after taking permission from the mothers, went to his leisurely Raj Bhawan, where there were separate Rajmahals for each of his sixteen thousand wives. The wives were very happy and got lost in that happiness. They even forgot the normal protocol to be observed and were fully absorbed in their husband. They embraced him and tears of happiness flowed down their cheeks despite all restraint. They were very happy to meet Lord Krishna although Lord Krishna was always with them when they were alone—must be spiritually. Shri Krishna had, without handling any armaments, conquered many rajas by creating division between them and thus making them fight with each other and in the process killing lakhs of sainiks of those rajas. With this, Krishna became the overall Lord of them all and they all became his vassals. Modern concept of 'Divide and Rule' followed by English during their rule in India, had always been followed in India in the past too. Ram had made Bali and Sugreeva fight with each other and having given refuge to Vibheeshan, conquered Ravan having known all his secrets. Krishna had used it immensely in his period. He had practically become overall Lord only by creating division in various Rajas and making them fight with each other and subsequently conquering the winner. Thus creating all his vassals. In Rajput period it was the division between Jaichand and Prithvi Raj, which is responsible for Mohammed Ghori's victory and consequently establishment of Muslim rule in India. Subsequently also all Muslim invaders had taken advantage of division in various rajas in India and established their rule. English of course were very expert in this technique. They won the battle of Plassy—their first ever victory with an Indian ruler—by winning over Siraj ud-daula's (the ruler) commander-in-chief and subsequently uprooting him too.

Subsequently also they made one Raja fight against the other and in the process became overall Lord. Even at the time of first war of Independence in 1857 (mutiny) when English had virtually been defeated in Delhi and UP and were practically being thrown out of the country, they, with the help of Sikhs and Panjabi soldiers (whom they hard made loyal to themselves) won over the forces in Delhi and captured Red Fort and subsequently slowly and slowly suppressed other revolting forces in Jhansi, Mysore etc. and once again established British rule in India to rule for a further period of about 90 years. During this 90 years' period too, they ruled by creating a division amongst the Indians on the basis of religion and caste and creed. This division on the basis of religion had led to the division of the subcontinent, which would have become a great force combined of present India, Pakistan and Bangladesh. English had realised this fact and, therefore, they created a gulf between Hindus and Muslims and encouraged Muslims to ask for creation of a country for themselves *e.g.* Pakistan. Most unfortunate part of the theory of 'Divide and Rule' is its application in present day India by the ruling party by creating a gulf on the basis of not only religion but also caste and creed and provincialism for their benefit without caring for the integration of the country. Be as it may, Lord Krishna had created division amongst the Rajas with a view to annihilate the rajas, who were asuras (bad rulers) as also to finish the small kingdoms and uniting them into bigger kingdoms under Chakraborty Emperor Ugarsen, Yudhisthra, etc. but the present division is virtually leading to smaller inlets within the country. Further, Lord Krishna, being an almighty God, was neither attracted by the wealth and women gathered from various rajas by defeating them nor involved in the same as he otherwise was overall Lord of the entire universe and a small number of rajas of India and their wealth and passion of a few thousand women had no meaning for him.

Coming to Hastinapur, Parikshit having been saved by Shri Krishna in womb had born as successor of throne. Yudhisthra had been ruling considering the entire praja like his children as a king should do. He had divested himself of all worldly passions as per Lord Krishna's sermon. This is what is Plato's theory of state in which the best managed state would be when the king has no selfish interest so that he keeps himself divested of all interests. He is not even allowed to marry and have his children so that he does not develop any vested interest. Similar was the set- up in Ram Rajya, where Ram had even separated from Sita and his sons for the satisfaction of the public at large. Similar was the start of Yudhisthra's rule. He being an overall Chakravarty king of many vassals, had lot of wealth. He had performed many yagnas. He was liked by his praja. Inspite of all wealth and leisures and pleasures available, Yudhisthra could only think of God and not getting absorbed in the worldly passions/ambitions.

अपीपलद्धर्मराजः पितृवद् रंजयन् प्रजाः,
निःस्पृहः सर्वकामेभ्यः कृष्णपादाब्जसेवया। (1-12-4)

It is said that Yudhisthra was so much caring for the state and not using a single penny of the state for himself that once he thought of performing Aswamedh yagya but found that in the exchequer, there was no money except that collected from public as land tax and he could not spent anything for such a yagya from such money. He was upset and subsequently his people found some wealth left by Raja Marut of Panjab on which he had the right and with that money only he performed the yagya. In those days Raja Marut of Panjab had held a yagya in which all utensils used were made of gold. After the yagya, the raja threw all those utensils in the kingdom of Yudhisthra. Also the alms given in the yagya to brahmins were so many that they could not carry these all and threw a major part towards Yudhisthra's kingdom. Yudhisthra's people collected all these and with these only, performed the yagya as on such thrown-away wealth, the first right is that of the king. Even now this rule is followed and all things under the earth belong to the state only.

Before Mahabharat, Vidur had left Hastinapur. After having attained gyan through Maitriya Rishi after redressal of all his doubts (Redressal of all doubts in way of attainment of gyan is a must as without it, there is no possibility of full belief and consequently no vairagya). That is why the need of a guru is indicated, who could remove all doubts. So Vidur after having redressal of all doubts in way of attainment of vairagya, came back to Hastinapur. In Hastinapur, every one was very happy. Kunti, Yudhisthra, Dharitrastra etc. all went to receive him as per protocol; he being the brother of Pandva and Dharitrastra and more enlightened. He met every one by embracing, bowing, blessing as required by protocol in each case. Yudhisthra made him sit on sinhasan. This too was a protocol to offer the sinhasan to guru and elders like guru. He paid respects to Vidur and served meals and made him take rest. Vidur stayed there for a long time. During his stay once he told Dharitrastra that his end was nearing. He, therefore, should quit this universe and adopt sanyas as prescribed in vedas. Further, living at the mercy of the killers of his sons was a curse.

अहो महीयसी जन्तोर्जीविताशा यया भवान्,
भीमापवर्जितं पिण्डमादत्ते गृहपालवत्। (1-13-22)

One should not get involved in the universe and have desire to live long in this universe even humiliating oneself to the extent Dharitrastra was living at the mercy of Pandvas. He, therefore, advised Dharitrastra to secretly depart from that place and go to Himalayas, where he should live for the rest of his life devoting the same to the cause of almighty. Dharitrastra got enlightened and left for Himalayas. Vidur here acted as a guru to Dharitrastra. When one is strayed, then someone, by slightest enlightenment can put him out of that straying. Gandhari too followed him. Next day when Yudhisthra could not find Dharitrastra, Gandhari and Vidur, he enquired about their whereabouts from everyone and was thinking that he must have caused some humiliation to them as a result of which they left. The great persons owe responsibility to themselves for any wrong happened in the state rather than finding some scapegoat for thrusting the cause on him. Then by chance Narad appeared on the scene. On having been asked about the whereabouts of the three, Narad told that meeting of the various persons and their separation is all already written in fortune and one should not care for the same. Here Narad had even indicated the concept of "bigger fish eating the smaller ones".

अहस्तानि सहस्तानाम पदानि चतुष्पदाम
फल्गूनि तत्र महतां जीवो जीवस्य जीवनम्। (1-13-46)

This is how the God plays his part in running the universe. Here none is above the other one and God is the greatest of the fishes, who controls all creatures. He told that Dharitrastra, Gandhari and Vidur had gone to Himalaya for performing Bhagwad bhakti. They had already been absolved of all their sins and involvements. Narad also told that in Himalayas itself, after a few days, Dharitrastra will leave his body followed by Gandhari and then Vidur would leave for pilgrimage. This consoled Yudhisthra.

Arjun had gone to Dwarka to meet Shri Krishna. When he did not return for several months, Yudhisthra started having fears and bad omens. People had started becoming unpious and irreligious and the wealths were not regular. The mutual relations had come to an end and each one was quarrelling with the other. Such things start happening when bad times come. Narad had told that Shri Krishna would wind up all his family. Yudhisthra doubted if that time had come. He, therefore, felt some havoc to take place in the circumstances. Meantime Arjun returned from Dwarka but he was quite sad. Yudhisthra enquired whether all in Dwarka was peaceful and whether anyone had insulted him there as he was quite upset. Arjun was already upset in separation from Shri Krishna and then Yudhisthra had put so many questions. He could not reply. He somehow consoled himself and told that Shri Krishna had snatched all his strength because of separation from him. He had because of the blessing of Shri Krishna married Daropadi; conquered the gods, including Inder; killed lacs of soldiers in Mahabharat and won the battle and had conquered many rajas, who presented all their valuables to the Rajya. But now without Shri Krishna's blessings, he had been rendered helpless. On return from Dwarka, he had been escorting some of Shri Krishna's wives but on the way the tribals defeated him and he could not protect those ladies. He was same Arjun, with same Gandeeva Dhanush and same chariot, before whom even the bravest could not stay, but could not even defeat the tribals. The family of Krishna in Dwarka had been cursed by brahmins that it would vanish. So they took excessive drinks and fought amongst themselves killing each other. All have, therefore, been annihilated. This infact is the spiritual power (maya) of the almighty that the people, whom he creates and brings them up, fight and kill each other like God creates, brings up and annihilates the creatures. This is also like the motto of "Big fish eating the smaller one". The braves kill the weaks and poors. At first Krishna was able to kill many rajas through his sons etc. and in the end same Krishna had been responsible for the killing of all Yaduvanshis in Dwarka. Thinking every time of Krishna Lila, Arjun had become fully devoted to Krishna and had been absolved of all materialistic involvements. He remembered the Gita Gyan sermonised by Krishna at the beginning of Mahabharat. He attained Brahm gyan and was free from the effect of 'maya'. Then he told that Shri Krishna too had gone to his loka. After hearing all this, Yudhisthra thought that their time to enjoy worldly leisures and pleasures had gone and decided to adopt sanyas. Kunti too after hearing the entire episode got herself absorbed in Brahma and left the universe by dint of her bhakti. With Krishna having left the universe, the Kalyug stepped in with all its clutches, *e.g.* spread of greed, violence (हिंसा), deception, and irreligiousness amongst the people. Yudhisthra handed over the rajya to his grand son Parikshit, and adopted Sanyas, leaving the grihastha. He left all his belongings and had become detached from the materialistic world. Arjun, Bhima etc. brothers too, followed Yudhisthra. They became fully devoted to Lord Krishna and ultimately got absorbed in him, leaving the universe.

The poet has here tried to say that there is an intimate relation between the man and the God and whatever man does is with the blessings of the God only. He only determines the path for each one of us and makes us walk on that path; sometimes getting derailed and again entracking and so on. All achievements and failures are as per his direction only and he tries to keep the people happy in the universe but wishes that ultimately people can attain fulfilment after submitting themselves to him. This is the spiritual relation or protocol between man and God.

Parikshit started ruling the Kingdom as a Chakravarty Raja. He had four sons and held several Aswamedha yagyas establishing his suzerainty on the rajas under him as vassals. Kalyug had stepped in during his regime. Parikshit having known that Kalyug was entering, started to capture him. In the process he conquered all rajas in the west. He heard the goodness of Pandvaas and their affection for Shri Krishna. He was happy to hear all this. He developed more bhakti of Shri Krishna. He, during his Digvijya yatra, saw a shudra beating a cow and an ox. Parikshit challenged the shudra and told him that he had, by beating the cow and ox, incurred crime punishable by death. He also asked the ox whether as on ox he was actually dharma and the cow the Prithvi and the shudra the Kalyug. Parikshit said that the raja, in whose reign the people have fear of criminals, loses all his admiration, leisure, pleasure in this life and the next life too. The raja had to protect all his subject from all kinds of ailments—

यस्य राष्ट्रे प्रजाः सर्वास्त्रस्यन्ते साध्व्यसाधुभिः,
तस्य मत्तस्य नश्यन्ति कीर्तिरायुर्भगो गतिः। (1-17-10)

Dharma told that being the successor of Pandvas, it was apt for him to assure like that. He further told that the people, who did believe in dualism (द्वैत), considered themselves responsible for all evil happenings. Some say it was in fortune, whereas the others attribute it to their karma; some say these are because of their temperaments and some say these are God-gifted only. Some people even feel that a reason for good or bad happening could not always be given. Parikshit consoled the dharma and the Prithvi (cow and ox) and undertook to annihilate Kalyug before he entered his kingdom. Kalyug also having seen Parikshit duly committed, begged to be pardoned. Parikshit rather than killing him only told him to go away from his kingdom in view of the Kalyug having sought refuse under him. Kalyug then told that since Parikshit was the overall Lord of entire universe, no place was left where he could go. Parikshit then told him to live at four places *e.g.* gambling dens, drinking places, love-making places, and places where violence was committed. On Kalyug's request Parikshit allowed him to live in wealth too. Kalyug, therefore, started living in these five places, which symbolised untruthfulness, pride, passion, cruelty and greed. The poet has by mentioning this episode, warned the people not to get involved in these five places. Dharma and Prithvi then left the place and Parikshit went to his Rajmahal.

Once Raja Parikshit had gone to forest for hunting. On the way he became very thirsty. He could not get water anywhere. He then found an Ashram of a rishi. He went there and asked for water but the rishi was in samadhi and so could neither see the raja having come there nor could listen to what he said. On this raja thought that rishi was only pretending to be in samadhi and was not actually so. So he got enraged and left the place. While going he saw a dead snake lying there. He took that snake and put it in rishis neck and went away. The rishi's son had gone to take bath in the river. Some of rishi's disciples told the son of what had happened. Without knowing, who that person was, he cursed that he would die after 7 days due to the biting by a snake (Takshka). When the rishi came to know of the son having passed on the curse on the raja, he rebuked his son that he should not have passed such a curse without knowing on whom and for what that curse was being passed on.

Here several concepts of social protocol come into play—

(1) The raja should not be so much proud of his position as to dishonour the rishis whom they always respected and worshipped.

(2) Even if the raja got enraged, he should not have thrown the dead snake in the neck of the rishi as it caused the rishi's dishonour.

(3) Parikshit himself was quite knowledgeable of all these concepts but it has to be accepted that the coming

events make the man oblivious of what he had been doing (under Hari 'Maya').

(4) As per Hinduism's fundamental, brahmin is a respected person and each person has to act as per dharma of his varna and wherever there has been a departure from such following, there has been great loss.

(5) The brahmin (especially the rishi) should be able to pardon anyone for any fault and leave it to the raja or the almighty, as the case may be, to punish him for the default and should not become the judge on the crime committed by someone.

(6) One should not pass on the curse (particularly a rishi) as it finishes one's tapsya, being down with rage, on a person without first knowing the facts and circumstances and the personality of the person on whom the curse was being passed on.

(7) The job of the raja is to protect the subjects for any wrong being done to them and should not as such cause any wrong to anyone himself.

(8) The rishi after knowing that his son had passed on the curse on the raja, did not appreciate his son's action and said that he had punished the raja, who always cared for the subjects so much, so heavily for a small omission on his part. He should not have considered the raja as an ordinary person as on raja devolves the well-being of crores of people. Around raja devolves so may other aspects of human life also like :

(a) Under raja's protection, the public at large is safe.

(b) If there is no raja, there would be chaos and anarchy and the people would vanish killing each other.

(c) In the absence of a raja, the thieves and dacoits would raise their heads as then there would be none to punish them.

(d) The women, children, wealth, etc. would not be safe.

(e) The institution of varna and ashram would collapse resulting in the collapse of the entire system.

(f) People would indulge in all kinds of vices as there would be none to check them.

(9) Parikshit was fully devoted to Lord Krishna and had performed several Aswamedha yagyas. He had come to the ashram upset with hunger and thirst and on his having come to the ashram, it was their duty to have entertained him. The raja got enraged because he was not attended to by anyone at the ashram. Serving water atleast is what should have been done in the ashram. There was, therefore, a lapse on the part of the residents of the ashram only for which he had to face the curse.

(10) The rishi only prayed to God to excuse his son for having done such a great sin in having passed on the curse on such a noble raja. Rishi's son too regretted his having passed the curse on the raja.

(11) The rishi rather than finding fault in others for the wrongs done to them, tried to find the fault within themselves resulting in the other party getting enraged and having done the bad deed.

(12) On the other hand the raja, after reaching the capital, when recollected what he had done, during the day to the rishi, he very much regretted and expected some bad consequence of the same and the raja too wished it to enable him to atone for the wrong done by him and promised never to repeat it. This was the protocolic approach of a raja toward praja for any wrong having been done by him. Meantime raja came to know of his being bitten by Takshka snake after a week due to the curse of the rishi's son on what raja had done to the rishi. The raja was happy to know it as this had given him a chance to leave the universe and become a sanyasi.

The raja handed over the rajya to his son and went in sanyas to Ganga for Krishna bhakti. Many rishis too came there with their disciples. Even Atri, Vashistha, Viswamitra,

Bhirgu,Gautam etc. great munis, dev-rishis, brahm-rishis and raj-rishis had come there. As per protocol, the raja welcomed them all and told of what he intended doing. He felt obliged in having the darshan of all rishis etc. and praised the rishi for the curse passed on him. He told that he had submitted completely to the Lord Krishna and was now not afraid of being bitten by Takshka as now his body belonged to Krishna only. He prayed to be blessed that in whatever specie he comes on rebirth, he would wish to be Krishna bhakta. All rishis appreciated his determination and undertook to stay there till raja got salvation. The raja asked them to advise him (1) the best task to be undertaken by all in such a situation and (2) the task particularly to be completed in short span of time available before death.

सर्वात्मना म्रिय माणैश्च कृत्यं,
शुद्धंच तत्रामृशताभियुक्ताः। (1-19-24)

At that time Shukdeva Rishi of his own reached there. He was above the concept of varna and ashram and was self contented. Here the poet has tried to make out that although the institutions of varan and ashram were in existence at that time, yet the people could reach above these too by dint of great tapsya. In other words these concepts were not a must for everyone to follow for ultimate fulfilment like even Viswamitra although an kshatriya, had become a Brahm-rishi by dint of his tapsya. Karan (although originally Kunti's son) a son of Radhey (shudra) had become a great warrior and the Raja of Anga Desh. Although he had come there unproclaimed yet the rishis recognised him and all stood in his honour as per protocol. Raja too bowed his head in honour and worshipped him. Having been honoured by all, Shukdeva took his seat. Raja then got up and after praising him for having come there to help him attain salvation, requested him to advise him what a person should do, who is likely to die shortly and also to advise what jap, tap etc. should be performed by public at large. Shukdeva ji then started replying the questions.

Skandh – II

This chapter contains the spiritual protocol between man and God and how with the fulfilment of this protocol one can attain salvation.

Shukdeva stated that whatever Parikshit had asked was of great public interest. The grihastha spends, rather wastes, his time in thinking and doing so many things with which he is concerned in that situation. Such persons are always after wealth and women, although these all fulfil the mortal vices only. A man should make himself such that atleast at the time of death, he remembered God.The rishi told that although he fully believed in the Nirguna God, yet after studying Shrimad Bhagwat written by his father, he had converted himself into a Saguna bhakta. People,who have belief in him (Lord Krishna) get absorbed in him after listening to Bhagwat, and attain salvation. Raj-rishi Khatwanga had attained salvation within two hours before his death by submitting himself to God. One should not, therefore, have fear of dying. One should rather get rid of worldly ambitions and vices and sit at a lonely place in solitude in memory of Shri Krishna. He should remember "अ उ म". He should concentrate his mind on this jap removing himself from the thinking of all evil matters, and absorb himself in God. Even if the mind still does not get concentrated, he should not get afraid and again try to concentrate. This effort will by and by take him out of all vices. One should, therefore, attain control on all his ambitions (passions) and get absorbed in Saguna Bhagwan. He will find all world already in God. Infact God is already in the innermost of the human beings, consisting of water, air, space, earth, fire, nature and the most import gradient the God. One, therefore, has to recognise oneself only. This would lead to the attainment of almighty. The air, rivers, mountains, vedas, sun, moon, universe, brahmlok, all gods, all directions, earth, fire, Brahma, Shiva, trees, day and night, the animals and lands, human beings and gandharva, asuras, brahmins, kshatriyas, vaishas, and shudras, etc. all combinedly constitute the almighty God. One, therefore, should worship only that God, who is a compound of everything seen and thought of.

Brahma, in the beginning of this creation, thought of the God and got from him the art of creating the universe. People read vedas but these are so deep to be understood and one gets confused and does not attain salvation. One should rather lessen one's desires to the utmost minimum and in this way when one gets detached from the wordly materials and subsequently by remembering the God with all concentration, one would get absorbed in him (God). It is easier for the human being, to, in the first instance, concentrate on Vishnu Bhagwan in the complete Chaturbhuj form. This should be started at first from one part and then, concentrating on other parts one-by-one.This is the almighty God—both Nirguna and Saguna and by concentrating on this Saguna Chaturbhuj, one reaches the Nirguna God Itself. When one reaches this stage, one is above all the three, satva, rajo and tamo gunas. The poet has also told the way in which one should end his life. This shows the extent of spiritualism existing in India, and shows how to live, how to die and how to concentrate in memory of God and ultimately get absorbed in God. By practice this is all possible although unless tried, this all appears only mythological. This in fact is the most practical approach for a grihast to attain salvation in the end and does not then come again in this universe in any form. This, the rishi indicated, is the way narrated in vedas and shastras and is tedious to be followed by the people in Kalyug. He, therefore, stated that in Kalyug, where the grihast does not want to adopt these rather tougher methods, Krishna bhakti in Saguna form, is the only other easier way, which could be followed by any one but for this too, one will have to divest himself from all worldly desires/vices/belongings and then only the concentration in Shri Krishna would be possible. One should, therefore, constantly, at all times and in all situations and with all the might at his disposal, keep oneself busy in listening to, reading and speaking of the Krishna leela (conduct) narrated by saints. The worship of particular god is in respect of what that god can give such as Indra can give all materialistic pleasures, Shiva can give strength and so on but the bhakti of Krishna awards everything including salvation and this bhakti is possible only by listening to Bhagwat.

अकामः सर्वकामो वा मोक्षकाम उदारधीः,
तीव्रेण भक्तियोगेन यजेत पुरुषं परम्। (2-3-10)

The entire Bhagwat is a dialogue between Raja Parikshit and Muni Shukdeva as both were Krishna bhaktas right from the childhood. To afford confirmation to the katha, it is said to have been narrated by either God himself or a respected muni. Ramcharit Manas is a narration of Ramkatha by Shiva to Parvati. Shiva, also redressed all the doubts in the mind of Parvati about bonafides of Ram's lila as incarnation of God. At places even Ram had explained the fundamentals *e.g.* creator and creature (ब्रह्म-जीव) relation etc. Similarly, Srimad Bhagwat has been narrated by Muni Shukdeva, who is also said to be a Bhagwan himself, to Raja Parikshit, when Parikshit had a notice of seven days to die and here too in these seven days entire Bhagwat had been narrated redressing all doubts which arose in the mind of Parikshit for the satisfaction and developing belief in the minds of public at large. After hearing the ingredients of Krishna lila, Parikshit, already absolved of all wordly attachments, fully devoted himself to God to listen to the narration by Muni Shukdeva. Full submission to God is necessary to understand him. Parikshit thus raised the basic question of how Bhagwan creates the universe; how does he bring up and how in the end he annihilates it. Also when Bhagwan also exists in the creature, then how he can annihilate his ownself and how a creator annihilates his own creation.

On this question having been asked, as per protocol, Shukdeva remembered Krishna before starting narration of his katha. Then he mentioned the various actions of God as creator, maintainer and annihilater of universe; the innermost of all his bhaktas, the creator of vedas, shastras and the one being worshipped by all. Similar question had been raised by Narad to Brahma and the God had replied to that question. Here the poet, even not satisfied with what Shukdeva would have said for creating more belief in people, has narrated the situation through the medium of God himself on the following questions having been asked by Narad—

(1) What the universe has been created for ?

(2) What is the basis of this universe ?

(3) Who had created the universe ?

(4) Who causes annihilation of the universe ?

(5) Who holds it up for creation to annihilation ?

(6) What in fact this universe is ?

(7) How does the God exist ?

(8) Is there anyone, who controls even God ?

(9) What is the shape and the features of God ?

(10) Why inspite of being God himself, Brahma had performed serious tapsya, which would indicate that there is someone above Brahma too. If so, then who he is?

Brahma told Narad that he had raised these questions for the well-being of the people of the universe. He also told that unless one is able to know, who above Brahma is, one cannot know, who in fact Brahama is?

(1) God created universe to make him appear in many forms.

(2) For this purpose he saw within himself the kal, karma and swabhava (काल, कर्म और स्वभाव). Kal is responsible for creation of the three—tamoguna, rajoguna and satvaguna—swabhava transforms these three gunas from one to another and karma is responsible for this transformation.

(3) The universe was initially like an egg lying in water. God gave life to that egg by virtue of his powers of

kal, karma and swabhava. From the egg was born a person with thousands of hands, legs, mouths etc. Brahmins are the mouth of that person; kshatriyas are the arms, vaishas are abdomen and thighs and shudras are legs. This almighty person is the combination of all worldly things eg. the foodgrains, juices, water, air, fire, medicines, smells, sun, moon, beauty, yagyas, cloud, all metals, electricity, and the lokpals to protect the universe comprising of human beings, animals, birds etc. Since these all things in universe are creation of God, they are the part of that self. When Brahma was born out of that almighty, he attained all his ingredients from that almighty. He also collected the things of use in the universe for him only and from these the universe had been created by Brahma.

(4) Having created the universe and further causing more and more creations, question arose that a part should be continued to be annihilated also. God, therefore, by his another power (शक्ति) owned the job of annihilation of the universe. (by and by).

(5) It is only the God, who by his shakti Brahma created the universe and then he himself holds it up (brings it up) and ultimately by his third power *i.e.* Shiva annihilates it. God, therefore, by his three different powers causes creation, maintenance and annihilation of universe.

(6) The universe is nothing but the combination of many species of creatures and the things needed for their maintenance in the universe. These things have been created for the use of various kinds of creatures suiting their requirements such as trees and their products for birds, grass, plants, and earthly products for the animals and all these and other products for the human beings.

(7) God with all his forms, exists in this universe comprising of earth, patal and akash.

(8) As already indicated, God runs the universe by his three shaktis of creation, maintenance and

annihilation and the one, who monitors these three shaktis, is God himself. There is none above him. In fact these shaktis of God also act on his behalf and are, therefore, considered as Gods themselves and since these powers owe themselves to the almighty, that almighty is overall God. Here we also find the principle of division of labour even existing in the realm of God like the one in present day universe and governance and continuing as such from the time of the creation of the universe.

(9) As already indicated, God from within himself at first created his three shaktis of creation, maintenance and annihilation and then for creating further creatures in the universe, he, from out of himself, created earth, water, space, air and fire which go into the making of the creatures. Then these creatures required something to live up on in this universe. So, for that purpose he created, trees, foodgrains,metals, medicines, fruits, etc. Since all these things are the creation of God from within himself, these can be said to be part of the almighty and hence the almighty lives in all these things.

(10) As already indicated, almighty God,wanted assistance of someone to create, maintain and annihilate this universe. So he created Brahma, Vishnu and Mahesh for these purposes. Therefore, Brahma, Vishnu and Mahesh are the three Shaktis of that almighty God, who controls the action of all these three shaktis and there is none above that almighty God.

Although the almighty God created the universe through his shakti Brahma, maintains the same through Vishnu and annihilates through Mahesh, the universe having once been created, the creatures started doing actions which were not being tolerated by others and in this way an anarchy or chaos started taking place in the universe. To remove that chaos and put the universe on right path as enshrined in vedas by the almighty, the almighty God had to come as incarnate in one of the forms created by him and vanishing after doing that job. In this chain did the God come incarnation as :

(1) Vraha to kill Hirnakshya, the first asura,who created anarchy and then started living in water. So God came as Vraha and killed Hirnakshya in water itself.

(2) Second was as Suyagya, also named Hari when he created God and annihilated asuras from the universe.

(3) Third was as Kapil.

(4) Fourth was Dattatreya when he lead to salvation, Raja Yadu and Suhasra Arjun.

(5) Fifth was as Sanak, Sanandan, Santan, and Sanat Kumar when he saved the earth from devastation and coached the rishis of self realisation gyan (आत्मज्ञान).

(6) Sixth was Nar and Narayan.

(7) As Prithu.

(8) Risabh Deva.

(9) Hayagriva.

(10) Matsya, when he, through a boat, saved the universe from being sunk.

(11) Kachhyap (कच्छप) when he served Amrit to gods and poison to asuras.

(12) Narsingha, when he saved Prahlad by killing Harinakshyap.

(13) As Vaman, when he measured the entire universe in 3 steps and in this way killed the pride of Raja Bali. Bali was fully devout of God. God, therefore, could not harm him but the gods and Indra were afraid of his tapsya and yagya. They, therefore, went and requested the almighty God to save them. God, therefore, had to go to Raja Bali as a beggar only as otherwise he had no cause of killing him, being fully devoted to God. In this way he proved that where one has no alternative to defeat anyone, one has to resort to begging by dint of which, he could be captured, although not defeated.

(14) As Parsuram, he killed all kshatriyas, who had left their dharma of prajapalan and had started indulging

in worldly passions creating anarchy for others. So, to kill such kshatriya rajas, God came as incarnate as Parsurama.

(15) As Shri Ram along with Bharat, Lakshman and Strughana to kill the rakshasas like Ravan etc. and restore faith and belief in his bhaktas.

(16) As Krishna and Balram to kill Kansa, Shishupal and other asuras and ultimately culminating in Mahabharat.

(17) Next would be as Budha and then.

(18) As Kali Avtar when in Kalyug people would start doing irreligious jobs and creating anarchy and chaos in the universe.

Apart from these Avtaras (incarnations) of Vishnu, Brahma and Shiva too had incarnated for the purpose of creation of universe and for annihilation of certain Asuras themselves. Devotion to anyone of the God incarnations, reading/listening to his actions (लीला) in that incarnation leads the human being to attainment of salvation. Every action of human beings reaches him and he always strikes balance between the good and bad actions to determine the form/specie in which he would again come in this universe unless one gets absorbed in him by dint of his devotion or bhakti. Bhagwat is what Almighty God had narrated to Brahma and Brahma in turn to Narad and Narad to Vyas and then from Vyas, Shukdeva listened and then Shukdeva narrated to Parikshit for the well being of the people in this universe. For this purpose, Parikshit, who had already divested himself from all worldly involvements, desired to be told about how he could absorb himself in Shri Krishna. He also requested for redressal of some of his doubts in this regard. Muni Shukdeva narrated the entire protocol between the creator and the creature in a consolidated from. Bhagwan controls the creature through 'Maya'. 'Maya' has many forms and one gets indulged in one form or the other of 'Maya'. After this, he starts telling "This is me" and "This is mine". He thus gets involved in the universe but when one gets absolved of these forms of 'Maya' then he gets rid of "this is me" and "this is mine" too and in that case the effect of 'Maya' does not devolve on him and he attains salvation otherwise he continues to come in one specie or the other on each death and rebirth.

Even Brahma was not above Bhagwan's maya and he was advised of the ultimate attainment by Bhagwan after Brahma had performed a selfless long tapsya. Brahma had asked how he could know the Nirguna and Saguna forms of the almighty. He recognised that by help of 'Maya', the almighty created, naintained and annihilated the universe but how it was done was requested to be told by Brahma. The Almighty God told Brahma that, he existed even before the creation of this universe. In the universe too after its creation it was all God only. Like the body which is made of five ingredients earth, water, air, fire and space (पृथ्वी, जल, वायु, अग्नि, और आकाश), but separately in these ingredients, body cannot be seen, almighty God is available in all atmas but he cannot be seen as such in any atma and it is by gyan only that God can be seen in atma. Therefore, it proves that God is there everywhere and everytime. Bhagwan then vanished and Brahma started creating universe. He first created Narad, who had put to Brahma same question as Parikshit had put to Shukdeva and Brahma had told him Bhagwat Puran, which Bhagwan had narrated to Brahma. Subsequently Narad muni narrated the same Bhagwat to Vyas muni. From Ved Vyas, Shukdeva had learnt Bhagwat, which contains replies to all the doubts that can arise in the mind of any human being eager to know the creator of universe. The Bhagwat defines Sarga (सर्ग), Visarga (विसर्ग), Place (स्थान), Maintenance (पोषण) Uti (अति), Manwantra (मन्वन्तर), Isanukatha (ईशानुकथा), Nirodha (निरोध), Mukti (मुक्ति), and Ashray (आश्रय). Sarg includes the five element (भूमि, आकाश, आदि), Senses (इन्द्रियां) Pride (अहंकार). The mortals and immortals in the universe are Visarga. The God's art in saving the universe from chaos is place (स्थान). God's grace in his bhaktas is maintenance (पोषण). The vedas and shastras, which define dharma are Manvantras (मन्वन्तर). The passion of the people is Uti (अति). The description of God in various incarnation is Iskatha (ईशकथा). Man's getting absorbed in God is Nirodha. Finishing one's self and joining God is Mukti. The Brahm or God is one, who creates and annihilates this universe and that is Ashrya (आश्रय). The God first created water. God then created the universe. Thus for the creatures in universe, he created sensuous power, moral strength and bodily force. Then various tastes were created, which were helpful in feeding the various instincts in human being, like power to speak, walk, touch, smell, hear, see, passion etc. and other parts of the body and other needs of the people to live in the universe. These needs continued to rise as per advancement of the society and increased ambition to "Have" of the human beings. All mortals and immortals in the universe are, therefore, the various forms of God himself. One becomes God with the attainment of salvation and human being with increased rajoguna and remaim in tamoguna, when there is no virtue at all. When tamoguna increases in human beings, chaos takes place so much that even the God become fearful. In that situation God comes as incarnate in any form.

Skandh – III

Srimad Bhagwat although explains about all such incarnations, it mainly devolves around Krishna avtar in Duapur, when he killed many Asur rajas and established kingdom in Dwarka culminating in Mahabharat. Shri Krishna awarded the Paramdham to the asuras killed by him or who were killed in Mahabharat by Arjun and gave away their lives while seeing Lord Krishna in the battle field. Therefore, in a way even such asuras, as were anti Shri Krishna, were Krishna bhaktas as they had always been remembering him although with a view to harming him and, therefore, had been granted Paramdham.

Shri Krishna had thousands of queens and he had been with all of them in the night with as many forms doing justice to each of them with his company. About ten sons had born from each one of them. Having been indulged in grihastha ashram for a long time, Shri Krishna developed detachment from them and attained vairagya. These worldly lusts are the 'maya' of Ishwar and the human being too is under Ishwar's 'maya'. When even Krishna developed detachment from these lusts then how his bhakta could have belief in such lusts and worldly involvements.

तस्यैवं रममाणस्य सवतंत्सरगणान बहून्,
गृहमेधेषु योगेषु विरागः समजायत।
and दैवाधीनेषु कामेषु दैवाधीनः स्वयं पुमानः
को विस्त्रम्भेत योगेन योगेश्वर मनुव्रतः। (3-3-22/23)

Here the poet has tried to inculcate in the minds of people that too much of indulgence in any worldly lust is bad and even through the media of Shri Krishna, he has tried to establish that having possessed so many wives, ultimately he felt detatched from them and developed vairagya. Therefore, the human beings should not indulge much in worldly lusts and keep these lusts under control otherwise it would lead to excess and ultimately complete detachment. As happened in the case of Krishna, after detachment all such belongings get wasted out. It is, therefore, better to keep oneself aloof from these lusts so that one may not later on regret on their getting wasted out. All Yaduvanshis had been killed by drinking madira, which spoiled their brain and intellect and they all died killing one another. The poet has here warned against drinking saying that it not only kills the individual, it also causes loss of all relations and belongings by (1) wasting wealth and (2) then killing one's people having been blind of the addiction and influence of Madira. After all his family members had died, Shri Krishna was sitting alone in a solitude under a peepal tree when Udhava came there. Shri Krishna being in lonely place narrated to Udhava the 'Bhagwat' which would help attain salvation to the people born after Lord Krishna had left. From protocolic point of view, one can have the best coaching from the guru, when he is free from all worldly involvements and is free to spare time for the disciples. The disciples should, therefore, be on the look out for such occasion. In Ramcharit Manas too Shri Ram sitting free in solitude narrated to Lakshman on his having asked the Ishwar—Jeeva relation and how Ishwar controlled the universe. Again Shri Ram narrated to all the three brothers and Hanuman the difference between saint, non-saint and other fundamentals in Ishwar-Jeeva relation when one day they had gone out of Awadh and were sitting freely in a garden.

Udhava told Krishna that having attained Krishna bhakti, he had no desire to have any of the four attainments e.g. dharma, wealth, satisfaction of all desires, and ultimately salvation (धर्म, अर्थ, काम, मोक्ष) and that he only wanted his bhakti. Further, when Vidur wanted to know the Bhakta Darshan narrated to Udhava by Krishna, Udhava told him that the proper person for this purpose was Maitreya Rishi and he should serve him for achieving the desired narration. Here the poet has indicated the principle of —

(1) only proper person, as was having specialisation, should be approached for any particular job.

(2) such proper person only can redress all the doubts in that regard and satisfy the listeners.

(3) To have the knowledge of such competent person, one would have to serve him enough to please him to narrate the desired knowledge to the incumbent.

(4) One, having such knowledge, particularly Bhagwad bhakti, should not himself narrate it to others as he loses the effect and only the persons authorised to part with such knowledge, should share it with others.

Udhava, therefore, advised Vidur to go to Maitreya Rishi, serve him adequately and then only request him to impart such gyan to him. As per Shri Krishna's advice Udhava went to Badrinarayana and lived there involved in Shri Krishna's bhakti. Shri Krishna had created entire Dwarka and his family to help him annihilate all asuras and after the asuras had been killed, he did not feel necessity of his family members to continue to live in the universe and, therefore, managed for their annihilation through madira. The poet has tried to say that one should live in the universe as long as he has not completed his purpose and the moment it is over, one should step out otherwise it would lead to discomfort to others and in that case one would have to leave the universe in bad taste. Having reached Maitreya Rishi's ashram, Vidur, although he was since clear about the Bhagwad bhakti, requested the rishi for the general well-being of the people only, as the great men generally do, to clarify what one should do in the universe as all people in the universe work to attain peace/pleasure but they neither achieve that pleasure nor are able to get rid of the worldly troubles rather such troubles go on incresing as the man tries to get rid of the same. Vidur, therefore, requested to narrate the method to get absorbed in Bhagwan to have real peace and pleasure. Now realising that Vidur had already got himself detached from the universe and had requested him to narrate the above clarification in the interest of the public at large, Maitreya Rishi conceded to his request taking it as a public well-being cause. In our constitution and modern concept of judiciary too, there is a provision for anyone to raise Public Interest Litigation without any cost to him in any High Court or Supreme Court. The courts too deliberate on such litigation keeping the general well-being of the public at large in view. Similarly in old days too, rishis, munis, gurus and even gods used to entertain such requests considering the same for the benefit of general public and bestowed all they knew to the incumbent of such requests. Such is the reason behind Vyas Muni writing Bhagwat, Valmiki writing Ramayan, Tulsidas writing Ramcharit Manas, Shukdeva narrating Bhagwat to Parikshit, redressing all his doubts as would normally arise in the mind of people at large while going through the contents of Bhagwat. Similarly, in the context here, Maitreya Rishi entertained Vidurji as he had asked the question to be replied in public interest and he started replying to the questions after telling that he was replying to the questions as the same were for public consumption and not for Vidurji himself as he had already got himself absorbed in Bhagwad bhakti and did not need anything more.

Maitreya Rishi told that before the creation of the universe, the almighty God was alone. He then thought of creating the universe. For this purpose he at first created earth, water, fire, air and space (पृथ्वी, जल, अग्नि, वायु और आकाश) necessary for the formation of any creature in the universe. Then created the tamsic, rajasik and satwik gunas to be inculcated in the creatures as per their requirement and then the Maya to control the creatures and have a protocolic link between the creator and the creature. At first almighty God created the small gods (देवता) with satogun inculcated in them. They praised God almighty and requested for being told what they could do in the job of the creation of the universe by the almighty God. Here even in this mythological narration, the poet has indicated the Parkinson Law according to which a person, generally desires to create more jobs, then the persons to monitor those jobs, then some more persons to monitor all the jobs and so on. Here also God almighty having thought of creating the universe, first created the gods to assist him. For this purpose he created the five ingredients—earth, fire, water, air and space—in formulating the gods and then 'Maya' to control them in doing the further job entrusted to them. After creation of gods, the Almighty created the creatures by assembling the above ingredients with pride, heart and parts of various gods and a part of himself too. Thus he created Atma in each creature as his part and also the God's initial incarnate with hands, feet, eyes, ears, mouth, tongue, heart, brain, etc. and having the three gunas—sato, rajo and tamo. Subsequently he left it to individuals as to which of the three gunans became primary for each of them. One became god with extra satoguna, human being with rajoguna and animal etc. with tamoguna. God then created vedas and varna-ashramas. Four varnas were Brahmin, Kshatriya, Vaish and Shudra. Here again the division in varnas was as per the extent of gunas in individuals. This human being, with part of the almighty, has been trying to find the 'whole' but has not been able to get him and ultimately only got absorbed in remembering the lila of God in various forms and listening to Harikatha from the learned persons.

Vidurji further asked how is it that God with his 'maya' creates, maintains and annihilates the human beings and how the human being, who is never without God within himself, is effected by the influence of God's maya. Maitreya told that although it appears contradictory within itself but this infact is the effect of 'maya' controlled by God. The human being is constantly under the influence of maya, as a result of which he is not able to make use of God within himself. This can be done by realising God through his bhakti and after getting absorbed in him. The one more one gets absorbed in him, the more one is away from the influence of 'maya'. Therefore, although both maya and God, are within one's ownself, yet who of them overpower the other depend upon. the effort of the individual, who, if rises above the influence of 'maya' *i.e.* he gets out of worldly ambitions, he would be nearer to God and one who is abosrbed in worldly ambitions/wishes/involvement, he is away from God. The result, therefore, is that only one, either 'maya' or God rules the human instinct. A person, who is down with the influence of 'maya' is always upset and sufferer and one who is absorbed in God after getting out of maya's influence is deemed to have attained the fulfilment and is happy. When one sees almighty God in everything and everywhere, he is considered to have attained gyan and when with the existence of gyan, he gets rid of the influence of all passions and worldly desires, one gets absorbed in God and attains salvation. But this all is achieved with God's grace only. One, therefore, have to have full belief in him forgetting everything else.

यदा तु सर्वभूतेषु दारुष्वग्निमिव स्थितम्,
प्रतिचक्षीत मा लोको जह्यात्तर्ह्येव कश्मलम्।
यदा रहितात्मानं भूतेन्द्रिय गुणाशयैः,
स्वरूपेण मयोपेतं पश्यन् स्वाराज्यमृच्छति। (3-9-32-33)

To have full belief and for getting abosrbed in almighty God, one have to know first how the universe has come into existence. At first there was one almighty God. He once sitting in solitude thought, there should be a universe, full of all kinds of creatures. In that direction, he first created Brahma. Brahma, after having known the purpose of his existence from the almighty God after a long tapsya, that he was to create the universe, started creating the ingredients first which went into the creation of universe. He cretaed ten such systems :

(1) The supreme truth
(2) Self
(3) Five essential ingredients—earth, water, air, space and fire
(4) Senses
(5) Heart and other selfish elements
(6) Worldly involvements like passion, rage, greed, affection etc.
(7) Trees, plants and medicines
(8) Birds and animals—due to the excess of tamoguna

these creatures only eat, drink, sleep and have passion. They neither have any thinking power nor any far-sightdness.

(9) The human being—he generally finds happiness in worldly pleasures which actually ultimately lead to unhappiness

(10) Rishis, munis, gods etc.

All these creations are actually the assembly of many atoms. The theory of atoms is stated to be the invention of modern science but in our vedas, shastras and even in Bhagwat, which had been written about 5000 years back, the word atom (प्रमाणु) has been used and this is defined as the minutest form of earth etc., which cannot be further divided and which has not come into operation and which has not so far merged with other atoms, is called atom. All things in this universe created by the Almighty is the assembly of many such atoms. This definition of atom is even on date accepted and atomic power is the result of the atom having been put into operation. This formula was available in our Bhagwat itself in ancient times too. Atom is the minutest and most powerful element. Two atoms combined make one molecule. These atoms go into making the entire universe. In the universe after its creation, first was Satyayug when human beings did not have any vices and it was total dharma only. In subsequent yugas—Tretra, Duapur and Kalyug—the dharma started remaining in the background and adharma came forward and threatened the people. As a result, asuras came into being, who were completely adharmic only.

Brahma first created four munis Sanak, Sanandan Sanatan and Sanat kumar and asked them to create the beings further but they became busy in the attainment of salvation and did not care for Brahma's order. Brahma then created a person and for his living created heart, senses, life, space, air, water, fire, earth, sun, moon and tap. He then created his wife also and asked him to produce children. he produced persons, who were always enraged and started spoiling whatever was available. Brahma then stopped such production and produced further ten persons and ordered them to produce further offspring. They produced many rishis including Vashistha, Pulastya, Atri, Bharigu, Daksha, Narad etc. Then all the vices were produced to influence the offspring of these rishis. Brahma also produced four vedas, varnas, ashramas and then other shastras, puranas etc. Still not satisfied with the pace of creation, Brahma created the first man 'Manu' and his wife Shatroopa. They indulged in marital relation as a result of which offspring started coming up. Then Manu asked for a place to live in as the entire universe was at that time sunk in water. Brahma then remembered the almighty God, who came incarnate as Varaha (वराह). From here started the incarnation of God.

All religions consider the prophet as the incarnate of God. Such a person is born to guide the people in the universe. Further, all religions tell of ultimate attainment, the salvation in one form or the other. Also all religions consider the start of universe from one couple—whether they are Manu and Shatroopa or Adam and Eve etc. This uniformity in all religions confirms the facts of nature. All were surprised to see Varaha but realising that it would be God only, the munis/rishis started praising him. The Varaha entered the water and located earth in it and brought it out of the water by the fore of his mouth. While bringing the earth out of the water, Varaha had to face Hirnaksh, a rakshas, who challenged Varaha but the Varaha killed him. Then Brahma etc. were satisfied that it was Bhagwan only as the incarnate and praised him. In this way God killed the rakshas and brought the earth out of water for Brahma to create creatures to live threreupon. After that Varaha went to his loka.

In another incarnate Kashyap's wife Diti, had a desire to have a son as brilliant as Kashyap himself. She, therefore, requested for fulfilling her wish. Kashyap, who was a great tapsavi, agreed to fulfil her wish, saying that:

> "Wife is, as per Hindu tradition, half of the couple (अर्धाङ्गनी)." Even in English culture, wife is called better half. Therefore, at least the concept of 'half' is there too.

यामाहुरात्मानो ह्यर्धं श्रेयस्कामस्य मानिनि,
यस्याम् स्वधुरमध्यस्य पुमांश्चरति विज्वर:। (3-14-18)

Further, Kashyap Muni had accepted that the husband could entrust the job of running the household to the lady. This concept is also prevalent throughout the universe in all religions these days also. Also Kashyap had accepted and pronounced that in grihastha ashram too, by living according to religious tenets, one can achieve the three—religion, wealth and satisfaction of all senses—of the four goals of life. The fourth *i.e.*, Mukti can be attained after leaving grihastha and passing life as a sanyasi, fully detached from all worldly ambitions. He also said that through wife one can have the satisfaction of all senses. In exchange, the husband has to satisfy the thirst of the wife of have offspring. But he said she would have to wait for a fortnight as that fortnight was not auspicious for conception. The effect of stars on the offspring, when it comes into universe, is accepted throughout the world even today. In India even the time of conception was treated as auspicious or otherwise. India, therefore, excelled in this art. Even today India is at the top in Jyotish Vidya. But inspite of Kashyap having asked his wife to wait for a fortnight, she did not and insisted on having conception then and there. Kashyap then remembering Brahma God and after taking bath etc. had marital relation with her. Diti conceived but was repentent on what she had done inspite of Kashyap declining to accede to her request. Kashyap then by yoga came to know that Diti would give birth to two persons who would be rakshasas and do all kinds of crimes on earth. When the crime became intolerable then God will come incarnate and finish them. But then Kashyap told that in view of Diti's belief in God Shiva and her husband, one of her grandsons would be of world fame equal to God himself. The poet has tried to convey that:

(1) The circumstantial environ effects the offspring at the time of conception, and

(2) The virtues of the husband and wife donot go unrewarded and genetically in further offspring some

of the children would have those virtues imbibed in them.

(3) After having done some action, contrary to the wishes of the great person, if one regrets for having done so, the effect of the curse gets reduced. Diti felt satisfied by hearing that firstly her sons would be killed by incarnation of God himself and one of the grand sons would be a great Hari bhakta.

On the other side, Sankadik Rishis had gone to see Vishnu Lok. They went there but were checked by the dwarpals of Vishnu. The rishis taking it as their insult cursed the dwarpals to become rakshasas but on their being repentent, the rishis milded the curse and said that even when they would become rakshasas, some element of Hari bhakti would continue to remain in their minds. These dwarpals—Jaya and Vijaya—became Hirnakshya and Hirnakshyap and the latter's son was Prahlad. When Vishnu came to know of his dwarpals having been cursed, he came and agreed with the curse having been passed on dwarpals. He also stated that anyone insulting the brahmins had to face their curse. Brahmins have been made superiormost in all varnas. They learn and then coach others to become learned. They perform seflless tapasya and devote themselves to the cause of the almighty. From this they attain power, even recognised by God himself and if such persons are insulted, the person responsible for causing such insult has to suffer. Brahmins, therefore, deserved to be respected and worshipped by people of all other varnas. These Jaya and Vijaya entered Diti's conception and were born. At first they became Hirnakshya and Hirnakashyap. When they were born there was anarchy and chaos all around and all bad omens were evident. Hirnakshya was killed by Vishnu as Varaha incarnate. Brahma had told Vishnu (Varaha) that Hirnakshya had become powerful because of his blessings. As already indicated, Hirnakshya had become very powerful asura but he did not forget Bhagwan as a part of the curse of Sankadik. So by his tapsya, Hirnakshya had got the blessing of Brahma not to be defeated by any god/human being. Now Brahma was repentent on his having given that blessing and requested

Vishnu (Varaha) to make the blessing ineffective. It is in this situation that Vishnu had to come as incarnate in Varaha. There was fight between Hirnakshya and Varaha. The fight was with clubs (गदा). During the battle, the Varaha's gada fell down after it was knocked by asura's gada. The asura had a good chance of attacking the enemy at that time but he did not as according to dharma, the enemy without armament cannot he attacked. Here the poet has indicated that:

(1) There were Laws of War at that time and all warriors even the rakshasas—abided by these laws.

(2) According to law, the enemy cannot be attacked when he is without proper armament:

(3) The battle between the two enemies was one to one. Here on the one side there was Varaha and on the other the rakshas and there were no asistants/sainiks/ helpers on either side.

(4) Even God (Varaha) appreciated the thinking,of the rakshas not to attack Varaha without gada.

स तदा लब्धतीर्थोऽपि न बबाधे निरायुधम,
मानयन् स मृधे धर्मं विष्वक्सेनं प्रकोपयन्। (3-19-4)

Bhagwan then got hold of his chakra but he did not use chakra as the enemy did not have it. So there was again one to one battle. This time the rakshas's gada fell on earth and Varaha did not attack him and allowed him to pick up the gada, again following the law of battle. Again the gada of the rakshas fell down but this time rather than picking up the gada, the rakshas used a trishul and threw it on Varaha. Bhagwan cut the trishul into pieces by his chakra and then threw his chakra on the enemy, who died. The gods became happy and praised God as usual. The Varaha went to his loka. Then the universe was taken out of the ocean and given to Manu for his offspring to live in.

Once Manu and his wife Satroopa and his daughter Devahuti came at Bindusar River. There was Kardam Muni's ashram on the bank of that river. Manu went to the ashram. As per protocol, Manu bowed his head in respect before the muni. The muni in turn gave him his blessing and honoured him as a guest as per requisite protocol. After that Manu sat on an asan (आसन). The muni praised Manu as an incarnate of God himself, who had been wandering about in the universe as per direction of Brahma and Vishnu. Manu was also the king of the universe which had been taken out by Varaha from the ocean and handed over to Manu. As a king it was incumbunt upon him to:

(1) Protect the universe and the people.

(2) For this purpose he had to create an army to protect him and his people.

(3) Varna and ashram institutions hard already been established at that time and the king had to see that these institutions were being monitored as per tenets of dharma ; each person acting as per his dharma according to the varna in which he was born and the ashram in which he presently was.

(4) If the king ignored his duties, then there would be chaos and anarchy in the universe.

(5) The muni asked for any job for which he could be considered capable and the purpose for which he had come to the ashram.

(6) The king felt obliged to the muni for having indirectly narrated to the king his duties.

(7) The girls had at that time been chosing the grooms for them after hearing the capability of a particular person and then it was incumbunt on the father to arrange that marriage. In a way in those days the marriages were by love and arrangement.

(8) The muni accepted the proposal of the king for marrying his daughter, who had chosen the muni as her husband saying that if a passion gets automatically fulfilled then one should not mind such fulfilment even though he may be a detached person from the universe because if he rejects such fulfilment, when available, he would have to beg for it in course of time and that would be at the cost of his image being spoiled.

उद्यतस्यहि कामस्य प्रतिवादो न शस्यते,
अपि निर्मुक्त सगंस्य कामरक्तस्यकिं पुनः। (3-22-12)

(9) The marriages were performed as per vedic process, after both boy and the girl agreed for the marriage and it was acceptable to the fathers of the boy and the girl.

(10) The detached person too accepted marital relation and grihastha dharma as well but after fulfilling the requirements of the grihastha dharma, such people again opted for sanyas as the ultimate attainment of salvation lied in sanyas only and this is what is provided in the ashram dharma as well,

(11) The daughter was given in marriage to the groom by the mother and father of the bride.

(12) As per protocol, many valuable clothes, ornaments and other things like utensils etc., required in the household, were given in dowry. This indicates that the institution of dowry in Hindus has been in existence even when the universe was started and is continuing till date. The dowry is given by the parents of the bride with a view to see that their daugher was able to establish the house after marriage. Such dowry, however, it appears, was restricted to clothes, ornaments, utensils and other things of use in the household and not the cash part of it as earning of cash for running the household was the ordained duty of the husband.

(13) After marriage, Manu and Satroopa went from that place after taking permission of the son-in-law.

(14) On return of the king to the kingdom, the people would come out of the houses to welcome and receive him as per protocol.

(15) The king lived as per prescribed process of attaining dharma, wealth, fulfilment of senses and ultimately attainment of salvation.

(16) Bhagwat-katha and hymns were being uttered in God's praise everywhere.

After marriage, Rishi Kardam and Devhuti started living together. As per dharma or protocol between husband and wife in Hindus, the wife has to :—

(1) Serve the husband to the best of her ability.

(2) Her sole aim should be to please the husband and this pleasure could be for the wife to detach herself from all greed, pride jealousy, attachment toward the parents and their family and serving the husband with utmost care and devotion

(3) She has to win the confidence, trust and please the husband by love, service, piety, and sweet words.

(4) The husband having been pleased has to express his pleasure/satisfaction for the service done. He even offers half of the dharma, he had earned during that period,which had been possible because of her service without any vices.

(5) The wife and husband then have to plan for having children. For this purpose, they have to take proper meals, use perfumes, other creams to keep the body attractive.

(6) A proper house duly furnished is to be arranged in leading the grihastha life.

(7) A means of transport to move about is arranged.

(8) The house should be properly decorated to suit the occasion.

(9) The husband and wife should take bath, wear attractive clothes and ornaments, use all perfumes etc. and perform such action as may make the atmosphere attractive for arousing passion.

Kardam Muni being as such, had full control on his senses and even after seeing Devhuti, very charming and attractive, he did not lose control of senses. They then spent some time in Himalayas and returned to the ashram and had marital relation for some years. They had a daughter. After that, Kardam Muni had to become sanyasi as per agreement before marriage. At that time Devhuti requested that although as per agreement, he had to now adopt sanyas but he should also see and care for the maintenance of his family and arrange for marriage of the daughters as well. Even today the maintenance of the family is a duty of the husband and in case of divorce as well (adoption of sanyas by husband is nothing less than divorce of the present day) the husband has to pay for the maintenance of wife and family, including marriage of daughters.

ब्रह्मन्दुहितृभिस्तुभ्यं विमृग्याः पतयः समाः
कश्चित्स्यान्मे विशोकाय त्वयि प्रव्रजिते बनम् । (3-24-52)

Kardam Muni then told Devhuti that God will himself come incarnate as her child. She should, therefore, continue her bhakti, control, tap etc. He will then grant her salvation. She, believing in what her husband had told, continued remembering Ishwar. After sometime, God came incarnate as Kapil Muni to write Sankhya shastra. At that time, Brahma told Kardam to give his daughters in marriage to Marich etc. rishis as per their temperament and capability. For marriage of a daugher (योग्य वर), a proper groom has to be searched. The groom should be such as to be comparable to the temperament and capability of the girl. Even now the kundlis of the boy and girl are tallied with a view to find if the life of the pair after marriage would be happy or otherwise. Brahma also told that Hari himself had born in their house. Then Brahma went away. Thereafter Kardam married the daughters to Marich and other munis as directed by Brahma, according to the tenets of vedas. Muni Kardam then proceeded for sanyas. Kapil muni wrote and taught to his disciples the Sankhya Shastra, which narrates the gyan of self realisation. Kapil Muni had been living with his mother in the ashram. Devhuti knew her son was God incarnate. One day when Kapil Muni was sitting in peace, Devhuti asked him, not as her son, but as incarnate of God, to tell her the way by which she could attain salvation as so far she had been indulging in worldly passions only which too was because of the God's maya itself. Kapil Muni told her mother as God that spiritual gyan and vairagya (आध्यात्मिक ज्ञान और वैराग्य) only can lead the person to attainment of salvation.

योग आध्यात्मिकः पुंसां मतो निःश्रेयसाय मे,
अत्यन्तो परतिर्यत्र दुःखस्य च सुखस्य च। (3-25-13)

He also said that mind is what is responsible for good and bad deeds or for worldly involvement or salvation. This is analogous to the present saying "Nothing is bad or good but thinking makes it so". When the aspect of 'me and mine' enters one's mind, the person is influenced by the effect of God's maya and gets involved in worldly vices. When one gets detached from worldly involvements, one attains salvation. Further, for one's mind to be detached from worldy involvement, one has to be in the company of sadhus and resort to Bhagwad bhakti. This only is the way to reach the ultimate goal of salvation. Now for the benefit of the people at large like her (specially woman), involved in worldly passions, Devhuti asked for the way suiting such person to reach the goal of salvation. Kapil Muni told that the persons, who are devoted to God and think that whatever they were doing was as per the orders of God and surrender the same to God himself, become his bhaktas and can easily get absorbed in him. Although such people do not expect salvation since they are not fully detached from universe but having reached God's Dham, and having been absorbed in him, one automatically attains salvation. Kapil Muni, therefore, told, that the best way for the persons in the universe, who do not leave universe, to attain the ultimte goal, is that their mind should, by way of bhakti, get absorbed in Him.

Kapil Muni further told in general that self-realisation is the sure way of attaining salvation, because God is in one's atma and realisation of atma is the realisation of God himself and realisation of God is salvation. Devhuti asked further that man and nature are dependent on each other. It is by dint of nature only that man becomes satvik, rajsik or tamsik. Now since nature and man cannot be set apart, there should be some method following which, even involved in worldly belongings, one could reach salvation. That method, she requested, be told for such people. Kapil Muni told that as the wood after producing fire herself gets burnt. In the same way if one leads his life in normal way following all tenets of dharma selflessly, one's mind becomes pure and with this followed by—

(1) listening to Bhagwad katha;

(2) achieving self-realisation ;

(3) vairagya;

(4) remembering him in isolation by concentrating one's mind, one gets detached from worldly vices, slowly and slowly, and gets absorbed in God;

(5) as far as possible following one's dharma as per tenets of shastras and to detach onself from all non-shastriya things;

(6) getting rid of all vices;

(7) not annoying any creature by speach, action, and mind;

(8) telling truth; Non-accumulation of material more than one's requirement;

(9) reading the shastras and acting according to what is provided in these shastras;

(10) always thinking of Hari leela;

(11) concentrating the mind slowly and slowly and thinking of God only;

(12) thinking of the Bhagwad idol; at first of some parts and subsequently the entireself;

(13) not having a biased, enraged, violent or jealous mind as the people with these vices are called 'tamsik';

(14) not even having in mind at the time of bhakti, the desire of earning name, earning wealth and doing bhakti with self-interest as such people are rajsi bhaktas.

(15) performing Bhagwad bhakti to redress oneself of the sins, worshipping God as a matter of service and submitting oneself to the cause of God as such bhakti is satvik bhakti.

(16) The bhakti could be by seeing the idol of God, touching the idol, praising God, seeing God in all creatures, taking shelter of vairagya, respecting the rishis, munis etc.. having control on all vices; having

company of saints or listening to Bhagwad leela/katha.

(17) The worldly belongings are all vanishable. One takes them as the source of all pleasures. The fact, however, is that the pleasure lies in getting detached from these and the more one gets detached, the more livable life shall he lead.

(18) For bad actions, one gets punishment even after death through the Yamraj. People even say that Swaraga and Naraka (स्वर्ग/नरक) have to be faced in this universe itself.

अत्रैव नरकः स्वर्ग इति मातः प्रचक्षते,
या यातना वै नारक्यस्ता इहाप्युपलक्षिताः। (3-30-29)

In our ancient days even biological science was at its peak. People in those days knew what doctors have been able to know after research for years using ultrasonic devices etc. In Tretayug the best of medicines were available. Hanuman could bring Sanjeevni booti and cure Lakshmana through the diagnosis by Vaid Sukhen. Such treatments may not be available even today. Bhagwat explains how after conception, the semen (mixture of male and female semens) develop into a being with all human parts; the periodicity with which these come into being and how after six months of pregnancy, the creature starts feeling very upset in mother's womb and requests the God to bring him out and this time he would do all virtuous actions. But on coming into the universe, he forgets everything that happened even since his previous death and again starts his life under the influence of Hari 'maya' and continues like this in this universe transmigrating from one specie to another. At the infant stage, the child faces many difficulties but he cannot express the difficulties and others cannot know the same. Subsequently when he grows up into youth, he develops all kinds of senses and waits to satisfy those senses. Non-fulfilment of the same leads to his getting enraged and subsequently falling into all kinds of vices. He tries to find life amidst those vices and is unable to find truth unless he comes across some saint/guru. The biggest vice in the universe is the company of wife and production of children thereafter.

बलं मे पश्य मायायाः स्त्रीमय्या जयिनो दिशाम् ,
या क्रोति पदाक्रान्तान् भ्रूविजृम्भेण केवलम्। (3-31-38)

One should, therefore, at this stage remember the God and involve in his bhakti after getting oneself detached from all worldly involvements. This, in essence, is what is prescribed in the institution of four ashramas—brahmcharya, grihastha, vanprastha and sanyas. This is the sole path of attaining salvation even after having been indulged in worldly vices. The salvation can be through the path of attaining gyan and devotion to Nirguna Brahma (God) and also through Bhagwad bhakti. The earlier path is tedious and the later is convenient. This path only is prescribed for the people of Kalyug as they cannot understand the devotion to Nirguna Brahma (God). Having listened all this form Kapil Muni (God), Devhuti started feeling detached from the universe and bowed before Kapil Muni, as God and not as her son, as according to protocol, a mother cannot bow before her son. Here the relation, is that of a bhakta and Bhagwan and, therefore, the protocol of bhakta and Bhagwan has to be followed. When Ram had killed Ravan, then Raja Dasratha, who had already died and was not able to attain salvation, as he had died in affection of son and so was not detached from worldly involvements, had come and praised Ram (as God and not as his son) and then attained salvation after getting rid of the Bhagwad maya and getting absorbed in Ram as God. After that, Kapil Muni took permission of mother and left the ashram. Devhuti too started Bhagwad bhakti as told by Kapil Muni getting detached from the very luxurious life provided by Kardam Rishi, as already explained, and attained salvation. Kapil God too went away and after giving the Sankhya Shastra (yogmaya) Gyan to the universe, he had his smadhi and left the universe telling the world the way to get detached from worldly vices and involving onself in selfless bhakti.

Skandh – IV

As already indicated protocol is followed even in gods and anyone not following it is negated in the gatherings. Manu had married his daughter Prasuti to Brahma's son Prajapati Daksha. Daksha had 16 daughters from Prasuti. He married 13 daughters to Dharma, one to Agni, one to Pitrigan and one to Bhagwan Shankar. Once all gods had gathered in a yagya by Prajapatis. All gods including Brahma and Shiva had come there. When all had come Prajapati Daksha, who was a senior Prajapati, entered (there is a seniority list in the realm of gods too like the one in each of the Departments today) the Sabha. All those, sitting there stood in honour of Daksha as per protocol except Brahma and Shiva. Brahma and Shiva did not stand as they were the Bhagwans and above all Prajapatis. Daksha then paid respect to Brahma, beng his father but did not pay any respects to Shiva. He rather pronounced in the Sabha that there were some gods in the Sabha (referring to Shiva) who did not even observe the well laid tenets of discipline. He said:

श्रूयताम् ब्रह्मर्षयो मे सहदेवाः सहाग्नयः
साधुनाम् ब्रुवतो वृत्तं नाज्ञानान्न च मत्सरात्।
अयं तु लोक पालानां यशोध्नो निरपत्रपः,
सद्भिराचरितः पन्था येन स्तब्धेन दूषितः। (4-2-9/10)

This indicated that

(1) There was an order of precedent in the gods at that time, according to which they respected and honoured according to individual's position.

(2) There was a code of conduct laid down in the shastras according to which each god conducted himself in meetings and gatherings.

(3) As is even today, when a senior comes, all already present stand up in honour, so was the system in those days too.

(4) In the Sabha, when Daksha came, since he was senior to all others, they all stood in honour but then Brahma and Shiva were Bhagwans and above all Prajapatis, as per order of precedent, they did not stand up in honour of Daksha. There was in this way nothing wrong in it as it was a meeting of all gods and amongst the gods, rishis, and Prajapatis, Brahma, Vishnu and Mahesh were the superior most in gods and in fact the only Gods—others being Devtas only. They, therefore, were not to honour a Prajapati. On the other hand, Daksha bowed before Brahma (God) who was his father but did not pay respect to Shiva (another God) thinking that he was his son-in-law and wished Shiva (as his son) should have stood in honour of the father-in-law. But the order of protocol differs from place to place. Here it was a gathering of all Devtas, Prajapatis and Gods. In that gathering, Gods (Brahma and Shiva) were superior most. Therefore, according by the protocol all had to act as per their position in the Sabha.

(5) In the social gathering of Daksha and his family, Shiva was obliged to pay respects to his father-in-law (Daksha). Daksha was expecting the same respect from Shiva (as his son-in-law) forgetting that he was the God in the Sabha and deserved to be respected by Prajapatis. Daksha thought it as his insult and pronounced Shiva as indisciplined, crude etc.

(6) As a mark of respect for the father-in-Law, however, Shiva did not offer any rejoinder as all others present there understood the position of Shiva as God in that gathering.

(7) Further, there were the various methods of offering respects—by bowing, when elders are involved and by

speech, when equals are involved. Similarly in present days also, the different methods of honouring the guests are prescribed—by guns, by bugle, by parade, by just wishing, etc. Daksha complained that, rather than standing in his honour, Shiva did not even wish him by speech.

"प्रत्युत्थानाभिवादार्हे वाचाप्यकृत नोचितम्।" (4-2-12)

(8) Since Shiva, out of respect did not give any rejoinder, Daksha took it otherwise as further insult to him and he got enraged so much that he passed curse (शाप) on Shiva that Shiva being a mean amongst Gods would not be entitled to any share in yagyas, havanas along with Indra and other gods. In the Sabha of Prajapatis, rishis, and gods, one should not get enraged but again Daksha was under the influence of Hari 'maya', so he passed this curse on Shiva starting a quarrel with him.

(9) There was a system that in all havans, yagyas etc., there was prescribed share for each god, including Indra etc. and what asuras had been doing is to deny these gods their share in havans thereby starving them and annoying them, compelling them to resort to refuge under the almighty, who invariably helped them by annihilating the asuras.

(10) Others, who were present, checked Daksha for passing this curse but he did not pay any heed and did press on the curse.

(11) Now after passing the curse in opposition of all present there, Daksha could not dare sit in the Sabha and left abruptly.

(12) Shiva's followers having come to know that Daksha had passed curse on Shiva, passed a curse on Daksha as a tit for tat that one who opposes Shiva (meant for Daksha) would be deprived of self-realisation gyan. He would be included in woman and would have the mouth like lamb. He would be in the process of transmigration of soul and would not attain salvation, and would wander about in universe for begging and becoming slave of worldly passions/vices.

(13) This led to the brahmins getting enraged and then Bhrigu in turn passed on the curse that all Shiva bhaktas would become bereft of conduct enunciated in shastras and their followers would be pisach, rakhdhari (राखधारी) and devils (भूत) evil spirits. Shiva, however, then left the place with his followers.

The mutual opposition/offence/ continued thereafter between Shiva and Daksha. Meantime Brahma promoted Daksha from Prajapati to Head of all Prajapatis, indicating that there is a *system of promotion* amongst the rishis, devtas, gods too. On his elevation as Head Prajapati, Daksha held a yagya in which all gods, rishis, munis, devtas and his daughters etc. had been invited except Brahma, Shiva, Vishnu and his daughter Sati (because she was Shiva's wife). Sati, saw all gods with their wives going to Daksha's place via Kailash. She checked up where they had been going and finding about the yagya being held by her father, she too requested Shiva to attend the yagya, where she could collect clothes ornaments etc. to be given by her parents to the daughters and sons-in-law as a mark of respect in honour of holding the yagya. The writer has indicated here the tradition of father setting apart clothes, ornaments etc. for both daughters and sons-in-law at all important functions held in that house. This tradition continues as a social protocol even today. The daughter too, even though quite rich and contented, always looks forward for such presents. In modern terms, it is called "Stridhan", otherwise why even as highly placed as Sati (Shiva's wife) could think in those terms, when Shiva was the owner of entire universe even admitted so by Sati herself here.

अहम् च तस्मिन् भवताभिकामये,
सहोपनीतं परिबर्हमर्हितुम्। (4-3-9)

To cover the lapse in protocol committed by Sati's father in not having invited them to the function, Sati told that as per vedic tenets, one could even go without having been invited to the house of husband, guru, parents and other close relations.

अनाहुता अत्यभियन्ति सौहृदं,
भर्तुर्गुरोर्देहकृतश्च केतनम्। (4-3-13)

Thinking of Daksha, Shiva also remembered the abuses he had hailed on Shiva in the meeting of Prajapatis and told Sati that she was alright in saying that one could go to the house of husband, guru, parents etc. without invitation but this could be done only when they are not proud, enraged and biased toward the incumbents. Education, tap, wealth, health, youth and birth in high caste are virtues of gentlemen but these become vices when in possession of evil-minded persons as then these give rise to pride, and kills the right-thinking. He told that one would feel better if injured by the arrows of enemy than to face the abuses by one's own near relations. He further told that although she was very favourite of her father but she had lost that regard being his wife as her father hated her badly in view of what had happened in the meeting of the Prajapatis. Question then arose as to what was the ego-hurt caused to them both in the meeting of Prajapatis. It was necessary for Shiva to tell as Sati was not there as witness to it. Shiva, therefore, stated that the protocolic requirement like going before any person in respect, showing respect to him, bowing before him are all followed in society and followed in a better way by the persons adept in self-realisation. Such people bow before the almighty Krishna, who is in everybody's heart and not to the proud human beings. Shiva said that he, therefore, bowed only before Krishna and none else (because he only is above Shiva). Shiva accordingly advised Sati that she should not even think of going to the yagya being performed by her father, when Shiva had not been honoured. If she still went there, she would have to face consequences, which would not be welcome to her and may lead to ultimate death. After that Sati got confused—whether or not to go to the father's house. If she goes, Shiva would mind it and if she does not go then she would not be able to meet all her family men. She was upset because of rage and shock and ultimately left Shiva and went to her father's house. Shiva then sent some of his followers to accompany her and made all necessary protocolic arrangements for her departure. As expected, Sati was ignored by the father on reaching his house and out of fear for Daksha, others too did not welcome her (including her sisters). Only her mother was affectionate to her and embraced her. Having been ignored by the father, Sati did not accept the honour granted by the mother. Then Sati saw that there was no provision for Shiva amongst the gods to share the 'Havi' and her father Daksha had insulted Shiva. Sati got enraged and said that Shiva was the greatest of all gods and he has no foes at all and still he was being insulted. She, therefore, could not live with the body granted by such a father and, thereafter, left this universe through yog-agni. All gods, present there, made noise after seeing Sati leaving the universe. The followers of Sati (sent by Shiva to accompany her) started spoiling the yagya. On the other side, Bhrigu Rishi produced some asuras out of fire and there was big fighting. When Shiva came to know of it, he produced one brave man (Virbhadra) and ordered him to destroy the yagya as Shiva's representative. Seeing Virbhadra coming like a storm, all present in the yagya, became shocked. Shiva's men destroyed the yagya from all sides, arrested Bhrigu and killed Daksha and arrested other gods present there and went to report back to Lord Shiva. The gods reported the matter to Brahma. Brahma already knew this to happen. That is why he did not go to the yagya. Brahma told that one cannot harm a capable man even if he commits some crime and he rather has to suffer.

तदाकर्ण्य विभुः प्राह तेजीयसि कृतागसि,
क्षेमाय तत्र सा भूयान्न प्रायेण बभूषताम्। (4-6-4)

Now, he advised the gods, to go and beg pardon from Shiva. Shiva gets pleased early so he would excuse them all for having done wrong in having joined the yagya, where Shiva was being insulted. Then Brahma along with the gods went to Kailash. The munis and gods accompanying Brahma paid respects to Lord Shiva and Shiva's men and Shiva bowed before Brahma as per protocol. Brahma then praised Shiva since Brahma had come to gain some favour from Shiva. Brahma requested Shiva to allow the yagya being completed and to enliven the dead Daksha; restore eyesight to Bhag-devta and Bhrigu to have his beard and moustaches,which had been uprooted by Virbhadra and the gods to recover from injuries caused to them in the quarrel. The yagya would be with his share. Shiva replied that Daksha would now have the mouth of a lamb as his own has been burnt. Other gods too would recover from injuries and Bhrigu would have beard and moustaches like that of a lamb. Brahma and other gods felt obliged to the response from Shiva. Daksha became alive and worshipped Shiva and after that started the unfinished yagya. In the yagya, all gods and Brahma and Shiva had come. When the yagya came to an end, Vishnu Bhagwan too reached there. Seeing him, all gods and Brahma and Shiva stood in respect as per protocol even followed by other gods. They started praising the almighty God. Since here Daksha was the host, he brought the Pooja samagri first and worshipped the God. Daksha and others praised God. Shiva separately praised and then Brahma praised the God. All rishis, vedas, yogeshwars, Agni, Gandharvas, Lokpal etc. praised Vishnu in an order. This indicates that an order, like the order of precedence in our times is available even in the realm of God and gods. Since Brahma, Vishnu, Mahesh and all other gods etc. were present at the yagya, it would be advisable to indicate the order in which they all worshipped Vishnu Bhagwan:

(1) Vishnu Bhagwan is at the top as he was being worshipped by all.
(2) Daksha, is at no. 2 as he was the host and had to first worship Vishnu.
(3) Daksha's men—Ritwij (ऋत्विज) and other members responsible for holding the yagya.
(4) Shiva
(5) Brahma
(6) Bhrigu
(7) Indra
(8) Wives of those holding yagya
(9) Rishis
(10) Sidhas

(11) Wives of yajman (यजमान)
(12) Lokpalas
(13) Yogeshwaras
(14) Vedas
(15) Fire (अग्नि)
(16) Other gods
(17) Gandharvas
(18) Vidyadharas
(19) Brahmins

After the yagya was finished, Vishnu proclaimed that he was the almighty God. He only controls 'maya' responsible for operating the entire universe, including creation, maintenance and annihilation. He himself signifies Brahma, Vishnu and Mahesh. No one should, therefore, differentiate between the forms of the same almighty God. This was with a view to mend Daksha, who had been under-estimating the might of Shiva, leading to all the trouble. Daksha finished the yagya from which each God, Brahma, Vishnu, Mahesh etc. had been given their share of Havi (हवि). All the gods then offered their blessings to Daksha, as demanded by protocol, and went away to their respective places.

Sati, who left the universe in the yagya, was born as Parvati in the house of Himalaya and Maina and after a lot of tapsya again got Shiva as her husband.

As already told, Manu and Satroopa had two sons—Priyavrat and Uttanpada. Uttanpada had two queens—Suruchi and Suniti. Raja loved Suruchi more. Poet has tried to make out that rather than differentiating amongst various wives, the raja should have only one wife. Dasratha had to suffer because he had three wives and Ram thereafter established the principle of one man one wife. He did not marry second time even when Sita had been sent to forests and Ram was having difficulty in performing puja in Aswamedha yagyas, where presence of wife was considered necessary. Uttanpada too had to pay for having two wives as he loved Suruchi more and hence had to be more affectionate to her son (Uttama) rather than Suniti's son (Dhruva). Dhruva left and achieved the goal of having the almighty God as his father but then Uttanpad had to regret for it. Hearing the unpleasant talks of the step mother Suruchi, Dhruva went to her mother crying but she could not do anything except to advise him to take refuge under the almighty and she even mentioned that all big persons became big because of Hari bhakti only. Dhruva left the kingdom in search of God. On the way Narad met him. He tried to dissuade Dhruva from this tough approach but Dhruva stuck to it. Ultimately Narad told him the Vishnu mantra to enable Dhruva to reach him. It shows nothing is impossible in the world, one should have the determination and right approach. Narad had even told Dhruva that these were all ways of God and an intelligent person should yield before the will of God. Narad further told that as a matter of principle, one should feel happy in meeting the persons more capable than himself; should have mercy on less capable and should develop friendship with the persons of equal capability. All this, however, did not have any effect on Dhruvaa as he was determined to reach his goal of attaining the singhasan through the almighty, where even his father could not reach *i.e.* in the heart of God almighty. Narad then agreed and told him that his mother had put him on correct path. Narad told him the mantra—"ॐ नमो भगवते वासुदेवाय". He also told the procedure for conducting Bhagwad Puja by offering flowers, leaves, water, vastra, as available in forest etc. It shows the comprehensiveness in Hindu dharma. For every job detailed procedure has been prescribed in the shastras and the yagya, puja etc. become readily acceptable to God, if done properly. It is not that God wants all these procedures to be adopted to reach him, he is only fond of love "रामहि केवल प्रेम पिआरा". But the procedures prescribed are with a view to ensure that the incumbent, if follows all this procedural aspect, gets absorbed in the almighty easily than just starting remembering him abruptly. Dhruva, after hearing from Narad, had a round of Narad, and bowed before him as per tradition. Narad went away and Dhruva too proceeded further. He started worshipping God as per procedure. After very tough tapsya, God came to him. Dhruva bowed before him and praised him and prayed for the grant of singhasan and constant bhakti. God granted Dhruva the highest honour ever had by any rishi etc. *i.e.* 'The Dhurva Loka' at the top of all stars. Bhagwan left after blessing Dhruva and Dhruva too left for his home. Although Dhruva was having the bad feeling about his step-mother even when God had come, God fulfilled his wish. After God had left, Dhruva felt why he made a wish for worldly involvement only and not the mukti when God had himself appeared before him.

When Raja Uttanpada came to know that Dhruva was returning, he went out of the town to receive him with all royal protocol, taking along with him all munis, his advisers, elders, mahajans, brahmins, purohit, guru, etc. along with two queens and son Uttama. Meeting Dhruva, raja embraced him. Dhruva bowed before his father, mother, step-mother—all blessed him. One whom God loves, is loved by all.

यस्य प्रसन्नो भगवान् गुणैर्मैत्र्यादिभिर्हरिः
तस्मै नमन्ति भूतानि निम्नमाप इव स्वयम्। (4-9-4)

Then Dhruvaa met all others with respect and got blessings from all. The entire town had been decorated in his honour as is done even today when a foreign head of state comes. There were the customs and traditions of decorating the town at such occasions. This would indicate how in ancient India, protocol was followed and laid down even for the minutest occasion. All streets were decorated with bandanwars, perfumes, banners, etc.; persons were standing at both sides of the roads/streets throwing flowers on Dhruva and shouting jaykara. The mahal too had been decorated to suit the occasion. Raja, finding Dhruva, capable of holding the rajya, coronated him and he himself went to forests having seen that he was already in banprasth age as prescribed in the institution of ashrams.

Dhruva had been ruling as per the tenets of dharma. Once his brother Uttama had gone to forest for hunting, where he was killed by yakshas. His mother also died in forest, when she went in search of her son. On this, Dhruva got enraged and attacked the yakshas. He killed most of them, when his grand father Manu came from Swarga and advised him to stop the battle as for the killing of his brother by one yaksha, he had already killed lakhs of them and should now stop it. He further advised that the yakshas were followers of Kuber but they were not the killers of his brother as the God only is the creator, maintainer annihilater of the creature.

न चैते पुत्रक भ्रातुर्हन्तारो धनदानुगाः,
विसर्गादानयोस्तात पुंसो दैवं हि कारणम। (4-12-24)

After listening to what Manu had told, Dhurva came back to his kingdom. Then Yaksh, Kuber etc. came to Dhruva and praised him and Kuber told Dhruva that he was happy on his having ended the war with yakshas and offered to ask for any boon. Dhruva only asked that he should constantly remember Shri Hari so that he ultimately attained salvation. Kuber acceded to the request and went away.

Dhruva came back to his home and performed many yagyas. He fully earned and enjoyed dharma, wealth and worldly passions/ambitions and after a long rule, handed over the rajya to his son Utkal and went to Badrikashram in sanyas as was adopted by everyone towards the end of life. There, Dhruva performed tapsya and ultimately went to Dhruva Lok. At that time he remembered his mother Suniti but was told that Suniti too was being taken along with him on a different plane (Viman). Dhruva wished to take revenge from his step-mother and God fulfilled that wish and made Dhruva the king. Subsequently, Dhruva during sanyas again performed bhakti and then got the paramgati. This shows that God fulfils the wishes of the bhaktas as they have and for which they worship God.

तांस्तान् कामान् हरिर्दद्याद्यान् यान् कामयते जनः
आराधितो तथैवैष यता पुंसां फलोदयः। (4-13-24)

Dhruva had handed over the rajya to his son Utkal but Utkal was always lost in Hari bhakti and was not looking into the rajya management. The praja, therefore, made another son Anga as the raja. This would indicate that democracy was in full play even in those days of monarchy and the praja had full powers to even dethrone a king and coronate another—but from the same royal dynasty of kshatriyas as the right of rule rested in kshatriyas only as per institution of the varna. Whereas the praja had a right to chAngae the king, this right was not so automatic and had to be resorted to only after all other channels/efforts had failed to work. That is why according to vedic tenets, the king had to care for the protection and well-being of the praja and the praja too excused the raja even if he commits some crime as within raja are imbibed the gods.

नावध्येय: प्रजापाल: प्रजाभिरघवानपि,
यदसौ लोक पालानां बिभर्त्योज: स्वेतजसा। (4-13-23)

After Raja Anga went for sanyas, there was none in the dynasty to succeed. Anga had one very rude son Bain. But seeing none to succeed, the praja made him raja. By his crude methods, he annoyed everyone and had indulged in all sorts of vices. The elders of the kingdom pondered over the matter and rather than dethroning him, they thought it fit to persuade him first to behave. They accordingly went and coached him thoroughly about the duties of a raja as per dharma but Bain told them that the raja comprised of all gods including Brahma, Vishnu and Mahesh and they should, therefore, not interfere in his way of ruling. The elders got infuriated and killed him. There was at that time none in the dynasty except one chid Prithu. The public made him their raja. Prithu was the incarnate of God Vishnu. All people, brahmins etc. praised Prithu and after collecting all the requisites for coronation, they coronated him the raja.

"सोऽभषिक्तो महाराज: सुवासा: साध्वलकृंत:" (4-15-13)

The coronation was performed as per vedic pronouncements. Like the present day when coronation is performed with all pump and show, in the olden days too, the coronation was as per laid down procedure in vedas with all celebrations. This procedure has been continuing from ancient time to Maurya period, Gupta period and subsequently in Rajputs too. After Rajputs in Muslims too the celebration of coronation of the king was in the public like Shivaji. So followed in British Empire as well. The coronation of Queen Elizabeth II was celebrated not only in England but in all English colonies (including India) too.

When the public started showering praise on Raja Prithu, he checked them saying that so far he had nothing to be praised about and that they should praise only after he had become praise-worthy. The public then, rather than praising him, started telling him what he would be as an emperor in future. He would be a Chakravarty raja, ruling as per tenets of vedas and shastras, respecting cow, brahmin and the people of various varnas and ashramas. Some of the important ingredients of a capable raja were:

(1) To rule as per dharma.

(2) To protect the praja from outside invasion and internal crimes.

(3) To punish the criminals.

(4) To always think and work for the well-being of the public.

(5) To perform yagyas from time to time so that the fire, Indra, etc. are happy and allowing rains, production etc. in a natural way.

(6) He should believe and act in equity and equality for all.

(7) He would collect wealth and spend the same for the well–being of the public at large.

(8) He should be very kind-hearted and respectful to all elders and benevolent to others.

(9) To arrange for relief to public when there is no rain or there is famine by pleasing the concerned god.

(10) Should have a strong force to enable face the outside invaders. He himself too should be a brave man, a good administrator and a good treasurer.

(11) Hold Aswamedha yagya to establish his supremacy on the rajas dependent and vassals under him.

During Raja Prithu's time (in fact in his father Bain's time there was no production of food-grains due to the crime committed by him) there was shortage of food-grains and the people were dying of starvation. Raja thought it would be because of something wrong with the production system. In Bhagwat it is mentioned that Raja Prithu took his bow and arrow and went to kill Prithvi, who was not giving food-grains. Prithvi fumbled and got frightened. She said that Pirthu was a noble and dharma-prayan raja, then he should not kill a woman (Prithvi is feminine gender).

प्रहरन्ति न वै स्त्रीषु कृतागः स्वपि जन्तवः
किमुत त्वद्विधा राजन् करुणा दीनवत्सलाः। (4-17-20)

The Raja, however, stated hat she had, by hiding all food-grains, starved the people and, therefore, there was no sin in killing a person, who lived for himself and was cruel to others, even if it were a male or female or eunuch. Prithvi then yielded and then raja milched her. Through the media of the Prithvi and cow, the poet has actually narrated that to produce food-grains/milk, lot of labour had to be done. When during Bain's time the raja was seeking pleasure only and the public had been living on loot, no one put any labour in producing food-grains. Raja Prithu could understand this fact. He, therefore, made his people put labour in producing food-grains and bringing up cows to produce milk. In this way both food-grains and milk were produced and the public could be saved from starvation. This is proved by what Prithvi had told also that in old days the rishis, who were aware of all supreme truths and realities had done research in agriculture and other fields and had prescribed methods of bringing about rains and producing food-grains giving maximum yield. The raja, therefore, should trace those shastras and act on that research. Such methods had eloped during the period of Raja Bain, when none followed them as a result of which the land had gone barren. This could again be made fertile by ploughing, sowing etc. and bringing rain by havans (Rains could be brought by havans also indicates that as today artificial rain can be had, in those days too some system of such rains would be available which is stated to be through havans.). The Prithvi had also told Prithu that for obtaining food-grains, he would have to smoothen the earth. This is nothing but ploughing the earth for producing food-grains.

समां च कुरु मां राजन्देव वृष्टं यथा पयः
अपर्तावपि भद्रं ते उपावर्तेत मे विभो। (4-18-11)

Raja acted accordingly and put his men in ploughing and sowing the land and arranged rains too and obtained all kinds of products from land. The people became prosperous. Raja then created many inhabitations for the public and animals in the form of villages, towns, cowherds, gaushalas, cantonments, and mines. This only indicates that the public was divided to live in villages/towns etc. and the people of each profession lived together. He also arrangaed to build houses for them. Hereafter all these jobs came in the charge of the ruler. He also performed many Aswamedha yagyas. As already indicated, such a yagya was performed to establish the sovereignty (overall lordship on smaller rajas and vassals) by the Chakravarty Raja/ Emperor. Also the holding of Aswamedha yagya was with a view to collect lot of wealth by the emperor from his vassals in the form of presents and all such collected wealth was spent on the welfare works for the public. Such works continued to be undertaken by the emperors during the regime of Mauryas, Guptas, Rajputs, Muslims and then in British rule too. In Prithu's time, the production was in plenty; rains were in time; the trees' production was maximum, the oceans gave jewels/pearls etc. There was Mines Department to extract metals/minerals from the earth.

Prithu performed 99 Aswamedha yagyas. When he wanted to hold the 100th yagya, Indra got frightened and he created disturbance. There was a great fight and Indra created one mischief after another. Prithu then wanted to kill him but as usual then Brahma came to his rescue. In the realm of God too, the smaller gods Indra, Varuna etc. live under the protection of overall Lord Brahma and all gods, including Brahma and Shiva, live under the protection of almighty God, Vishnu. There is accordingly a multi-tier system of administration in the realm of God like the one in public administration. Brahma advised Prithu not to insist on holding the hundredth Aswamedhaa yagya as it was said that one, who performed 100th Aswamedha yagya, he would become the ruler of Swarga too snatching Swarga from Indra. Therefore, whosoever attained supremacy in yagya, tapsya etc. it was Indra, who became frightened of losing his kingship and would request Brahma for help. Since Brahma had himself advised Prithu not to hold the 100th Aswamedha yagya, he had to agree. Then Brahma told Prithu that Indra was regretting for having caused disturbance in 100th yagya. He may now be excused and Prithu may enter into an agreement with him. He told that great persons do not develop enmity with others as this body is not all in all and for the sake of Atma (a part of Paramatama), one should learn to excuse others. Otherwise one would be considered to be under the influence of 'maya' only.

सुधियः साधवो लोके नरदेव नरोत्तमाः,
नाभिद्रुह्यन्ति भूतेभ्योयर्हि नात्मा कलेवरम्। (4-20-3)

Atma is different from the body and intelligent persons care for the well-being of atma and not the body and the well-being of atma lies in its getting absorbed in Parmatma. In a way Brahama (God) advised Prithu now to leave the universe and resort to sanyas as is the tradition in Hindu dharma. Prithu fell in feet of the God and surrendered to his will. God picked him up and embraced him. Prithu requested God that he already had enough of dharma, wealth, satisfaction of worldly ambitions/passions (धर्म, अर्थ और काम) and he was not interested in salvation (मोक्ष) too. He only wished his ears to continue listening to Shiva and Hari leela (हरि चरितं) for all times to come, as also to serve them only. God asked him to rule till he desired as per dharma and then surrender himself to him, who will take care further. Blessing the king, God went away from there. King honoured all gods, rishis etc., who had gathered there after which they all went to their respective places. Here the God himself has narrated the jobs of a king and that he should limit himself to his sphere only and not to enter the other's realm as it would create trouble. In a way God did the job of maintaining the checks and balances between various kings, kings and gods and within gods too. The same theory of checks and balances is applied even in modern diplomatic relations and within the three fundamental ingredients of public administration viz Legislative, Executive and Judiciary. These all would appear to have come down from the ancient Hindu system of management.

Prithu's praja was prosperous and in peace during his regime. They all came out to welcome/receive the raja, when he came back to the kingdom in the traditional attire and form of shouting slogans of Jayakara, displaying banners and flower, garlands etc., Raja too in turn distributed alms and prizes to the subjects. The grant of award/jagirs/ reward by the Govt. to deserving persons in various spheres has been coming down from the ancient system mentioned in Hindu shastras. The tradition of producing food-grains and putting labour in the job for earning his livelihood by the raja came down to be followed by subsequent rulers of India, including the Muslim rulers. It is said that in Islam, everybody, including king, has to toil for himself to earn his livehood. All fundamentalist Muslims, therefore, do something to earn their livelihood. Even Aurangzeb is said to be preparing caps etc. in his idle time to have a semblance of earning his livelihood by labour. This also puts the concept of 'Labour' above all methods of earnings.

"आरब्धानेव बुभुजे भोगान् पुण्यजिहासया" (4-21-11)

To redress the public grievances, Raja Prithu had also been holding public audiences from time to time. This kept the bureaucrats at their toes and did not allow kings-men to harass public or act against the rules. This was followed by subsequent rajas in India, including the Muslim and British rulers—Jahangir's Darbar is famous. The kings, therefore, had in their palaces/forts, one enclosure called Diwan-e-aam (enclosure for meeting the general public) and another Diwan-e-khas (enclosure for holding meetings with his consultants, ministers or advisors). In one such meeting, Prithu proclaimed that all right-thinking people should come forward with their suggestions (complaints) in respect of the management by the king, protection and well-being of the public by the ruler and in arranging for their livelihood. He told that one of the jobs of ruler is to put the public on correct path of dharma and not simply collect tax from them. All subjects should give suggestions, complaints and also act as per tenets of dharma, included in the concept of varnas and ashramas. The king also advised about the ultimate salvation of the public by Bhagwad bhakti. In other words, the king cared for all the four achievements of public—dharma, wealth, satisfaction of worldly ambitions/passions and ultimately salvation (धर्म, अर्थ, काम और मोक्ष). In modern concept of governance, however, the king is to devote only in the spheres of regulating wealth and fulfilment of worldly desires (अर्थ और काम). King's above pronouncement made all gods, rishis, brahmins and public very happy and satisfied and praised the king. Ram too, during his rule, collected people and told them the way for attaining salvation.

When the King had finished his proclamation to public, four Munishwaras came there. As per tradition, king worshipped, honoured and respected them and then asked them to tell how a human being could attain salvation. Since the Munishwaras were the representatives of Brahma, the writer has chosen them to give reply to the king's query to make it more believable. The Munishwaras told that devotion to God is the sole way of attaining salvation. This relieves the men from worldly involvements, divest them from bodily attachment and inculcates vairagya in their minds leading to absorption in the almighty God. This, therefore, is the only way of attaining salvation, the Munishwaras told. The king felt grateful for their advice. Now when the rishis etc. came to Raj Bhawan, it was incumbent on the raja to offer presents to them. Here too the king placed himself, his wife, son, all wealth and kingdom at their disposal and requested for accepting anything out of it although they were all already fully content. They blessed the king to keep thinking of the well-being of his subjects as per his dharma. King praised them and after that the Munishwaras left for their abode.

King Prithu after ruling the kingdom for a long time as per the tenets of Rajdharma, handed over the kingship to his son and proceeded on sanyas as prescribed in the system of ashramas. In vanprastha and subsequently in sanyas, the king performed tapsya and ended up in attainment of salvation. His wife Archi had acccompanied the king to forests. Although she had never even stepped on land, she served her husband in the forests so that he did not face any difficulty in his conducting bhakti. After Prithu's death, the wife also resorted to sati with the husband. The concept of sati was existing in ancient period but it was only self-sacrifice thinking there was nothing left in the universe for the wife after husband had left, particularly for a wife, who was fully devoted to husband. Subsequently, some ill-ways cropped in the tradition and the people started burning the wives on death of husband forcefully in the garb of sati, either to grab their wealth or to eliminate the dynasty or to avoid the wife from entering into second marriage and so on.

After Prithu, his eldest son Antardhian succeeded him. He had four brothers. He, therefore, divided the kingdom into four and made each of his brothers, the ruler of each part. Although according to the tradition at that time, the eldest son succeeded the father, but it was upto him to keep his brothers with him to assist him in doing the Rajkarya or to divide the kingdom into parts entrusting each part to each of them. In Ram's period, Shri Ram was Chakravarty Raja and his brothers were with him in Ayodhya to assist him in the discharge of royal duties but after Shatrughan defeated the asur raja of Mathura, he continued to stay there to rule that area although it had been merged with Ayodhya. Similarly, the king of Hastinapur, Raja Dharitrastra had given a part of his kingdom to Pandavas to rule and Yudhisthra ruled making Indraprastha as his kingdom's capital. After the defeat of Pandavas in gambling, Indraprastha was annexed with

Hastinapur and after the return from forests, Pandvas had asked for the return of Indraprastha but Duryodhan refused leading to the war of Mahabharat. So here Raja Antardhian had divided his kingdom into four and made each of his brothers, raja of each of the 4 kingdoms. Further, here the writer has also indicated the main jobs of a raja as:

(1) To see that all people act as per varna-ashram dharma.

(2) Protection of praja from external aggressions.

(3) Perform acts of well-being of praja.

(4) To perform yagyas to keep all gods in his favour so that there was rain in time, foodgrain, milk, metals etc. production as per scheduled requirement.

(5) Manage the finances of the kingdom and control the central exchequer.

(6) To punish the criminals.

(7) To impose penalties for wrongs done and arranging their receipt and accountal.

(8) To receive the general tax—a part of the produce from the public.

This would indicate that detailed duties of people of all varnas had been prescribed in shastras.

राज्ञां वृत्तिं करादान दण्ड शुल्कादि दारुणाम्,
मन्यमानो दीर्घस्त्र व्याजेन विससर्ज ह। (4-24-6)

Thinking the jobs entrusted to the raja as cumbersome and tough, Raja Antardhian left the kingship and went away to forests. Then his sons etc. succeeded him and ruled for a long time. During their rule, one of them came across Bhagwan Shankar after tapsya. Shankar appeared before him and told that a grihastha person should perform his duties as per varna and ashram dharma and in doing so he would attain salvation. He also indicated that a person, who devotes himself to the bhakti of Vasudeva Bhagwan is quite affectionate to him. The writer has clearly told to remove any differences between Shaivites and Vishnuvites that bhakti of Shiva or Vishnu is of same almighty, whose three functions of creation, maintenance and annihilation are performed by the three forms viz. Brahma, Vishnu and Mahesh, of the same almighty God.

अथ भागवतां यूयं प्रियाःस्थ भगवान् यथा,
न मद्भागवतानां च प्रेयानन्योऽस्ति कर्हिचित्। (4-24-30)

Then Bhagwan Shiva alongwith the rajkumars praised the almighty God Vishnu. During Bhagwan's praise, Shiva said that the human being fully involved in worldly passions/ambitions is always worried of one job or the other and is busy in one thing or the other. Thus he gets more and more involved in these worldly passions but God is always alert. He, whereas puts the human being under the influence of his maya, also alerts him to keep away from worldly involvement. The differences between Shaivites and Vishnuvites existed in Ram period too and continued thereafter so much so that these differences further escalated even between the believers of Ram and Krishna. Goswami Tulsidas felt these differences and even, he, being the worshipper of Ram, initially did not believe in Krishna and it was only after he visited his brother, who was a Krishna bhakta and he prayed before the idol of Krishna that Tulsi would bow only when the Lord Krishna had dhanusban.

तुलसी मस्तक तब नवै धनुष बाण लो हाथ।

It is said that the idol of Krishna then appeared with dhanushban and Tulsidas became believer of Krishna too and thereafter wrote Krishna Geetawali. Therefore, trying to extinguish the difference between Krishnaites and Ramaites and again by making Ram say

"शिवद्रोही मम दास न होई" (मानस)

Shiva curser cannot be Ram bhakta, Tulsidas even finished differences between Shaivites and Vishnuaites as well.

Shiva after preaching the rajkumars about the importance of God-worship, went away to his place. The rajkumars were human beings, very much involved in the satisfaction of worldly passions and thought that satisfaction of these passions could be only in grihastha ashram.

धर्मो ह्यत्रार्थकामौ च प्रजानन्दोऽमृतं यशः

लोका विशोका विरजायान् न केवलिनो विदुः। (4-25-39)

But our ancient period did put checks on the actions while in grihastha dharma as well and even on the rajas such as the raja, while going out for hunting in forests was not allowed to kill many animals and even the non-vegetarian rajas were allowed to kill the animals to meet his requirement and not more than that.

तीर्थेषु प्रतिदृष्टेषु राजा मेध्यान् पशून् बने,

यावदर्थमलं लुब्धो हन्यादिति नियम्यते। (4-26-6)

Such detailed restrictions have been imposed on the vicious tasks undertaken by all, including the rulers. This was the protocol existing not only between the raja and praja but between the raja and all creatures as well. Killing of animals without requirement led one to be cruel towards animals, birds and then towards human beings too. Such a raja could, therefore, not think of well-being of the praja and would always think of extraction out of them. The people fall under the influence of 'Maya' and get involved in worldly passions. But all this 'bhog' is done by the body and for the body. The 'bhog' actions by the body are left over here on death and it is only the Bhagwad bhakti, which accompanies a person and that is the deciding factor for the subsequent formations. Body of a person performs all actions but there is some one else to give direction to the body for doing certain jobs. That someone is the 'mind' (मन) and the mind is a form of the atma itself. Thus mind or atma goes to Parloka after death and the atma or mind has to face the consequences of the doings by the body in this universe.

येनैवारभते कर्म तेनैवामुत्र तत्पुमान्

भुंकते ह्यव्यवधानेन लिंगेन मनसा स्वयं।

शयानमिममुत्सृज्य श्वसन्तं पुरुषो यथा,

कर्मात्मन्याहितं भुक्ंते तादृशेनेतरेण वा। (4-29-60/61)

It is this mind which under the influence of 'Maya' differentiates between 'me', 'mine' and 'you' ,'yours' and keeps involved in the worldly ambitions, which go on escalating every now and then and if the same mind comes out of the worldly involvements, it, after self-realisation, gets absorbed in God leading to salvation. Both things—involvement in worldly passions and absorption in God do not, therefore, go together. This in fact is the spiritual protocol guiding the relation of creature and the creator. The mind, therefore, is mainly responsible for operating the human body in the fashion, it likes. One can harvest as sown. Similarly the mind has to face the ultimate harvest of its doings—good or bad, as the case may be. All the senses, which want to enjoy worldly life, are monitored by the mind. The mind, can direct the hands to do puja or crime; directs the eyes to see God idol or a prostitute (वैश्या); the ears in listening to Bhagwat Katha or worldly abuses. Further, if the mind gets involved in worldly passions, it expects more and more for satisfaction of such passions. Similarly, a mind, busy in listening to Hari katha starts getting enjoyment more and move in listening to such katha, and ultimately leading to absorption in Hari himself. According to these actions only the human being gets one specie or the other or gets salvation and unless a mind (आत्मा) gets hold of another body (formation/specie), it does not leave the previous one. This is the concept of transmigration of soul accepted in Hindus and also accepted by other religions too in one form or the other.

Skandh – V

As already indicated Manu had two sons—Uttanpada and Priyavrat. The conduct of Uttanpada and his family has already been explained. Priyavrat was great Bhagwad bhakta but still he adopted and accepted and passed through grihastha ashram as per the tenets of dharma. He had wife, sons and home but ultimately attained salvation too. The reason for such an achievement is the Bhagwad Prem in earlier life. One who once gets absorbed in Bhagwad bhakti, he does not absolve himself completely from that path inspite of diversions caused to him due to the worldly involvement.

Priyavrat had received the Bhagwad bhakti gyan through Narad and the dharma of a raja (as ruler) and of a grihastha through his father Manu. He, therefore, was a composit of both grihastha and Bhagwad involvement. It was his father Manu, who ordered him to become raja as he had been fully trained in that trade. But with the fear that after getting involved in rajya, he would be deprived of Bhagwad bhakti, he was reluctant in accepting what the father had ordered. But Brahma desired Priyavrat to involve himself in the creation of universe for which purpose Manu had born. He, therefore, came to Priyavrat. Narad also came there at that time. Narad, Manu and Priyavrat paid respects to Brahma, worshipped him and praised him. Brahma then advised him that no one should have any atheistic thinking. Every one is created to follow his sermons to live in the universe and help create further. Also the creature has to perform his best in the form he is born. Brahma, therefore, advised him to get involved in the worldly passions and enjoy that life and meantime not to cut himself off from memory of almighty God too. Priyavrat accepted what Brahma ordained. He then worshipped Brahma. After entrusting the kingdom to Priyavrat, Manu adopted sanyas. Priyavrat married Brihasmati and had 10 sons, who were equally brave, diligent, intelligent, handsome and with all virtues. His rule was completely as per tenets of dharma and the entire praja followed the same. He divided the universe into seven continents and seven oceans. Same geographical division still exists. All the continents are surrounded by the oceans.

Once, after having ruled for many years, he met Narad Muni and realised that he had involved himself too much in the universe. He then left his wife, sons, kingdom etc. to be ruled by his sons and proceeded on sanyas as usual according to ashramas concept. Subsequently following what Priyavrat had been doing during his regime viz. creation of seven continents and seven oceans, the sons also continued creating further countries out of the continents and thus established the concept of various countries and their inhabitants. Then followed the concept of their inter-relation which is the present form of international laws and international relations. Subsequently the laws of war, peace, varan, ashram, dharma etc. were introduced and detailed rules on each concept prescribed in various vedas, shastras etc. These are the fundamentals of human faculties even to date.

Priyavrat's son Agnidhar had his son Nabhi. He succeeded the throne. But he did not have any offspring. He held a yagya to have a son. Vishnu Bhagwan appeared in the yagyashala. Nabhi requested him to give a boon that he would have a son like God himself. God said he did not have any of his like. He, therefore, will come as incarnate himself. Nabhi, therefore, had a son, who was named Risabh Bhagwan. Nabhi, in course of time, handed over the rajya to him and went to follow sanyas dharma. Praja was very much impressed with Risabha. He ruled for many years according to the tenets of dharma and provided all kinds of reforms for the well-being of the public. He had one hundred sons including the one named 'Bharat'. India was named as 'Bharatvrasha' after his name during his rule. All the sons were intelligent and learned in various vocations. Bharat, being the eldest, succeeded the throne. Risabha coached the people, the gyan of self-realisation and the ultimate attainment of salvation. He also told his sons to rise above self and sacrificing the worldly involvements of having wife, sons, home, wealth etc., the attractions of the materialistic world. One should not indulge in these as these are the 'maya part' of the almighty, which carry the human beings away from the achievement of ultimate goal of nirvan. 'Me' and 'Mine' are the cults which one has to get rid of. One should, therefore, be very alert in this universe and have Bhagwad bhakti through which he would be absorbed in him and attain salvation. Ultimately Rishabha Deva handed over the rajya to the eldest son Bharat and adopted sanyas dharma like the ordinary person to show that the concept of varnas and ashramas was sancrocent and had to be followed by all in India.

Bharat was a great ruler and Bhagwad bhakta. It is observed that in ancient India, all rulers had been Bhagwad bhaktas too and if there was any who was with asura's instincts, he could not live long. Either he was killed by praja or God's incarnate as during those days India being in Satya yug, there was constant affinity between the rishis/munis of India and the almighty God through yog/bhakti or self-realisation. India, which was so far called "Ajnabhvarsh" became Bharatvarsha after the name of ruler, Bharat. Bharat, like his predecessors, held many yagyas establishing his sovereignty on the entire universe. One thing to be seen is that all these rulers were Chakravarty emperors having their kingdom through the entire universe. Even in havans/yagyas etc., the gods used to accept the ahutis by personal appearance.

In course of time after many years of rule, Raja Bharat distributed his kingdom amongst his sons and went out to an ashram adopting sanyas.

"स्वतनयेभ्यो रिक्थं पितृपैतामहं यथादायं विभाज्य स्वयं सकल—
सम्पन्निकेतात्सवनिकेतात पुलशश्रम प्रवव्राज"। (5-7-8)

So far the tradition had been to handover the throne to the eldest son if he was not incapable to hold the charge according to the rule of 'PRIMOGENITOR' but here the mention is that the emperor Bharat had distributed his kingdom amongst his sons. This seem to be a departure from the set tradition. Here it is also indicated that the kingdom was distributed amongst his sons by the raja according to their capability (यथायोग्य). It is not explained how he departed from the tradition. But one reason might be that the kingdom was very vast (entire universe) which could not be ruled by one son and, therefore, Raja Bharat would have distributed it amongst his sons according to the capability of each of them. There is instance of such distribution by Ram too when he made Shatrughan, an independent raja of Mathura after he conquered it from an asur raja after killing him whereas all other brothers lived together in Awadh, assisting Ram in the governance of the kingdom.

While in sanyas, one day Bharat was sitting by the side of a river after taking morning bath etc. He saw a she deer coming to the river to take water. At that time she heard the lion roaring. Out of fear she jumped in the river. She was pregnant at that time and during the jump she delivered off the baby deer and died. King brought the baby deer out of mercy to his ashram and kept it very affectionately, so much so that in bringing up the baby deer, he even started missing his daily programme of bhakti etc. thinking that the baby deer having been alone in the universe, there was none to bring him up. He also thought that the baby too had been considering Bharat his all in all. He had always been thinking of the deer only protecting him from all other animals; arranging for his meals etc. But the deer, one day left the ashram. After all the animal loved to live independently in the forest along with other animals only and could not live with Bharat even though he loved him immensely. Bharat started feeling the separation of the deer so much that at the time of his death too he had been thinking of the baby dear only. After death he could not attain salvation as he, rather than getting absorbed in

Bhagwad bhakti, was absorbed in the affection of the baby deer and unless one gets rid of the worldly affections, one can not attain salvation. Bharat in next birth, became deer as he had been thinking of the deer only at the time of his death. But in view of his past Bhagwad bhakti, he continued to have vairagya from the worldly involvements. Bharat's life span confirms—

(1) The king had to rule as per the tenets of dharma.

(2) He was to expand his kingdom; collect wealth for the kingdom from other rajas; keep them as his vassals.

(3) Holding Aswamedha and other yagyas from time to time to establish his supremacy amongst the vassals under him and also for the well-being of the praja.

(4) The rajas after a long rule, when found themselves unable to continue ruling, would handover the rajya to his sons and proceed to adopt sanyas, to attain ultimate salvation.

(5) Although the concept of succession to the throne by the eldest son *i.e.* the rule of primogenitor was existing in those days, it was the prerogative of the king to handover the kingdom to any of the sons, as may be considered capable of governance. Even Raja Dasratha had said, when Kaikayee asked for handing over rajya to Bharat and sending Ram to forest for 14 years, that he was handing over the rajya to Ram as he was the eldest and capable of holding it otherwise as per his prerogative, he could hand it over to Bharat too. Raja, accordingly as per that prerogative divided the kingdom amongst has various sons according to their capacity and capability.

(6) During sanyas one should not get attached to materialistic worldly things. Raja Bharat, although had divested himself of the affection of his wife and sons and after handing over kingdom to his sons had proceeded for sanyas and was doing all actions of a sanyasi, fell in affection of the baby deer and forgot all his duties toward God and his dharma as a sanyasi.

(7) The king could not attain salvation as he had not detached himself from worldly vices of affection etc. One, therefore, has to detach himself completely from the worldly vices and get absorbed in the almighty to attain salvation.

(8) One descends on rebirth according to one's thinking at the time of death. The king had been thinking of the baby deer only at that time, so he became deer in the next birth.

(9) The theory of transmigration of soul is established along with the concept that a human being could come in any specie and not necessarily of a human being only as per his actions in life. The king Bharat at first became a deer and in the next birth he was born as brahmin in view of his tapsya as Bharat. As a brahmin he again resorted to Bhagwad bhakti and got salvation.

(10) One can come in any form on rebirth taking into account his doings not only in the immediate last life but on the reckoning of his previous lives as well.

On his birth as a brahmin, Bharat remembered the doings of his previous lives and had everytime a fear in his mind that he might again be put to same kind of formations as before. Due to this perception, he did not take interest in his studies inspite of best efforts of his father and brother. As per protocol, it was the duty of the father to make his sons educated but he died without any success in his mission. People started taking him as a 'mental' case. He used to eat whatever others gave him. He had attained some sort of self-realisation (आत्मज्ञान) as a result of which he never minded his happiness/sadness etc. He would not even take bath or take interest in any worldly/ personal needs. One day, the people of a shudra Raja, were searching for someone to be offered as human sacrifice (नर बली) to Chandi Goddess. They got hold of this brahmin and prepared him for the sacrifice, although as per law the killing of a human being is forbidden except in emergency and even then the killing of a brahmin is not allowed at all. Seeing a brahmin having been brought for sacrifice, the Goddess came in motion from the idol. She was enraged and looked quite furious. She killed all the people, who wanted to sacrifice the brahmin. She, in this way, had shown that any crime on the saints falls back on the crime-doer itself.

एवमेव खलु महदाभिचाराति क्रमः कार्त्स्न्येनात्मने फलति। (5-9-19)

Thereafter once Raja Rahugana of Sindhu Sauvir country was passing on his palki. The palki carriers needed one person for carrying palki. They came across the brahmin (Bharat) and put him to carry the palki. He was not able to keep pace with other carriers. When the palki was not being carried smoothly, the Raja ordered them to walk evenly. The carriers felt afraid since the Raja was not happy. They told the raja that they were walking in order but this new carrier was not able to keep pace with them. The raja thought that one bad man in the group could spoil the others if not set right in time. The Raja, sarcastically told the brahmin that he was tired having carried the palki alone, being not quite strong enough for this purpose. The brahmin did not, however, mind, what raja had said as the brahmin had realised the Atma-Parmatma relation and had absorbed himself in the almighty. The palki was still moving unevenly. The raja got enraged and threatened him of dire punishment if he did not mend himself. The brahmin did not still mind it and told him that whatever he had said was correct because the palki had to be carried by the carriers; the path was to walk on, the fatness too belonged to the body and not to the atma. The rage, wishes, threat, fear, pride, love, lethargy, old age etc. were all relevant to the person, proud of his body and that these were not there in him. So far as the question of life and death was concerned, this happens to all mortals. He was not afraid of that too. He was a raja and the brahmin was his subject. He did not, therefore, see any room for objecting to what the raja had said. He was prepared to do whatever the raja wanted him to do but there would be no use punishing him. The brahmin stopped talking after saying all this and continued to carry the palki but the raja hearing these fundamentals of shastras from the brahmin got down from the palki and fell in his feet and recognising him as brahmin requested him to tell, who he was as he was afraid of having insulted a brahmin, more than of anything else. Brahmin accepted that being a Raja he had said all good things and had to tell him without knowing that he was a brahmin and now begged to be excused. The brahmin further coached the raja indicating the duties of a grihastha raja, etc. and the detailed vedic philosophy, God and creatures relation and the virtues and vices of the man in the universe. The raja bowed before him and requested him to coach him of the vedic philosophy in a simple way. The brahmin told him that firstly using the persons to carry his palki was only indicative of his being a proud raja, who boasted of helping his subject whereas here he was being cruel to them. All mortals and immortals were part of God himself and this could be known when one found God in all those things and got absorbed in God. The brahmin then told that in the past he was Raja Bharat and leaving the universe he adopted sanyas but then fell in love of a deer. He got that specie on next birth and now have become a brahmin after several transmigrations but due to his tapsya, he remembered the Bhagwad bhakti in each birth. Now he lives in isolation having been frightened by the behaviour of the human beings and waiting to get absorbed in almighty God. The raja got converted into Bhagwad bhakta and admitted that the satsang only could convert even an animal into a bhakta. The raja only by a few hours coaching of the brahmin became bhakta and realised the self.

King Bharat was the ruler of not only India but the entire universe. The universe had already been divided into seven continents and seven oceans. The seven continents were—

(1) Jambu Dweep. It included Indian sub continent surrounded by mountains in the north, north west and north east and by ocean in the south, south east and south west. Entire India is accordingly safe from all sides. It has many rivers and hills. The writer has mentioned many hills and many rivers. The hills and rivers exist even today. This would indicate that in

our ancient time there must have been comprehensive survey of the entire land. There is mention of the use of river water by the habitants along side these rivers. These rivers had also been tamed by the rulers for supply of water to the subjects, which proves the engineering fete of that period. Bharatvarsh being protected by mountains and ocean from all sides, there was no fear of external aggression. The battles were amongst the rajas of various kingdoms within India. The rajas were conducting yagyas etc. for timely rains. Infact in view of the vicinity of mountains and ocean, the rains must have been a natural phenomena in India. Further, the land being fertile and with the use of river waters which was available in plenty, there were no famines or shortage of foodgrains etc. The land being rich in minerals, there were departments of mines and forests, and the mines etc. were also fully exploited. People were, therefore, well off. God had been particularly happy on India in view of the fact that the rishis/munis could undertake undisturbed tapsya and all others too had been adopting vanprasth and sanyas in time. So Bhagwad bhakti was at the top. Rishis/munis were respected by all others. Therefore, by their tapsya, they could keep the gods pleased and always prayed for the well-being of the people of this country. The country being so well of and Bhagwad bhakti immensely prevailing, even the gods prayed for a birth in Bharatvarsha to enable them to resort to Bhagwad bhakti. Even the rishis/munis etc. rather than asking for salvation in boon from the God, they only wished to be Bhagwad bhakta in whatever form/specie they came on transmigration.

(2) Plux Dweep—This is also surrounded by oceans. This dweep had ample of forests in it. There were a few mountains and rivers too. There was ample of rain which enabled forests coming up.

(3) Kusha Dweep—This is also surrounded by oceans. There were herbs and small mountains in this dweep. Priyavrat's one son Hiranyareta ruled this place. He

had divided the continent into seven countries–each ruled by his seven sons.

(4) Karauncha Dweep—This is also surrounded by oceans. This dweep is mostly mountainous. There were many forests and gardens, full of flowers and fruits in this continent.

(5) Shak Dweep—Again surrounded by oceans, this was also ruled by one of Priyavrat's sons, who further divided it into seven countries. It contained many big forests. There were seven mountains and seven rivers.

(6) Pushkar Dweep—surrounded by oceans, it had many lakes full of kamals. It was ruled by Priyavrat's another son Ramnak.

(7) Beyond these dweeps there were two big dweeps fully covered by mountains and ice. These most be referring to the Poles of the present day having Antarctic and Arctic continents/oceans.

The above narration indicates that

(1) The emperors of India ruled the entire universe in those days.

(2) The universe had been properly divided into continents and countries with a view to have effective governance.

(3) The rivers/mountains etc. had been adequately exploited to the benefit of mankind.

(4) Proper survey of the entire universe had been undertaken. The continents/oceans mentioned even now testify their correctness.

(5) Mines and forests had been fully exploited that is why there were ample of jewels, diamonds, gold, other metals etc. in use in those days.

(6) The Rule of Law existed and all rulers followed these rules. These rules were nothing else than the vedic and other shastriya tenets.

(7) Not only the universe but also the entire space and other stars had been surveyed and there is narration of what exists in these stars also. The research in

present days is a very small fraction of what had been achieved in those days.

(8) Foodgrains were in plenty as rains were in time and to the extent of requirement.

(9) The kings were also able to undertake works for the well-being of their subjects.

(10) There were proper fortifications of the land to protect the kingdom from external aggression.

(11) There was research undertaken in geographical aspects too thereby explaining the change of seasons; formation of days and nights, months and years the speed and movement of stars and there inter-star effects, the weather conditions in various countries, including the poles.

(12) Lastly full research had been conducted in the "Man, his actions and results", thereby establishing that every person is faced with three kinds of temperaments viz., satvic, rajshi and tamshic. One who has primarily satvic temperaments, he conducts himself as per the dictates of dharma, does not annoy any one and is helpful to all; the one with rajshi temperament, lives for himself and the one with tamsic character loots others, annoys others and is a fear for each other. They do not at all conduct themselves as per dharma. After death too these persons meet with good or bad behaviour on behalf of the almighty. The concept of various Swargas and Narkas (heaven and hell) is also with reference to one's temperament and conduct in this universe—satvic, rajshi or tamsic. Whereas the persons with satvic conduct get salvation or ultimate Swaraga (Heaven); the rajshi persons get both good and bad conditions, heaven for some time and then hell. They are born in this universe in the specie determined as per their actions in the previous life (lives). The person with tamsic character and conduct gets very sever Naraka (Hell) and is born after passing through hell and undesirable species.

Skandh – VI

This part deals with the rituals, which, if followed, can save the person from all kinds of tortures after death. As already indicated, the man is born under the influence of 'maya'. Now it is upto him to fall or not to fall and the extent to which one falls under that influence depending upon his conduct in the universe. A man in grihastha is subject to all kinds of influences of maya in the form of passion, rage, pride, arrogance, greed etc. One feels that by dint of possessing these, he would be happy in his life but actually the effect is otherwise. The more one gets involved in the satisfaction of these instincts, the more one becomes prone to such inducement and it is only at a very late stage that one realises of the hollowness in all these vices. These vices are undertaken by a person through heart, action and speech (मन, कर्म, वचन), and unless one atones for this vicious conduct in this life span, one has to face the effect after death in determining the specie, one attains. A person resorts to vices in the universe under ignorance. Therefore, the effect of a bad action can be neutralised by a good action and so on. A person living as per the dictates of dharma, keeps control on all vices and then gets absorbed in almighty God resulting in the attainment of salvation. The vices can be eliminated by tap, control over passions, a strong will power, donation, truth and a pious life. Such a conduct finishes the vicious elements in one's life. Or one alternative to these is the Bhagwad bhakti, if one could resort to follow it by keeping the company of the sudhus. This is said to be best path for attaining salvation. One, who has learnt to get absorbed in the almighty God, all his sins are washed out and one becomes entitled to salvation. The story of Ajamil is an eye-opener in this context. Ajamil had been doing all sorts of crimes to bring up his family of 10 persons. His youngest son was 'Narayan'. He was fond of that son. At the time of death, he got frightened with the Yama's men and being frightened he called 'Narayan' for help. Since he had remembered 'Narayan', the God, at the time of death, the Yama's men went away and the angels came to take him after death. In this way, even if one submits to the mercy of God at the end of life, one becomes entitled to salvation. Ajamil too was initially leading his life according to the tenets of dharma but once he met a prostitute (वैश्या)in a naked form. His passions aroused and he fell for her. Thereafter he started doing all sorts of bad actions to get hold of money to please the vaisya and in the brought up of her family. He continued with this sort of life till death but then at the time of death he remembered 'Narayan' although through the medium of his son and because of that all his sins in the past were waived and he got salvation in view of the fact that at the time of his death on his calling 'Narayan' the angels had come and they narrated the 'Dharma' to the Yama's men. This narration was heard by Ajamil too and because of that he became a bhakta and got absorbed in God leading to salvation.

Here the question arose as to whether the Yamaraj is superior or there is someone else, who had the overall power to undo the actions of Yamaraj's men. It is here that the concept of VETO comes in. The concept of VETO which is used in present time for undoing the actions of the subordinates/juniors etc. exists in the realm of God too where God is the almighty with over all VETO in his powers and the smaller gods work under his overall control although they have been given autonomy within their fields. This is like the institution of federation in our times where the federating units have limited autonomy and the overall command rests with the federal Govt. In UNO too the five permanent members of Security Council have VETO power for undoing what has been decided by all others. In the realm of God too there is some such concept working. This is what was told by the Yamaraj on having been questioned by his men who had been forbidden from taking away Ajamil for punishing him for his vicious actions. Yamaraj told that there is one almighty God. He has three parts in Brahma, Vishnu and Mahesh, who create, maintain and annihilate the creatures of the universe. Under these three parts are various small gods like Indra, (the incharge of Swaraga), Varun (incharge of water) Kuber (incharge of treasury) Aditya (The Sun) Wind, Fire, Yamaraj etc. They all have some autonomy but are under the over-all control of the almighty God. These small gods too have further subordinates under them to assist the respective gods in the discharge of their duties. In this way their is a fool - proof multi-tier system of governance in the realm of almighty God with God having the VETO power to undo any action of the gods under him. Bhagwad dharma has been institutionalised by God only and the creature follow the tenets of dharma as per their understanding and to the best of their capability but the result is reckoned by the God only in his own way.That is why Shri Krishna had confirmed in Gita that man should go on doing actions and leave the result to him:

"कर्मण्येव अधिकारस्ते मा फलेषु कदाचन"। (गीता-2-47)

Bhagwad bhakti is, therefore, the only sure way of absorption in him and attainment of salvation by leaving the result to God.

Raja Prachinbarihi had ten sons born in sea. After coming out from sea, they saw the entire land covered by trees etc. They, therefore, created wind and fire to destroy the trees. The trees started getting burnt but then God saw that in this way all forests would be destroyed whereas these were neessary for the living of the creature. God told them to stop destroying the trees as the trees were meant for —

(1) providing fruits, flowers and medicines for the use of creatures;

(2) the trees provided the abode, and flowers and fruits for being eaten by birds;

(3) the animals like snakes and reptiles, the plants and their leaves and grass had been made;

(4) other animals, trees, creepers and plants had been made;

(5) human beings, foodgrains, fruits etc. have been made;

(6) animals like oxen, camels etc. are helpful in the growing of foodgrains etc.

The forests etc. therefore, have their use and are not to be annihilated particularly Prachinbarihi had been sent with the task of creating the universe and if the trees etc. are annihilated then how will the beings survive? This philosophy had been there behind the existence of the forests, trees, plants etc. Even though it is in existence today and the forests' existence is very much felt necessary but some greedy people cut off trees for filling their coffers without caring for the existing rules. As God had told the sons of Prachinbarihi, someone has to take in hand the survival of the forest today and punish the culprits. Pachetas then stopped burning the trees and after getting married, they produced off-spring. Raja/Prajapati Daksha was one of their sons. Daksha produced gods, rakshasas and human beings. He produced from his wife Asikni, ten thousand sons and 60 daughters. The daughters were married to Dharma, Moon, Kashyap, Bhoot, Pisacha etc. They produced further off-spring to add to the creatures of the universe. Most of the creation of earth is that from the union of Kashyap and his wives Aditi, Diti, Danu, Kastha, Arista, Sursa, Ila, Muni, Krodhvasha, Tamra, Surbhi, Sarma and Timi. Timi produced the creatures of water; Sarma produced animals like lions, tigers etc; Surbhi produced cattle; Tamra produced birds like eagle, duck etc; Muni produced apsras, Karodhvasha produced serpents, reptiles etc.; Ila produced trees, creepers; Sursa produced rakshasas; Arista produced Gandharvas; Kastha produced horses etc.; Danu produced 61 human beings; Aditi gave birth to almighty God's incarnate as Baman and Indra, Varuna/Dhates, Vidhata etc.–12 sons.

Indra got the wealth of all Lokas because of his tapsya. This included the rajya of Swargaa as well. Having got the rajya of Swaraga, he fell in the leisures and pleasures so much that once when he was rejoicing in Swaraga, Guru Brihaspati came and Indra did not pay respects to him. He did not even stand up on his coming. Brihaspati without saying any word, came out and went away. After he had left, Indra realised his mistake and went in his search but could not find him. Asuras were under the discipleship of Shukracharya. He came to know through his intelligence that there was some ill-feeling between Brihaspati and gods. Taking advantage of the situation, asuras invaded the gods and injured them badly. In that condition, in the absence of their Guru Brihaspati, they went to Brahma for help. Brahma at first condemned Indra's behaviour towards Brihaspati and then directed them to go to a Tapasvi Vishwarupa, who with his Vaishnavi knowledge managed to return the looted wealth of Indra to him. In this episode the writer has touched upon the following points of protocol:

(1) The principles of protocol are applicable not only to this universe but to Swarga Lok as well.

(2) One should not be proud and get lost after attaining wealth and kingship. In Ramcharit Manas too it is said that "जग बोराइ राजपदु पाएँ". Indra after attaining the kingship of Swarga, had been much proud and did not care for his guru even.

(3) The guru had to be respected in whatever position one might be. The principle that "The king should not leave the singhasan" does not apply when guru comes. Brihaspati was the guru of all gods but Indra did not pay respects when he came to his darbar.

(4) The greatness lies in excusing the guilty. Even when Indra did not pay respect to Brihaspati, he did not utter a word there and simply walked out of the Sabha.

(5) When one is insulted in any Sabha, one should not stay there at all.

(6) Even though an insulted guru does not do any harm to the disciple, the other people take advantage of

the rift in particular persons. Due to ill-feeling between Brihaspati and Indra, the asuras thought that Brihaspati would not help Indra and they took advantage of the situation and attacked on gods and defeated them. Similar situation arose in India when taking advantage of the dispute between Prithvi Raj and Jaichand, Mohammed Ghori invaded India and defeating Prithvi Raj established Muslim Rule in India. Subsequently taking advantage of the disputes amongst various rajas/nawabs of India, British established their kingdom defeating the rajas/nawabs one by one, and India have to pay for it till date.

(7) There was Intelligence Department existing in those days, working very efficiently. The ill-feeling between Indra and Brihaspati came to be known by the asuras and taking advantage of the same, they invaded the gods.

(8) One enemy should be on the look out for the weak points of the other and take advantage of the same at the appropriate time. There had always been battles between asuras and gods, sometimes gods won and the others asuras. So asuras were always on the lookout for a chance to conquer gods and loot the wealth of Swargaa.

(9) In case of difficulty, one should approach the immediate superior and in his absence only approach the next superior as a matter of protocol. The gods having been defeated by asuras, had always been approaching Brihaspati, their guru to help them but now since guru could not be traced, they had to go to the next superior. In other words the governance by channel exists in God's realm too.

(10) Such superior should not automatically entertain the aggrieved person but should at first make him realise his mistake of offending the immediate superior.

(11) The guru/elders have to be respected and the persons in a meeting have to stand up in respect for the guru when he comes to the meeting. Standing up is

considered as a sign of respect for the incumbent. Brihaspati felt insulted when Indra did not even stand up in the Sabha.

(12) The intelligent persons after having done a mistake atone for the same. Indra, although did not pay respect to Guru Brihaspati, yet immediately realised his mistake after guru left the Sabha and he atoned for the same. The intelligence of Guru Brihaspati lay in having left the sabha without uttering a word and that paid the premium as Indra on this, realised his mistake. If Brihaspati had said something then it would have resulted in quarrel between the two.

(13) On the asuras having defeated gods and looted them, the gods went to Viswarupa for help and Viswarupa by his Vaisnavi know-how obtained back the looted property. It shows that battle was not the only way of conquering someone but there were other methods too—might be some method of give and take to settle score without resorting to war. Even today many international disputes are resolved by such methods (i.e. execution of international agreements of give and take, rather than resorting to war).

(14) There were persons with specialisation in each vocation. Brahma directed the gods to Viswarupa, who was only a tapsvi and could not have helped the gods facing the asuras in battle but he must have specialised in mediating between the parties in disputes. So he helped the gods getting back the wealth looted by the asuras. The other aspects of the deal are not known. Its spiritual part is the repetition of two mantras ''ॐ नमो नारायणाय'' "Om Namo Narayanaya' and ''ॐ नमो भगवते वासुदेवाय'' "Om Namo Bhagwate Vasudevaya" sitting in a particular position. This mantra is called Narayan Kawach (नारायण कवच). Any one, who owns this Kawach, gets whatever he wants.

(15) The body, wealth and people of the universe are mortals and are of no use to oneself but are of use to

others. Therefore, a thing which is for being used by others can be had by others who are the actual owners.

अहो दैन्यमहोकष्टं पारक्यैः क्षणभङ्गुरैः,

यन्नोपकुर्यादस्वार्थैर्मर्त्यः स्वज्ञातिविग्रहैः। (6-10-10)

(16) Every one, who is born has to die. There is nothing that can save anyone from death. In such a condition one should opt for the best use of body before death. Two types of deaths are considered best—one by the yog when he is absorbed in Brahama and in that position he leaves the universe and another to die in battle field, while fighting with the enemy. This is the war strategy. The commander has to be a good inspirer. By inspiration he can put his running men to fight with enemy. Same was done here and such an inspiring lecture had its effect in the battle field.

(17) A wealthy person is most selfish in the universe. The more wealth he has, the more he becomes self-centered. Under the pride of wealth, Indra insulted his Guru Brihaspati and when asuras had defeated them, they made Viswarupa as their guru and Viswarupa by virtue of giving Narayan Kawach helped gods obtain their wealth back from the asuras. But Viswarup's mother being from Asura dynasty, he had also been helping the asuras in yagyas. This could not be tolerated by Indra, who deceitfully killed Viswarupa. Now here Indra was guilty of having killed a brahmin, who was guru too and also having killed him deceitfully. Having done this anti protocol job, Indra had been hiding himself and wandering from one place to another for over a year. Meantime when Viswarupa's father came to know of his son having been killed by Indra, he created an asura named Vritrasura. He was very brave and frightening. He attacked the gods and defeated them. They, as usual, worshipped Vishnu, who advised that Vritrasura could be killed by the Vajra (वज्र) made of the bones of Dadhichi Muni. They, therefore, should beg for the flesh of Dadhichi as beggers and then get one Vajra prepared out of his bones. The gods followed Vishnu's

advice and went and begged for the flesh of Dadhichi. Dadhichi was known as a donor. He could not refuse, although he had known that the gods had been sent by Vishnu. He killed himself by yog and offered himself to gods. Gods got Vajra prepared from his bones and then challenged Vritrasura. The gods defeated his army and also attacked him. It is at this time that he inspired his commanders to lose their lives in battlefield and earn good name rather than running away from the battlefield. Vritrasura knew that the Vajra had been made from Dadhichi's bones on the advice of Vishnu. He, therefore, submitted himself to the wish of Vishnu. He got absorbed in him and offered himself to be killed by Indra as he believed that conquest, wealth, and all virtues are available on the side which is helped by the almighty God.

तेनैव शत्रुं जहि विष्णुयन्त्रितो।
यतो हरिर्विजयः श्रीर्गुणास्ततः। (6-11-10)

It is rare that an asur had so much belief in the almighty God. He prayed to God to keep him in his service in whatever specie he was born after his death and that he did not have any wish for salvation etc. He preferred to die and get absorbed in the almighty God rather than conquering Indra and attaining the rajya of Swarga. Vritrasura attacked Indra by a Trishul. He got frightened and the Vajra also fell down from his hand but still Vritrasura did not kill Indra as it was against the laws of war to kill enemy without arms. He, therefore, permitted Indra to pick up the Vajra and then kill him. There cannot be a better example of :

(1) Belief in almighty God.

(2) Submission to the cause of God.

(3) Following the laws of war even though it involved his own death.

(4) There were the laws of war, which were followed even by the asuras what to speak of other rajas.

(5) There were frequent battles between the gods and the asuras on one pretext or the other.

(6) Indra was always afraid of any human being excelling in tapsya or bravery lest he should snatch the Swarga from him.

(7) The gods had always been going to the almighty God for protection in case of loss suffered by them due to the attack of asuras.

(8) Even the almighty God had been helping the gods in case of difficulty, even though such a difficulty was their own creation, as and when they went and prayed for protection. This only shows that even after incurring sins, if one goes and repents before the almighty, he forgives him and accedes to his request. Such a relief is there is all religions. Christianity specially believes that after causing any sin, if one goes to Christ and begs to be excused, he excuses him. Similarly such a belief is there in Muslims too.

(9) Although Vritrasura allowed Indra to pick up the Vajra from the earth and to kill him yet he believed that creation, maintenance and annihilation was only in the hands of the almighty God and Indra or anybody else, who takes the pride of having killed or saved anyone, is false.

(10) Vritrasura was such a learned person, knowing the entire vedantic philosophy, that an asura could not be expected to be. This was all blessing of God to him.

(11) Indra appreciated the benevolence on the part of Vritrasura for having allowed him to pick up the Vajra and to kill him and he recognised him not as asura but as a great saint as he had left all asura vices and got absorbed in the almighty God. Indra then after a lot of further fighting killed him.

(12) Aswamedha yagya was a panacea for all sins as in this yagya the almighty God is worshipped and on successful completion of the yagya, all sins are excused. Indra had been unhappy over Vritrasura's killing as it amounted to killing of a brahmin. But Aswamedha yagya wiped off that sin.

(13) Happiness of a raja depends on the well-being of some neessary ingredients—guru, mantri, kingdom, fort, treasury (exchequer), army, friends, praja, diwan, traders, vassal rajas and queen (s) and son (s). The king is restless when even one of these ingradients is lacking.

(14) An issueless raja could have sons by performing certain yagyas. Raja Dasratha got Ram, Lakshman, Bharat and Shatrughana with the help of the yagya. Pandu got all his sons with the help of Dharma, Sun, Indra, etc. Similarly Raja Chitraketu got a son by performing a yagya. The yagya in those days would indicate that their must be some high standard clinical operation/ medication which could improve fertility for the purpose of bearing offspring. For such a specialisation the name of yagya had been given. Indra was worshipped for rains. That would also indicate that some scientific method might be there to effect rains. Even today artificial rains can be caused by sprinkling some chemicals on clouds. By this method the rain can be had to the requirement. In past period too it is said that rain could be had to requirement, would only affirm this belief.

(15) The life and death is as per luck. Sometimes young children die whereas their elders are still alive. It is said such things did not happen in Ram Rajya and if such an occasion took place then Raja was held responsible for it. It was said if such deaths and births were to take place according to the fortune then where was the need of the existence of God to control all these deaths and births.

न हि क्रमश्चेदिह मृत्युजन्मनोः,
शरीरिणामस्तु तदाऽऽत्मकर्मभि। (6-14-55)

(16) In the case of death of Chitraketu's son obtained from yagya, Narad told the sad raja that the life and death are as per karma (कर्म) of the previous births/

future births. In this way we meet and disperse in this universe after finishing our respective jobs and this cycle goes on. A believer in God should not, therefore, get upset on the death of a close relation. One is at first upset when one does not have offspring and then more upset where one loses the offspring. Therefore, the best thing is to have a belief that the wife, sons, friends etc. are of momentary conjunction and bound to set apart. The earlier one reconciles to this situation, the better it is. To prove this, Narad made the dead son of Chitraketu alive. The son then told Raja of his past transmigrations and his relations in each form. Some were now old; some were young; some were yet to born etc. One, therefore, should not think that one particular body is only his son/father etc. as the relation changes with each transmigration. After telling all this, the son again died. The raja got enlightened and adopted vairagya (वैराज्ञ) thereafter. In fact it is the God, who is the atma in each body. He creates each body and enters into it. He maintains it till he wants it and then gets out of it when he has some other formation to adopt.

(17) As we say in English that "Nothing is good or bad but thinking makes it so", so did Chitraketu Raja say in his meeting with Shiva that the creature keeps on wandering about in the universe because of ignorance, passing through the sadness and happiness. In fact neither one creates sadness nor happiness for himself nor are these created by others. These come and go in cycle as per karma but the ignorant persons blame self or others for causing the same.

नैवात्मा न परश्चापि कर्तास्यात् सुखदुःखयोः
कर्तारम् मन्यतेऽप्राज्ञ आत्मानां परमेव च। (6-17-20)

(18) One, who has absorbed himself in God, does not have any fear from anyone as he takes it that sadness and happiness, birth and death, boon and curse etc. are all god-gifted and cannot be managed by creatures.

(19) God being in everyone, does not consider anyone very dear or very non-dear; everyone is same for him.

(20 On Parvati having passed on a curse on Chitraketu that he would be asura, Chitraketu accepted it otherwise in exchange he too could have passed on a curse on Parvati. Great men do not have an addiction of taking revenge but accept even the curses with obligation.

(21) Nobody can understand a woman; her face is like a lotus in full blossom; her talks are quite sweet like amrit but the heart is quite sharp. They are selfish and for their selfishness, they can even get their close relations killed.

Skandh – VII

From the narration so far, it is clear that the almighty God, who is considered to be non-partial to anyone, appears to have been partial in favour of Indra and other gods and impartial to asuras or in some cases even to the rishis/ munis where Indra had been frightened because of the tapsya done by them. God even waived all the ill-doings of Indra and punishing others, who had already been wronged by Indra and other gods. This appears something unprotocolic on the part of the almighty God.

As already indicated, all such clarifications have been given either by God himself or by his representative like Narad Muni etc., with a view to put some element of confirmation in it. Similar question had been asked by Yudhisthra when at the time Shishupal was killed by Lord Krishna, he got absorbed in Krishna himself. Then Narad had told that partiality, impartiality, insult, praise etc. all are relevant to the existence of body only and not to atma. The man indulges in all these good or bad things by dint of his selfishness. It is here that the God's maya comes into operation because of which man inculcates within himself "this is me", "this is mine" and "this is you", "this is yours" concept. From this only the entire universe operates, and one can get rid of this only on getting absorbed in God. Now absorption in God can be by bhakti or enmity. God's enemy is also Bhagwad bhakta as he too always remembers God and always thinks of him only. That is why Shishupal on death could get absorbed in Krishna. Similarly Kansa had been thinking of Krishna only out of fear that he was his killer; the rishis etc. remember God out of love or bhakti for him. Some rajas in the Krishna period remembered him out of jealousy. The family of Yaduvansh had been absorbed in Krishna out of their affectionate relation and the gopis had been in Krishna because of their love or intimacy with him.

After Hirnakshya had been killed by the God as incarnate Varaha, his brother Hirnakshyap consoled his mother that he would take revenge of his brother's death by the God. For this purpose, he at first performed tough tapsya. He, although an asur knew that God could not be met without bhakti and unless he met God, he would not be able to achieve the goal of securing a boon of becoming the strongest person on earth, who could not be killed by any one. This would indicate that:

(1) For any big achievement, bhakti was necessry as through bhakti only one could meet God and God only could grant the highest boon on earth.

(2) Even the asuras were initially having belief in God. Like Hirnakashyap, Ravan, and Kumbhkarna too had performed tapsya and got their desired boon from Brahma. Subsequently Ravan had even worshipped Shiva and presented his own heads as bali (बलि) on Shiva. It was only subsequently that they attained some rakshas character as a result of which they annoyed rishis/brahmin/cows etc.

(3) They knew that they could be killed by God only if they became treacherers of the first rank forcing God to incarnate to kill them.

(4) When such people performed tapsya, the gods became frightened.

(5) By great tapsya such asuras wanted to become overall Lords of the universe.

Hirnakashyap took a boon that he could not be killed by any human being, animal, any creature or non-creature, god or asura, neither in the house nor outside house; neither in day nor in night; by any astra-shastra; neither on land nor in space. He wanted to be overall lord of the universe and none should be able to defeat him in battle. Brahma acceded to his request. Hirnakshyap thus worshipped Brahma and became very strong. He conquered the entire universe and other gods' lokas and started living in Swarga. He had all things of leisure and pleasure available to him. He ordered all yagya bhag to be given to him. In other words he ordered to be worshipped by all like God. Every one was afraid of him. All gods prayed to God for annihilating him. God told that he was aware of his criminalities and would soon do something through the media of his son Prahlad, who would be Bhagwad bhakta and when annoyed by his father, he would go for his rescue.

Hirnakashyap had four sons, including one Prahlad. Prahlad was from birth itself a Bhagwad bhakta having full control on all his passions and having no vices. Hirnakashyap was naturally not happy with him. It is God's maya that in respect of rakshasas killed by the God's incarnate, someone in the family only was responsible. Kansa was killed by the son of his sister Devki. Ravan kidnapped Sita on excitement by his sister Sarupnakha. Here Hirnakashyap was killed because of his son Prahlad. Once Hirnakshyap had asked his son Prahlad as to what was the best thing he liked. This was with a view to involve him in such things of his desire so that he could indulge in vices, leaving aside the virtues. But Prahlad told him that he did not like the people indulging in 'my' and 'mine'. This was the basic thing liked by the asuras and not liked by Brahmama bhakta being Brahama's 'maya'. He held the guru responsible for such thinking and rebuked the guru to bring him up as he liked. Guruji asked Prahlad as to who had coached him that way. Then again Prahlad affirmed his conviction. Guru beat him. Guru taught him the education pertaining to dharma, artha and kam) (धर्म, अर्थ और काम) but Prahlad learnt all that was in vedas and shastras including the diplomatic policies of sam (peacefully), dam (by wealth), dand (by punishment) and bhed (by causing division) (साम, दाम, दंड और भेद). In fact these were the basic policies adopted by rajas for proper governance. The Hindu rajas had been following such policies. These had been adopted by prominent Muslim rulers like Akbar too. He created division in Rajputs by marrying the sister of Man Singh and then keeping some Rajputs on his side and making them fight with others not with him. In Aurangzeb's time too such a policy continued to be followed. Subsequently English had been following the same policy. In Plassy battle, (the first battle fought by English with Indian Nawabs) the English by 'dam' policy purchased Siraj-ud-daula's Commander-in-Chief and by bhed policy created division in his army. Thereafter having been successful in the battle by application of this policy, they applied it on other Muslim rulers and against Marathas, Sikhs and other rulers too resulting in having become supreme in India. Prahlad had mastered such policies in no time. Subsequently, when Hirnakashyap asked what he had further learnt in school (The father expected now he will mention about the type of education he wanted to be inculcated in Prahlad). Prahlad told about the nine kinds of Bhagwad bhakti. He again abused the guru although he was not responsible as he had not given such a coaching. He then started beating and ordering of the punishments to Prahlad, like causing injuries by spears, throwing him down from the hills, putting him under elephants' feet and ultimately by burning him in pier in the lap of his sister, who had a boon of not burning in fire. But the sister got burnt in fire and no harm was caused to Prahlad. Prahlad even started coaching the Bhagwad bhakti to his other class-fellows and citizens to get rid of the worldly passions and ambitions as these took the man to hollowness and wrong path. He, therefore, wanted them to come up above the concept of 'me' and 'mine'. This all education Prahlad had attained from Narad, when Prahlad was in the womb of his mother, who stayed in Narad's ashram for sometime. Similar education is stated to have been attained by Abhimanyu from his father Arjun, when he was in the womb of his mother Subhadra.

Seeing no way of mending Prahlad to bring him to his way of thinking, Hirnakashyap decided to kill him. He tied Prahlad to a pillar and wanted to kill him. Then a voice came from the pillar and God was born as Narsingha. This infuriated Hirnakashyap and he challanged the Narsingha Bhagwan. A battle ensued. Bhagwan took him at the door of the house, put him on his thighs and killed him by tearing him off with his nails. This way Bhagwan complied with all the conditions Hirnakashyap had asked in boon from Brahma e.g. not to be killed by either man or animal or god or asura, nor in the house or outside; neither in day nor in night; with no arm etc. At that time some other asuras also came to help him but Narsingha Bhagwan killed them all. All gods, Brahma, Shiva, Indra, rishis, sadhus etc. came and praised the almighty God for having killed the rakshas and saving the gods and rishis from his criminal clutches. Here again they had come and praised the almighty God in a protocolic system—the mightiest coming first and so on. They came in following sequence in order of priority (order of precedence) :

(1) Brahma (ब्रह्मा)
(2) Shiva (शिव)
(3) Indra (इन्द्र)
(4) Rishis (ऋषि)
(5) Pitras (पितर)
(6) Sidhas (सिद्ध)
(7) Vidyadharas (विद्याधर)
(8) Nagas (नाग)
(9) Manavas (मनुआ)
(10) Prajapatis (प्रजापति)
(11) Gandharvas (गंधर्व)
(12) Charanas (चारण)
(13) Yakshas (यक्ष)
(14) Kimpurush (किंपुरुष)
(15) Vaitalikas (वैतालिक)
(16) Kinnaras (किन्नर)

Narsingha Bhagwan could not be pleased by all the above gods etc. Then Prahlad came and praised him. Prahlad had inter alia stated that God could not be pleased by wealth, high caste, beauty, tap, education, image, strength, force, intelligence or yoga but can be pleased only by bhakti. So even a brahmin with above faculties but without bhakti is worse than a shudra, who had devoted himself to God and is absorbed in his bhakti. It is here that the flexibility in the institution of varnas and ashramas in Hindu Philosophy appears. Although the varana ashram dharma is required to be observed by all in whatever varana or ashram they are and whenever there had been breach in observing these principles, Hinduism has suffered. Yet there has been relaxation in these concepts in deserving cases such as by dint of his bhakti, Nishadraj (a shudra) became Ram's friend. Even Jatayu (a bird) came closer to Ram because he sacrified his life for the sake of Ram. Krishna himself was brought up in a family of gwalas (cow grazers) but he came up to be the Raja of Dwarka.

At the time of Sita swayambar in Ram kal, Raja Janak had made arrangement for seating the public not in order of brahmins first followed by kshatriyas, vaishas and sudras (as per known classification of society) but according to their capability.

उत्तम मध्यम नीच लघु, निज निज थल अनुहारि।

Like the modern order of precedence divided into Class I, Class II, Class III, Class IV etc. depending upon the rank and capability owned by each. This relaxation in the compliance of the varana-ashram has, therefore, been indicated here.

विप्राद् द्विषड्गुणयुतादरविन्दनाभ—
पादारविन्दविमुखाच्छ्वपचं वरिष्ठम्,
मन्ये तदर्पितमनोवचनेहितार्थ—
प्राणं पुनाति स कुलं न तु भूरिमानः। (7-9-10)

On the basis of Prahlad's praise (Prahlad was the son of an asura) Narsingha Bhagwan got pleased although he could not be pleased by Brahma, Shiva, rishis etc. God became happy and, as usual, asked Prahlad to ask for any boon. But Prahlad, having full devotion in God, did not ask for any boon as he was already all-satisfied and all-content. He only said that asking for any boon would confirm his mentality of being the offspring of an asura and any boon asked for is for satisfaction of worldly ambitions, which he did not have. He, therefore, said asking and giving boon is only the give and take contract like a transaction with a bania.

नान्यथा तेऽखिलगुरो घटेत करुणात्मनः
यस्त आशिष आशास्ते न स भृत्य सवै वणिक्। (7-10-4)

He, therefore, asked for a boon that should not have any ambitions at all.

Bhagwan accepted the version of Prahlad. This is the Bhagwan and bhakta protocol, not a give and take concept. Bhagwan asked him to keep thinking of Hari and listen to his katha, and that after having lived in this universe comfortably, he would attain salvation. Prahlad, being the obedient son of the father, inspite of the cruelties he showered on him, requested God to excuse his father for all his wrong thinkings about God. God told him that his father had already attained salvation by virtue of his having been killed by God himself. This is Hindu culture in which even when father is cruel, the son still continues to be obedient to him. Ram did not mind his having been sent to forests, rather than coronating him as pronounced. Similarly Ram always respected and took extra care to keep Kaikayee in good humour although she was instrumental in Ram's exile.

Prahlad thereafter was coronated and, as per protocol he gave alms to beggers, brahmins etc. Like any other boss, the protocol works in the realm of gods too. Narsingha Bhagwan warned Brahma not to agree to such boons as had been given to Hirnakashyap as such boon make the incumbent very rude and crime-infested without having any fear from anyone. This way the almighty God used to keep the gods under him at their proper places and used to point out their omissions, Narsingha Bhagwan was then worshipped by Brahma as a token of his mistakes having been corrected by God. In fact as already indicated, Hirnakashyap and Hirnakashya were the two rakshasas, who had become so as a result of curse by Sanakadik Munis to Bhagwan's Parshads (पार्षद) Jai and Vijaya and had now been granted mukti by having been killed by almighty God and took their previous charge of Parshads (पार्षद). Jai and Vijaya, however, had to had three formations. In the next formation they became Ravan and Kumbhkarna and had been killed by Ram (incarnate of God) and subsequently as Shishupal and Dantvaktra killed by Shri Krishna (incarnate of God).

A subsequent incident is of killing of Mayadanava Asura. After having achieved a boon from Lord Krishna, Mayadanava

(मयदानव) created three aeroplanes, which had been filled with arms and armaments and could annihilate any place. These planes were nothing but the fighter planes of present day. It shows that in ancient India too technology was at its peak. Even in Ram period there is mention of Ram having used an aeroplane in coming back from Lanka to Ayodhya. But what was prepared by Mayadanava were the fighter bombers. He annihilated all gods' hideouts with the help of these bombers.

Then gods went to Shiva for help. It is seen that whenever a boon is given to an asura by one of the Gods—Brahma, Vishnu and Mahesh—the gods approached the other one to undo its effect if the boon was used by the asura against the gods. Here since he got the shakti from Lord Krishna, it would have been, as a matter of protocol, not possible for undoing its effect by Vishnu. So the gods went to Shiva for help. In case of Hirnakashyap the boon was given by Brahma. Therefore, Vishnu had come as incarnate Narsingha Bhagwan and killed him. But here Shiva was not successful in his mission as Maya asura had an Amritkund in which all asuras killed by Shiva got new lives. Therefore, again Vishnu had to come to his help and he became a cow and Brahma became his calf and they drank the amrit from the kund. After that when Maya asura came to know that Vishnu had drank the amrit as a cow and the security men were helpless, Mayadanava asura told the security-men that whatever is in fate has to take place and even God, asura, human being or any other creature cannot mend what is in fate.

"देवोऽसुरो नरोऽन्यो वा नेश्वरोऽस्तीह कश्चन" (7-10-64)

Such a belief is universal in all religions and in fact it is because of such a belief in fate that a human being is able to cross the biggest tragedies in life. After killing Mayadanava asura, Shiva went to his abode.

After this, the writer, again through the media of a dialogue between Yudhisthra and Narad, tells about the varana and ashram institutions, which are fundamental to Hindu dharma. In Hindus nothing is left to chance but is all in black and white in shastras duly authenticated by rishis, munis, gods etc. Narad, although a rishi, narrated about these dharmas as he had listened from God himself in Badrinarayan Ashram to give further authentication to such a cult. This is spiritual protocol imbibed in Hindu society. In varnas, there are brahmin, kshatriya, vaish and sudra. Those who perform religious rituals are brahmins. They hold yagya, dan, tap, attain and impart education, taking alms (दान) and giving alms are all functions of brahmins. The kshatriyas have to protect the subjects from internal law and order problems and outside invasions. They punish the culprits and impose tax on subjects to make up for the expenses of national exchequer. The vaisyas have to serve the brahmins and involve themselves in cow breeding and protection, agriculture, trade and arrange for feeding all other varrnas' people. Shudras have to serve the people of all the other varnas. Their livelihood is dependent on these people only. The people were expected to act according to the dictates of their respective varana dharma. However, this was the general division of the society. One could attain parlance in others' field too like Viswamitra, being a kshatriya, had, by virtue of conducting tapsya, become Brahmrishi. Nishadraj, a shudra had become Rambhakta and so on. In such cases, the person was respected and recognised in the society as per his achievements and not as per his birth although birth did have its say in some cases like Daronacharya did not accept, as his pupil, anyone other than a kshatriya. Karan could not get married with Daropadi as his dynastic succession was not known. Still, by and large; the persons' present faculties had been recognised in the society. That is why in Sita swayamber, the arrangement for seating of public had been made not as per the known division into brahmin, kshatriya etc. but as per their prevalent capability.

उत्तम मध्यम नीच लघु निज निज थल अनुहारि (मानस)

That is why Viswamitra, although a kshatriya had been allotted the highest stage being a Brahmrishi at that time.

So far as the ashramas (आश्रम) are concerned. These were frour—brahmcharya upto 25 years of age; grihastha (गृहस्थ) upto 50 years of age; vanprastha (बानप्रस्थ) upto 75 years of age and sanyas (सन्यास) thereafter till death, presuming that the men lived for about one hundred years. Compliance with these ashram dharmas was considered as a social and spiritual necessity and were applicable to the persons of all varnas.

Brahmchari (ब्रह्मचारी) : This was the period spent on education. Everyone irrespective of the varana, he belonged to, had to go to Gurukul after about 5-6 years of age for education. Education was imparted by a brahmin guru according to one's dharma i.e. a brahmin pupil was taught about vedas and shastras, yagyas etc., a kshatriya was taught vedas etc. besides the laws of war, peace, international relations, use of various arms, law of governance etc. Vaish was taught about his vocations of trade, agriculture etc. Shudras generally did not attain any eduction as their dharma was only to serve the people of other three varnas. The pupil had to live in the Gurukul day and night and all pupils irrespective of varana, they belonged to, had to live alike. They had to beg for their fooding and that of the guru. Begging even by the rajkumars taught them to be humble to all. They had to live having control on all passions and according to the tenets of dharma, living in full discipline and fully obedient to guru. The Gurukuls were run by the raja. The gurus, however, did not have many requirements of worldly leisures and pleasures because if they lived in pleasure, they could not coach the pupil to live with control over their ambitions and passions.

Grihastha (गृहस्थ) : In grihastha, one should do all jobs of household and do all acts for the cause of the almighty. Here the jobs to be done by a Grihastha differ from varana to varana. A brahmin is not to accumulate wealth and feel satisfied in whatever is given in alms or collected by the pupils during begging (भिक्षा). The kshatriyas had been living during grihastha with all royal leisures and pleasures still doing their job of governance, protection of subjects from internal crime and external aggression, collection of revenue, tax, arranging for all kinds of yagyas etc. to enable the people live comfortably and peacefully. Similarly, vaishas were to do agriculture, trade, all industrial enterprises, whatever there were in those days; paying tax to the exchequer etc. and shudras in grihastha had only to serve the people of other varnas and live on whatever they got from them. But all had been remembering the almighty God everytime and acting according to the tenets of dharma. All had to get married and produce offspring and manage to earn livelihood for the family as per his vocation and spare the excess for donations, yagyas and to the causes of gods. During grihastha too, although the people were allowed all sorts of leisures and pleasures, they were to have all these actions under control and always keep on attending satsang etc.

Vanprastha (बानप्रस्थ आश्रम): After enjoying grihastha life upto 50 years of age ,one should divest oneself from the universe after handing over the charge of the household to the sons. The raja has to had over the kingdom to his eldest or other son, considered capable of ruling over the people. The vaish should make his son incharge of trade, agriculture etc. as was being handled by him. The brahmin generally already had the life of keeping themselves divested of worldly passions/ambitions. The shudras too were not forbidden from adopting vanprastha. During vanprastha, the people irrespective of the varana to which they belonged, had to live alike. They depended on bhiksha. They controlled all their passions/ambitions and devoted themselves fully to the cause of almighty God. Have satsang, company of rishis etc. and devoting the time in Bhagwad bhakti. They had to live on fruits etc. available in forests and not the foodgrain etc. obtained from their cultivation. They could set their own kutiyas to live in the parlance of other vanprasthais, sanyasis etc., wear clothes to the minimum possible requirements to cover the private parts only. They have to leave the concept of 'me' and 'mine' "You" and "Yours" and take it that everything belonged to God only. They should fully control all their sensual feelings, worldly passions/ambitions and live like tapsvis.

Sanyas Ashram (सन्यास आश्रम): In sanyas ashram, the people above 75 years of age get fully divested from universal attractions, which were started in vanprastha. The sanyasis are also supposed to coach the grihastha about the way to attain salvation and the Bhagwad bhakti. They themselves too have to keep fully devoted to the cause of almighty God and try to get themselves absorbed in God through the Bhagwad bhakti with the aim of attainment of salvation. They are not supposed to keep any connections with the people in grihastha or in the universe and all the time think of God only and leave the universe leading that sort of life in due course.

In this way the people could lead the life as a brahmchari, as a grihastha, vanprasthai and sanyasi. In Hinduism, the grihastha can live with all leisures and pleasures and can still attain salvation, if followed by vanprastha and sanyas requiring him to divest himself from all worldly attachments—wife, son, wealth, even sensual feelings etc. In Hinduism, therefore, there is a provision of vanprastha and sanyas for all to attain the ultimate goal of salvation. In all other religions only the mullas in Muslims and the priests in Christians are the custodians of religious discourses but in Hindus, everyone in vanprastha and sanyas is the coach of religious tenets in addition to the rishis, munis etc. Also in this way there is a change in the control over householding also. The rajkumars succeed to throne without having to do away with the father king after he became old since he himself would coronate the son and leave for vanprastha. In this way there would be no need to become Aurangzeb and arrest his father Shahjahan, and kill his brothers and sisters to coronate himself. Similarly, in vaishas also the sons become automatically incharge of trade, household etc. on the parents' departure for vanprastha and sanyas. Also in this percept of dharma, everyone, if followed religiously, becomes entitled to attain salvation and if not salvation, then to have the formation of human being on next birth and so on.

Skandh – VIII

Bhagwan Manu left for the forests alongwith his wife. He performed tapsya for hundreds of years. He said all mortals and immortals in the universe are the formation of almighty God only. Therefore, they should think as if everything belongs to him or nothing belongs to them. Either way they have to feel contented with their lot as there is no end either way. Having thought so, one comes up above the Bhagwad maya and the concept of 'me and mine', 'you and your' which is the influence of maya. God is always there to help the persons, who have risen above this maya, and absorbed in him.

In the context of God's incarnation to protect the elephant (गज) from being taken away by the crocodile, there is mention of all kinds of trees, plants etc. of coconut, rose, tad, chir, pakar, bergad, sandal, neem, lemon, amla, rudrax etc. and all kinds of flowers. This would indicated that in ancient times, the botanical knowledge was quite upto the mark. People used to grow, maintain and utilise these flowers, plants, trees etc. for the well-being of the mankind. In that forest, there lived an elephant. He was so strong that even lions, tigers etc. were afraid of that elephant. He once went to a lake with clean water. The elephant took bath in that lake. Bhagwad maya had been influencing the elephant as a result of which the elephant became proud. At that time a forceful crocodile caught hold of elephant's leg. The elephant tried to get rid of the catch but was unsuccessful. All the other elephants with him too left him in this time of despair. The elephant got frightened and then remembered God for help. He had in his previous life learnt the Bhagwad bhakti mantra which he still remembered. He repeated the same with concentration and praised God. God, having found the elephant in trouble, came there for help and killing the crocodile, he protected the elephant. As usual as a matter of protocol, the gods showered flowers and resounded Bhagwan's Jaykara. Bhagwan not only saved the elephant from the clutches of the crocodile but also granted him salvation. On the other side, having been killed by God himself, the crocodile too got salvation.

In another episode of Kachhap, incarnation of God, once all gods had been defeated by asuras and due to the curse of Durbasha Rishi, even Indra had lost all his force. Durbasha had passed a curse on Indra in view of the non-compliance of a protocol by him. Durbasha had offered him a necklace received by him with God's grace. Indra, however, without respecting it, passed it on to his elephant, who crushed it under his feet. On this, Durbasha, thinking Indra extra proud, passed on a curse on him that he would lose all his force. It was common in Hindus that rishi etc., if not honoured/respected, used to pass a curse on the incumbent to teach him a lesson, rather than entering into querrel with him. Now the gods having been defeated by asuras, as usual and through proper channel, they first went to Brahma for help. Brahma told them that almighty God could only help. They then with Brahma went to God. God being almighty could help them but then he had to put the gods too to some labour. He told them to enter into an agreement, as the time being favourable to asuras, it was not possible to conquer them in battle. After the agreement, the asuras and gods should start churning the ocean to take Amrit out of it. The gods had no alternative except to enter into an agreement with asuras.

"यात दानवदैतेयैस्तावत् सन्धिर्विधीयताम" (8-6-19)

and अरयोऽपि हि सन्धेयाः सति कार्यार्थगौर्वे। (8-6-20)

Whenever some big job is to be undertaken, then one should even agree to the enemy's terms. Gods were therefore, advised to agree to whatever terms the asuras offered. The gods came to asuras without arms. As per laws of war, a party to the battle, if approaches without arms, indicates that the enemy wants to come for entering into a peace alliance. This principle hold good even today. When the proposal of ocean churning and taking amrit out of it jointly was placed before the asuras, they agreed. Gods agreed because almighty God's help was with them and asuras would have thought that once amrit was churned out, they would take all and divest gods of it as gods had already been defeated by them. Then they brought Mandrachal for churning with Vasuki (a snake) to be used as the rope for churning and entered into another agreement of sharing amrit. Churning started. When Mandrachal was getting sunk in to the ocean, God came for help as Tortoise (कच्छप) incarnate. The Tortoise took the Mandrachal on his back. Churning again started. At first poison came out of it. Asuras refused to take it and entrusted it to the gods. Gods then thought of Shiva, who could digest poison. They requested him and Shiva agreed for the cause of all gods. He took the poison as a result of which Shivaa's neck became blue. Shiva said—

आसां प्राणपरीप्सूनां विधेयमभयं हिमे,
एतावान्हि प्रभोरर्थो यद् दीन परिपालनम्। (8-8-38)

The greatness lies in helping the poors in case of need when one was in a position to help them.

The churning again started. At first Kamdhenu came out, which was taken away by rishis. Then a horse came out, which was taken away by Bali. Then came out Kaustabha (कौस्तुभ) mani, which was taken by Vishnu. Then came out Apsaras, which went to gods. Then Lakshmi came out and was owned by Vishnu. Like this, all the things which came out during churning, were shared by asuras and gods as per agreement. The poet has tried to affirm that like the present day international agreements entered into by various nations, in ancient times too such agreements had been entered into between gods and asuras and each side had to abide by it. Then came out one person, whom Lakshmi wooed. He was infact Vishnu himself as incarnate 'Dhanwantri'. He was responsible for introduction of all medicines. He came out with the amrit kund in his hand. The amrit kund was snatched by the asuras. Gods became tense but almighty God consoled them. Vishnu then came in the form of a beautiful and charming lady. Asuras wanted to woo her and were attracted by her charms. The lady took away the amrit kund promising to distribute it between the gods and the asuras. She made them sit in separate queues and gave away the amrit to gods. Then only asuras realised the strategy. One of the asuras had entered the queue of gods and took amrit but when God came to know of it, he cut him with his chakra. Having already become amar, he could not be killed but became two parts. They are called RAHU and KETU. In this way gods having served and yielded before the almighty God, got the amrit through Vishnu by having done labour and asuras, being against the tenets of God, had to suffer in the bargain. God then left the place. The asuras attacked the gods. Now the gods having taken amrit and God being on their side, they won the fierce battle fought between gods and asuras. In this battle, there were gods and asuras on foot, on horses' back, or elephants' back, on chariots etc. and as per laws of war, then existing, the persons (gods and asuras) on chariot, fought within themselves; those an horses fought within themselves; those an elephants fought within themselves; those an foot within themselves. Furthermore, the persons with sword fought with sword; with bows and arrows fought with the other party too with bows and arrows and so on. In this way, the writer has tried to make out that there were detailed laws of war and these had been followed in letter and spirit by both the parties to the battle. Even gods had to follow such rules although pertaining to the universe. This indicated the universality of such rules/laws. The ingredients of these laws of war can in brief be indicated below. Such rules even hold good in present days to some extent :

(1) Enemy without armaments was not attacked and he was considered to have come for peace treaty.

(2) There was provision for arriving at peace treaty when the war was going on. For this purpose one block of the enemies used to surrender arms as is done even now-a-days.

(3) Peace treaties were drawn out giving all points of agreement as is in the case of international agreements these days.

(4) In the battles, all kinds of arms/armaments were used like trishul, arrows, bhallas, shaktis etc. and as per principles of battle, both enemies in field used to fight with same kinds of arms/armaments.

(5) Both the sides used to fight on the same kinds of means of transport like on elephants, on horses, on chariots, on foot etc.

(6) There was technological development upto the mark in as much as there were aeroplanes, rockets, fighter bombs etc. and all these were fully equipped with arms/armaments.

(7) Usually the battles were fought in pairs i.e. amongst one person from each side or army with army.

(8) After the war was over, proper treaty was executed, the winner dictating terms to the defeated one.

(9) Generally the war ended with the conqueror taking wealth from the defeated one and the kingdom was handed back to the defeated ruler.

(10) There were akashvanis too in existence like the present day wireless, T.V. etc.

(11) Like present Music band of army, in those days also music was displayed in battles.

In the battle, the gods were losing. They then, as usual, remembered the almighty God, who appeared on his gruda in the battle field and killed the asura leaders Kalnemi, Mali, Sumali and Malyawan. This encouraged the gods and demoralised the asuras. The gods now attacked with greater force. Fierce battle again took place and ultimately gods won it. The almighty God helped the gods in this battle from time to time, either by his presence in the battle field or by advising the gods through Dev-vani/Akaswani.

When Shiva came to know that Vishnu, as Mohini, had charmed all asuras and gave amrit to gods, he became anxious to see Vishnu Bhagwan as Mohini. This would indicate that even the gods like Shiva are not above the maya of almighty God. Shiva went to Vishnu and after praising him requested for showing him his Mohini form. Vishnu, acceding to his request, became a charming and attractive girl. Shiva was accompanied by Sati but forgetting her, he went after Mohini, having been entraped by her charms. In the process, he lost his semen. Then he realised that he had been overpowered by Vishnu's 'maya' and came back to Sati. Vishnu too came in his own form.

As already indicated, the war between the gods and asuras was a continuous process. Sometimes asuras won while at the other, the gods. It is also seen that gods always had victory over asuras with the help of almighty God only. After having been defeated by the gods after amrit distribution, asuras again gathered their strength and with the blessings of Bhrigu, brahmins and Shukracharya, their Guru, the asuras gained strength again and attacked the gods under the leadership of Asura Raja Bali. Gods, as usual, went to Brihaspati, their Guru. Brihaspati, however, told them that asuras had a favourable time and had blessings of Bhrigu and brahmins. They could not be defeated. He, therefore, proposed that gods vacate swaraga etc. and go in hiding. The gods acted accordingly and in the process, Bali became the overall Lord of the entire Brahmand (ब्रह्माण्ड). The gods went to next senior 'Brahma' but he too could not help and advised them to wait for the almighty God Vishnu's incarnation in the house of Aditi and Kashyap Muni. At the same time the mother of gods, Aditi was worried about her sons having lost all wealth and kingdom to Raja Bali. She worshipped Vishnu. Vishnu getting pleased, promised to take birth in her house. Vishnu then was born as Baman (बामन) Bhagwan in the house of Aditi and Kashyap on the sacred day of Vijay Dashmi. All the Hindu festivals are based on the incarnation of God or according to the importance of seasons. On his birth as Baman, alms were given to brahmins, and yagyas etc. were performed as laid down for such occasions. So all occasions in Hindus are celebrated according to a laid down protocol of observing vrat, havans, etc. Baman Bhagwan came to know that Raja Bali was performing an Aswamedha yagya. He departed for Bali's place. Baman's departure for

Bali's place, created some upheaval in the atmosphere. Bali's Guru Shukracharya and Bhrigu had been thinking as to what was going to happen. At that time, Baman Bhagwan entered the yagyashala as a Baman Brahmchari (बौणा ब्रह्मचारी). The brahmins stood up and welcomed and respected the Baman Brahmchari. Bali was happy to receive Baman brahmin and offered to him a stage to his standard as per protocolic requirement; washed his feet and worshipped him and offered to ask for anything so that the same could be presented. He thought that a brahmin would ask for cow, foodgrain, brahmin girl for marriage or say small amount of wealth or horse etc. So he offered anything to be given on askance. Whereas the protocol requires a raja to give anything to a brahmin on askance, it also requires the raja to at first verify the antecedents of the incumbent guest. Raja Bali failed here and without caring to know his antecedents, offered anything on earth to him. He, being the overall Lord of entire Brahmand, was in a position to meet any demand of an ordinary person or much so of a brahmin as brahmins do not have much requirement. Brahmins appreciated Raja Bali's response as being apt to the family he belonged to. In social protocol the legends of a family, had a greater say. Bali belonged to Prahlad's family, whose guru was Shukaracharya. They had always welcomed giving alms/donations to brahmins. So was the saying in Raghukul :

रघुकुल रीति सदा चलि आई
प्राण जाईं पर वचन न जाईं। (मानस)

Raja Dasratha had to accept sending Ram to forest and coronating Bharat as per the two boons given to Rani Kaikayee. So was the family of asuras, descending from Hirnakshyap, Prahlad to Bali, where anything could be given in alms. Hirnakashyap too, when undertook to kill Vishnu and he could not find him in any loka, immuned him saying that since Vishnu was not available anywhere, he must have gone to a place from where one does not come and in that case there was no use keeping enmity with him. Further there was no use enraging oneself for one who does not exist as ignorance and pride enhances rage.

वैरानुबन्ध एतावानामृत्योरिह देहिनाम्,
अज्ञानप्रभवो मन्युरहंमानोपवृंहितः। (8-19-13)

On this, Bali asked Baman brahmin to ask for whatever he wanted as he could even give continents in alm. Baman told that he only wanted land sufficient for three steps; that would suffice for him as one should collect only as much as is quite necessary. Now as per protocol, for fulfilling one's words, one had to enter into an agreement (संकल्प) taking water in hand as an evidence as for any agreement to have its worth, evidence must be there. Even today, evidence in necessary for any such undertaking/promissory note etc. In old days such agreements were entered into either having water or fire as witness. Ram had undertaken to help Sugreeva and vice versa, when Ram met Sugreeva in Kiskindha and such an agreement was entered into making fire as witness. Shukaracharya knew that it was almighty God himself and alerted Bali from entering into any such agreement as he did not know that under the cloak of there steps land, he would take his entire wealth etc. as he could measure everything in Brahmand in three steps and in that case not being able to fulfil his undertaking, he may have to go to hell and even otherwise one should not give in alms so much that one is not left even to make do his livelihood. Shukracharya even confirmed what he had told on the basis of what had been indicated in vedas but Raja Bali told him that having promised to give anything Baman wanted, he could not go back from his word. He was not afraid of poverty or going to hell as much as denying to fulfil the promise, particularly if the alms-seeker was Vishnu himself, who otherwise too was the owner of all in Brahmand. So giving a thing to its actual owner, is in fact no alms-giving at all. Having found that Raja Bali,his disciple, was not agreeing to what he had said, Sukracharya passed a curse on him that he, having insulted him, would lose all his wealth. Still Raja Bali took water in his hand and undertook to give three steps land in alm to Baman. Then the Baman, as God, started escalating so much that the entire universe, space, akash, patal etc. came within his self. Seeing him in that Virat form, all asuras got frightened. Then the Virat form became the form of Vishnu Bhagwan. He measured entire earth with one step by second step he measured Swarga, and could not find any place left for the third step. All gods and Brahma and Shiva worshipped Vishnu Bhagwan's step in Brahmlok/Swarga. The asuras seeing Vishnu taking everything in two steps, got enraged and got prepared to fight with Vishnu. Then a fight started between asuras and God's men. Raja Bali, however, checked his people from fighting saying that it was god's time, and asuras would again conquer, whatever is now lost, in due course. Bali was then arrested by God's men. God then asked Bali to fulfil his commitment of giving three steps land. So far he had given only two steps land and he should give third step land otherwise he would have to go to hell for non-compliance of the undertaking. This way, God wanted to confuse Bali but he stuck to his promise. He praised God almighty and offered the third step to be kept at his head. He was not afraid of going to hell or to face any difficulty, what he was afraid of was his image being spoiled. He told that the asuras accepted any punishment given by the almighty as it ultimately resulted in advantage only. Like Hirnakashyap having opposed God, had been killed by him and he in the transaction was benefitted as he get salvation having been killed by God. Ravan had also said so, when Sarupnakha, came and narrated to him how her ears and nose had been cut by a tapasvi, who subsequently also killed Khar-Doosan etc., that he was not an ordinary man as ordinary man could not have killed Khar-Doosan and since he was Brahma, he should develop enmity with him so that by being killed by him atleast, he could attain salvation, which was not otherwise possible as the other alternative of attaining salvation by jap, tap etc. was not within his capability to perform. Similarly, Bali also told Baman that any punishment by guru/Gobind was only to his advantage. Then Prahlad appeared there. Also came Brahma and Bali's wife. Everyone praised Lord Vishnu and requested him to release Bali from the captivity. God told Brahma that man forgets his self under the influence of wealth. Therefore, the first thing God does when he is kind to anyone is to snatch his wealth so that he realises self and God too and in the bargain getting absorbed in him, he attains salvation. God indicated that he was happy with Bali's devotion to God and sticking to his word and, therefore, had assigned to him the place not available to gods even. He only would be his Bhakta Upendra. Bali praised God as he was released from the captivity; bowed before almighty God, Brahma and Shiva and went to the assigned Loka. God gave Swaraga to Indra; Shukracharya finished the yagya left unfinished by Bali. Bali became Upendra. He was escorted by Indra to Swarg. Brahma, Shiva and other gods went to their respective places.

This shows that although God is sole owner of the universe yet for the protection of cows, brahmin, gods, sadhus, vedas, dharma and wealth, he comes incarnate.

गोविप्र सुर साधुनाम छन्दसामपि चेश्वरः
रक्षामिच्छंस्तनूर्धत्ते धर्मस्यार्थस्य चैवहि। (8-24-5·)

Skandh - IX

Raja Parikshit had so far heard all about the manvantras and the forceful conduct by almighty God in the regime of those manvantras. As already indicated, Srimad Bhagwat is the narration of all the incarnations of almighty God in the shape of questions and answers by Raja Parikshit and Shukdeva at the bank of Ganga. In fact all Hindu Granths are in this fashion only. Ramcharit Manas is what Parvati had asked and Shiva had narrated. Simultaneously Bhardwaj had asked and Yagvalka had narrated. Similarly Bhagwat has been narrated by Shukdeva to Raja Parikshit as a redressal of all his doubts about the various incarnations of God. There is not a single book available on all incarnations of God with emphasis on Shri Krishna as Shri Krishna had saved Raja Parikshit in the womb of his mother from the attack of Aswatthama.

In this part, Parikshit has asked about those who were born in Manu's dynasty; who are presently living, and those who are yet to born. Here one can telll about who had been and who are in the particular dynasty but who are yet to be is something unthinkable. This, however, has been replied to on the basis of some jyotish/calculation/ siddhi/bhavishya bani/darshan etc. which is available only in Hindus. This has also stood the test of time in future and come out to be correct.

ये भूता ये भविष्याश्च भवन्त्यद्यतनाश्च ये,
तेषां नः पुण्यकीर्तीनाम सर्वेषाम वद विक्रमान। (9-1-5)

Shukdeva then explained about Manu's dynasty in brief. As already explained, almighty God was the only survivor at the time of universal upheaval (प्रलय). Then God gave birth to Brahma and then from Brahma, Marich and his son Kashyap were born and from Kashyap was born Vivaswan and from him Manu. Manu gave birth to ten sons from his wife Shradha. Manu was at first not having any offspring. Then Vashistha Muni by a yagya, managed for the son to born but instead of a son, a daughter was born. Vashistha was surprised and then he came to know that the demand (संकल्प) given at the time of yagya was not correct. But then Vashistha converted the daughter into a son. This would indicate that :

(1) In our ancient days, there must be some clinical method by which offspring could be born. Raja Dasratha had also got sons by virtue of similar yagya (medication).

(2) Then the medication had to be correctly applied otherwise it could give reverse results too. Here a daughter was born instead of a son because of a wrong demand (medication).

(3) There was a system of changing the sex of the being as is prevalent in present days too by certain operations. Similar surgery must be available in our ancient times too as a result of which the daughter was converted into a son. He gave birth to a son Purarva. Suduman handed over rajya to his son Purarva and adopted vanprastha as per the concept of varna-ashram in Hindus.

Subsequently Manu got ten sons. Most of these ten sons had got converted to brahman, kshatriya, vaish, shudra etc. This would indicate that although the varna-ashram concept was followed by all but there were exceptions to this concept and by dint of his karma, one could get changed to another varna. Similarly in Ram period Viswamitra, who was a kshatriya became Brahmrishi and was reckoned as a rishi. Therefore, there was no strictness in the concept of varna-ashram and exceptions were there. Hindu dharma is accordingly based on *not so strict* adherence but had a scope for accommodation and relaxations in various concepts as situation warranted. Manu's one son Prishdhar had become shudra; another Kavi became a tapasvi; Dhrist became a brahmin; Nabhag became a vaish; and so on.

Manu had one son Raja Ambrish. He was a Bhagwad bhakta. He had performed many yagyas. At the time of completion of one of the yagyas, Darbasha Muni had come as a guest. He told raja that he was hungry. Raja worshipped him with full protocol, and offered food but he went to Yamuna to take bath. Meantime the yagya time was getting expired and he had to do last performance before expiry of the time. In this last rite, something is to be eaten but as per protocol, he could not eat till Darbasha had taken food. Seeing no alternative, he consulted brahmins as to what could be done in the situation. The brahmins advised him to take water and not food. This would amount to the fulfilment of the last rite of yagya. Subsequently when Darbasha returned, he found the yagya having been finished in his absence. This, he said, amounted to insult of the guest and created a jin to finish him. But Bhagwan who was happy with the performance of the yagya, helped the raja and killed the jin. After killing the jin, the Chakra of Bhagwan proceeded to kill Darbasha too. Darbasha tried to hide himself everywhere but everywhere he found the Chakra following him. He went to Brahma, Shankar etc. for helps but they advised that only almighty God could help him. He then went to Vishnu Bhagwan. Bhagwan told him that he had to protect his bhakta and so he was helpless. Since bhakta is wholly dependent on God, he could not think of anyone in preference, not even of himself or Lakshmi.

अहम् भक्तपराधीनो ह्यस्वतन्त्र इव द्विज,

साधुभिर्ग्रस्तहृदयो भक्तैभर्क्त जनप्रियः। (9-4-63)

This is the protocol between Bhagwan and the bhakta. Bhakta yields completely and makes himself dependent on Bhagwan only and in turn Bhagwan too takes care of the bhakta against any trouble on him. Bhagwan, therefore, advised Darbasha Muni to go and seek refuge under the raja only. He only could save him. Although tapsya and education are the sole achievements of a brahmin yet if the brahmin started misusing the same, then he gets reverse result too. In this way the writer has indicated the protocol between bhakta and Bhagwan :

(1) Bhakta yields his everything to the cause of God.

(2) God helps him against any difficulty which befall on him.

(3) God even punishes brahmin if he exceeds his powers and tries to harm a bhakta.

(4) This shows the inbuilt checks and balances in the powers attained and exercised by the people of each varna even those by brahmins.

(5) Brahmin, although is all-powerful, yet he too has to face the consequences for misusing his power to annoy an innocent person as Darbasha had to face for having unnecessarily punished raja Ambrish.

(6) For having done wrong even brahmins had to beg to be excused by the rajas as Darbasha had to do having failed to be protected by anyone against Bhagwan's Chakra. In such a case, the kshatriyas readily tried to help the regretful brahmin. Even Darbasha then had to praise the raja. Out of protocolic necessity, the raja had not taken his meals eversince Darbasha had fled frightened by the Chakra. Now only after paying respects to Darbasha, feeding him and giving him proper asan, raja too took his meals. This is the sacrifice and respect the people of other varnas had for the brahmins. In the end, raja Ambrish handed over the rajya to his son and adopted vanprastha.

In Manu's dynasty, Raja Harishchandra was born. He was known for his truthfulness so much so that he gave his rajya to Viswamitra for askance and had to suffer a lot alongwith his wife and son. Ultimately the truth had its reassurance and Harishchandra having been successful in the test of truthfulness got his rajya back. In succession, there was Raja Ansuman. He tried a lot for years to bring Ganga into India but he had not been successful. On his death, Dilip became raja. He too tried to bring Ganga but had been unsuccessful. His son Bhagiratha succeeded in course of time. He too continued the efforts to bring Ganga. Ganga appeared and told Bhagiratha, on his request to Ganga to come on earth, that

(1) her flow was too fast that the earth would not be able to stand it; and

(2) People would wash their dirt in Ganga which she would not be able to tolerate.

Bhagiratha told that Shankar Bhagwan would check its flow. Then Bhagiratha worshipped Shankar, who accepted the proposal and absorbed Ganga in his hairs. Then Shiva let out a small portion of Ganga on earth. This Ganga on the way enlivened the uncles of Bhagiratha who had been burnt by brahmins' curse, meaning thereby that Ganga's touch worked as panacea for the people of this earth. The entire story behind Ganga coming on earth (in India), would indicate that Ganga, in ancient period before Bhagiratha Raja, must be flowing to some other country from Himalayas and Raja Ansuman, then Dilip and then Bhagiratha would have worked to divert Ganga from that other country to Bharat by cutting mountains etc and this took them many years to do the job. Regarding the flow of Ganga, it may be stated that Ganga must at that time be rising from a huge lake and cutting of Himalayas widely would have involved a great-flow in India. Therefore,what Bhagiratha would have done is to check the flow of Ganga in mountains itself and to cut the mountains in such a way as to bring Ganga to India in a milder flow. Even the present flow is quite much for the country. Regarding its sacredity, it may be indicated that in the past all rivers were considered sacred and had been worshipped in India as they were a boon to the land through which they flowed and Ganga is particularly considered sacred as it has some chemical values in its water, which donot allow any germs to exist in its water. This fact is in existence even on date. Therefore, the sanctity and purity of Ganga has not perished till today even though the sewerage of many towns, falls in it.

Ram Avtar

In Raja Harishchandra and Bhagiratha's dynasty, Raja Khatwang succeeded. He was succeeded by Raja Deerghabahu and then Raghu, Aj and Dasratha. Raja Dasratha got four sons—Ram, Lakshman, Bharat and Shatrughan. They were all the incarnations (partially) of God and Ram was incarnation of Vishnu. After completing the education at the ashram of Guru Vashistha, the brothers started helping their father Raja Dasratha in the discharge of his royal duties. In those days, the education was at the Guru's ashram only and irrespective of whether one was a brahmin, kshatriya or vaish, he had to live on equal footing as co-disciples and the principle of equality got into their minds to make the disciples submissive and without any pride. They had to go to collect bhiksha (भिक्षा) and to live on it. Part of the bhiksha was also taken by guru. They were fully submissive to the dictates of the guru and guru too used to be well-versed in all vocations—knowledge of vedas, shastras; use of arms (sword, bow and arrow, gada etc.) diplomacy, rajneeti, international relations, laws of war, peace and international agreements, trade, agriculture, suiting the pupils for various walks of life. After the education, the pupils used to return to their respective houses. Since the Guru did not have much of worldly requirements, they used to devote themselves fully to the teaching of the pupils.

After the completion of education when Ram etc. started living at the house, Muni Viswamitra, who was not being allowed to perform yagya etc. by the rakshasas came to know that Ram had come as incarnate of Vishnu and he should be brought to kill the rakshasas. Muni Viswamitra was initially an kshatriya and he could have fought and killed the rakshasas but then he would have lost his tapsya in getting enraged and indulging in killing of human beings, since he had now become a Brahmrishi. So he decided to have Ram for this purpose. It is here that the principle of "Division of Labour" and each person doing his own job, comes into play. Since kshatriyas only were designed to fight with rakshasas, it was but fair to entrust the job to them. Even otherwise it is the duty of the raja of the area to protect the people from external invasion, internal disturbances etc. in exchange of taking the part of product (राज कर) from them. This was generally ten per cent of the produce. So detailed were our social and political laws that there was no difficulty to be faced by anyone if these were properly adhered to. Muni Viswamitra went to take Ram and Lakshman from Raja Dasratha. Raja was initially not inclined to agree to the Muni's request out of the affection for the sons, but then Guru Vashistha advised him to send Ram and Lakshman with Viswamitra. Guru's orders/advice could not be ignored by the raja as a matter of protocolic compulsion. So Ram and Lakshman went to the forests to protect Viswamitra from rakshasas. On the way, they first faced Tadka (a rakshasni). Ram killed her with one arrow. This infused the confidence in the Muni that Ram would be able to do the job. Viswamitra also coached Ram and Lakshman in the art of using bow and arrows (धनुर्विद्या) as was known to him. Ram and Lakshman, on reaching the ashram, asked the muni to perform his yagya etc. fearlessly. They killed Subahu and other rakshasas and threw away Marich to a distant place near Lanka.

At that time Raja Janak had fixed up Sita's marriage through a swayamber. This would indicate that the women in those days were quite intelligent and capable of selecting the groom for themselves. The concept of love marriage was also in vogue.

In fact Ram and Sita had fallen in love with each other on their first meeting in the garden before the swayamber itself and they had prayed to their respective Gods for making their love a success. Viswamitra took Ram and Lakshman to the Swayamber. In the swayamber, the condition of marriage was that anyone breaking the bow (dhanush) would many Sita. This dhanush (Shiva Dhanush) was so heavy that the rajas, who had gathered there to try their luck to have Sita, the most beautiful princess of the time, could not even move the dhanus. Then with Viswamitra's blessings, Ram broke it in a second. Then Parshuram, who was a Shiva Bhakta, came on knowing the dhanush having been broken, and challenged Ram.

He was proud of having annihilated kshatriyas from the universe several times. Ram accepted the challenge and finished his pride. He accepted Ram as his God.

After marriage, Ram and other brothers continued to live in Awadha. As per Hindu Dharma, concept of varna and ashram, one (even the rajas) had to think of leaving the home and proceed for vanprastha (बानप्रस्थ). During this period, one, after leaving all worldly attachments, had to live in forests and devote himself to the cause of God, fully. So, Raja Dasratha too thought of proceeding to vanprastha after handing over the rajya to his eldest son Ram. The theory of primogenitor was in vogue at that time according to which only the eldest son, if capable of handling the affairs, was coronated and the others were to assist him. He discussed the matter with Raj Guru Vashistha and other mantris, advisors, seniors in the Government. They readily agreed to the proposal, knowing the capability and popularity of Ram. This would indicate that :

(1) Renouncing the world and proceeding for vanprastha was necessary for everyone.

(2) The eldest son was coronated, if capable.

(3) The Raj Guru and other mantris/advisers had to be consulted before taking any major decision pertaining to governance. So, the democracy was in operation, although in a limited way, and the king was not fully autocrat.

The day for coronation of Ram was fixed but the mistake Raja Dasratha committed was that he took the decision when Bharat and Shatrughan were not there. Might be because Raja Dasratha did not expect any objection from them to Ram being coronated as he was the rightful successor and all brothers respected Ram but such a great celebration being without Bharat raised doubt in the mind of Raja Dasratha's queen Kaikayee (Bharat's mother), who made raja to agree to give too boons first and then asked for Bharat's coronation and Ram being sent to forests for 14 years. Ram, however, had no regret and happily proceeded to forests. Sita and Lakshman too accompanied him. Such was the spirit of abdication and element of renunciation of worldly riches at that time that nowhere could such sacrifice be seen. In Mohammedan rule, Aurangzeb killed his brothers and put his father in prison with a view to occupy the throne. Even in Hindus, there had been fights for the kingdom amongst brothers. But Ram's family was to set a precedent of protocol and maryada(मर्यादा).

In the forests, Bharat came to request Ram to rule Awadha but having come on father's orders to forests, he could not go back. As a via media Ram appear to have accepted the kingship of Awadha in absentia and appointed Bharat to rule Awadha defacto in his absence. For that Ram gave him the authority (mentioned as paduka in Ramayan). While in forests, Sarupnakha, the sister of Khar-Doosan and Ravan rakshasas saw Ram and Lakshman and got attracted towards them on their beauty and proposed herself but they could not accept the request and Lakshman had to cut her ears and nose. She complained to his brothers Khar-Doosan, who attacked Ram. Ram, however, defeated them in the battle and killed them. Sarupnakha then went to Ravan and narrated the entire episode to him. Ravan made a plan to kidnap Sita. For this, he did not want to develop a battle with Ram knowing fully well that he would not be able to win over him in the battle. He sent Marich, another rakshas in the guise of a golden deer. Ram went to kill the deer and the deer took Ram away. In his absence when Lakshman too had left the ashram to find out Ram, Ravan kidnapped Sita. On return to ashram, Ram and Lakshman having not found Sita there, had been wandering in forests in search of Sita, crying and enquiring from everyone if they had seen Sita. The poet has desired to indicate here that a person involved very much in the wife has to face such difficulties.

भ्रात्रा बने कृपणवत् प्रियया वियुक्तः,
स्त्री संगिनां गतिमिति प्रथयंश्चचार। (9-10-11)

Because of the involvement in Rani Kaikayee, Raja Dasratha had to send Ram to forests and lose his wife and Ram had to face difficulty in forests, when Sita had been kidnapped. Ram on the way found Jatayu, who had been wounded by Ravan, when he tried to save Sita from his clutches. He was at the brink of death, when Ram met him. After telling Ram that Ravan had taken Sita, he gave up his life. Ram performed Jatayu's last rites as a human being. This shows that Ram as God, loved not only his bhakta human beings but the other creatures as well. Ram granted him salvation too. Thereafter Ram met Sugreeva, who had been expelled by his brother Bali from kingdom. Ram developed friendship with him and entered into an agreement for mutual help. This would indicate about the concept of international relations and international agreements being executed amongst the rulers of various countries like the present day system, and each agreement had the sanctity by virtue of having been witnessed by fire (Agni) or water.Under this agreement, Ram killed Bali and restored Sugreeva to the throne of Kishkindha and thus fulfilled his part of the agreement and alerted Sugreeva not to forget to fulfil his part of the agreement viz. to search Sita and then to proceed further to take her back by defeating the kidnapper. After Hanuman located Sita in Lanka, Ram proceeded with Vanar Sena to Lanka. He arranged a bridge on ocean upto Lanka. This would indicate that in those days, proper survey was done and then the technology was so advanced that they could construct a bridge on the sea, without any steel work.

Shri Ram entered Lanka. Vibheeshan, who had been expelled by his brother Ravan from Lanka and had taken refuge under Ram, told about the strategy to be adopted in starting the battle with Ravan. Lanka had already been burnt by Hanuman and now the Vanar Sena further destroyed it. This was sufficient to spread fear wave in Lankans. Ravan held a meeting with all his advisers and sons etc. This would show that even the most autocrat king like Ravan, was not completely autocrat but used to consult his advisers, sons etc. before embarking upon any important mission/project. Ravan, even got his brother Kumbhkarna awoken. There was a fierce fighting amongst the armies of the two sides. When entire army and all sons of Ravan and his brother Kumbhkarna had been killed,

Ravan himself came to the battle field on his chariot. It is at this time that Indra sent his chariot with the Sarthy Matuli to be used by Ram so that he was able to fight in a better way on equal footing with Ravan. Again fierce battle between the two took place and ultimately Ram killed Ravan. On his death, there was hue and cry in Lanka.

Shri Ram asked Vibheeshan to perform last rites of Ravan and then arranged for coronating Vibheeshan and thereafter brought Sita from Ashoka Vatika after checking up her intention to join him.

Here we find some protocolic compliances :

(1) Ravan being on the chariot, Indra sent his chariot for being used by Ram as both the enemies have to be on equal footing in the battle.

(2) Ram had been fighting with Ravan for the sake of gods only. Therefore, it was for the gods in turn too to look after the convenience of Ram.

(3) After Ravan had been killed, Ram did not work in haste in calling Sita back. Since Sita had been kidnapped by the raja of Lanka, she was the property of that State. Ram, therefore, at first arranged for the coronation of Vibheeshan as the raja of Lanka as even otherwise a kingdom cannot be left without a raja even for a single day as such a situation could bring anarchy. Even now in a democratic set up when the prime minister loses the vote of confidence, he is obliged to resign but the President asks him to continue till alternative arrangements are made. So, with the concept of first work first, Shri Ram at first coronated Vibheeshan and then with his permission only brought Sita to his ashram.

By this time the period of 14 years had also expired. Ram etc., therefore, boarded the Pushpak viman of Vibheeshan to reach Awadha. But before arriving in Awadha Shri Ram got it verified (through Hanuman) whether Bharat and other people of Awadha actually wanted Ram to come back or not. Having found that in Ram's absence, Bharat had all along been living like a sanyasi only and had been anxiously waiting for Shri Ram to return to Awadha, Ram came to Awadha. This was necessary from protocolic point of view because if Ram had come to Awadha without checking up Bharat's intention and if Bharat desired to continue to rule Awadha having tasted the raj for 14 years, both Ram and Bharat would have been put in a very awkward position. When Bharat came to know that Ram had been coming back, he went out of the town to receive Ram alongwith Guru Vashistha, the mothers, mantris and other seniors of the town together with Ram's Padukas as required by protocol. These padukas were actually nothing but a comprehensive letter of authority given by Ram to enable Bharat to rule in Ram's absence for 14 years. Now on Ram's arrival back, Bharat decided to hand over the rajya to Shri Ram along with the letter of authority. Receiving Shri Ram by Guru, Bharat etc. outside the town is also the tradition then existing like what is available today too for receiving any foreign dignitary. Bharat and Ram met with great affection. Then Ram, Lakshman and Sita met the guru, brahmins, mothers and other seniors, who had come to receive them. Ram etc. came to Awadha with all the pump and show suiting the occasion. Guru Vashistha then arranged for their bath etc. and all arrangements for Ram's coronation were made. Coronation was done amidst all seniors, mantris etc. by the guru. After Ram was coronated, he started ruling the kingdom according to the tenets of dharma keeping the concept of varna and ashram into view. As already indicated, in Ram Rajya, every citizen had been doing the job as per his dharma laid down in varna-ashram institution and wherever such institutional requirements were fully fulfilled, there had been peace. In Ram rajya, all led life as ordained by vedas and shastras as a result of which—

(1) The forests, mountains, rivers and ocean all had been sparing their products for the use of public.

(2) Nobody was mentally tortured or was under any tension as the duties and wishes of everyone were properly laid down and fulfilled and everyone was happy and content doing the same. Once there was

no tension, there was no ailment too. Even one could evade death if he did not want to die then and wanted to live for some more time.

(3) Ram had already seen that Raja Dasratha had to suffer because of keeping multiple queens and in the bargain had to give up his life. He, therefore, decided to have only one wife and propagated for the same amongst his subjects too.

(4) The king has to keep in mind that the praja follows the king (यथा राजा तथा प्रजा). The king, therefore, had to lead a simple, pure, religious and restrained life so that the people also did the same.

(5) The wives were fully devoted to their husbands copying the living of Sita.

(6) Ram had held many yagyas including Aswamedha yagyas. These yagyas were held in which all dependent rajas (vassals) were present and offered presents to their monarch accepting his superiority over them. This is like the present concept of Suzerainty in which the vassal states have to provide particular presents to the monarch's exchequer and accept his superiority.

(7) Ram's brothers had been invading the rakshas rajas and after conquering them the booty was put in Awadha's exchequer. In this way, Bharat conquered Gandharvas; Shatrughan killed the Rakshas' Raja of Mathura and merged it with Awadha.

(8) As a part of king's duty to see that none in his rajya was having any complaint against the raja, Ram used to go incognito in nights to visit Awadha. Once he saw a washermen rebuking his wife, who had stayed out for the night, that he could not keep her in his house as Ram had kept Sita even after she had been in Lanka for a long period. This Ram listened from several persons. He held a meeting of the seniors and decided to renounce Sita. Such was the Raja-Praja relation (protocol) in those day. Whereas the raja always thought of well-being of the people, the people were free to criticise the raja and the raja

was guided by the majority opinion. In this way democracy and freedom of speech were in full play.

(9) Freedom of professional vocation was always there within the concept of the institution of varna-ashram.

(10) Ram had been leading his life in absence of Sita in great agony. This shows that the matrimony is the root cause of many distresses even for the persons leading saintly life like Ram and Sita, then what to speak of the persons, who are very much indulged in woman.

स्त्रीपुप्रसंग एतादृक्सर्वत्र त्रासमावहः,
अपीश्वराणां किमुत ग्राम्यस्य गृहचेतसः। (9-11-17)

Eventually Sita gave up her life and after that Ram ruled Awadha for many years without any attraction, distress etc. That is why in modern time, Plato had pleaded for the theory of State in which the king was not allowed to marry as in that case he would become selfish to take care of his wife and children and if he was alone, he would think of the well-being of his people only. So Ram lived like the platonic emperor. Ram became very popular and was liked and loved by all.

Pururva was also born in this dynasty. He was very handsome and brave raja. Urvasi, an apsra of Swarga fell for him and came to the earth. Pururva was also charmed by her beauty and they got married. From their union, six sons were born. This would indicate that in those days there were very frequent visits of the persons from swarga to the earth and vice versa. Also there were marriages taking place in the persons of different planets. Now the people are trying to search moon, Jupitor etc. but when and how much success is achieved has yet to be seen. After some time, Urvashi went back to swarga on Indra's orders, as Indra was against such unions.

Anyway, Urvashi had already given birth to six sons, who further had their offspring and one worth mentioning was Gadhi. His daughter was Satyawati. One Richik Rishi proposed himself to marry Satyawati but Raja Gadhi was not agreeable and at the same time he could not say no to the rishi as it would have offended the rishi involving serious consequences. He, therefore, put a difficult condition for marriage—delivery of one thousand horses, which should be white complexioned but with one black ear. Richik could know that such horses were available with god Varuna. He brought one thousand such horses from Varuna and on handing over the same to Gadhi, he married Satyawati (his daughter). This would indicate that :

(1) marriages generally took place within same varna *i.e.* brahmin, kshatriya, vaish, and shudra. This facilitated the offspring of such marriages knowing their dharma from the birth itself and were prepared for the duties of that dharma later in life.

(2) Even the bride's father could accept something in consideration of the marriage although as per general tradition, the bride's father used to give dowry in marriage to the groom's father as Raja Janak had given in Sita's marriage to Raja Dasratha. But here Gadhi, the bride's father had accepted one thousand horses in marriage of his daughter Satyawati to Richik, who was a muni.

(3) In exceptional cases, inter-varna marriages too took place like Gadhi married his daughter to Richik. Similarly, Raja Dasratha's daughter had been married to Sringi Rishi and so on. So flexibility too did exist in inter-varna marriages.

Satyawati gave birth to Jamadagni. Jamadagni married Renuka. From their union several sons were born; the youngest one being Parshuram. It is said that Parshuram was the incarnation of God himself. He was born to annihilate the kshatriyas, who had by then forgotten their dharma and by misusing the national exchequer and extracting more and more money from public, had started living lavishly. They had become cruel to brahmins and extractions from vaish and annoying the shudras. As already indicated, whenever the varna-ashram dharma was not followed in India, there was chaos and anarchy. At that time, because of the cruelty of kshatriyas on people of other varnas, Parshuram came as incarnate of God to eradicate the non-dharmik kshatriyas. Such cruelty was in fact ushered in only by the rajas, who had obtained boons from God by Tapsya. Raja Arjun of those days had performed tapsya and asked the boon of having one thousand hands and also not to be defeated by anyone in war. In those days performing tapsya and then asking for boons from the God, on his having been pleased, was a normal phenomena. Actually tapsya is such a thing that if one had known the modus-operandi, and become successful in getting any boon from God, he would pass on that method to others, who too would try the same. In this way, the performance of tapsya and achieving the desired wish had become common. God too having once agreed to award any boon was bound to fulfil the same, whatever might be the consequences. Similar cruel boons had been attained by Hirnakashyap and later on by Ravan and others too. Then God himself had to find out a way of annihilating such cruel persons. So Raja Arjun had attained all sidhis, force, wealth and image and became Sahasbahu Arjun. It is said tat once Sahasbahu was taking bath in a river with may beautiful ladies. He stopped the flow of river by his force. On the other side of the river, Ravan was taking bath. When he could not get water, he got infuriated (after all he too considered himself as a great warrior). He came to Sahasbahu and started abusing him. Sahasbahu caught hold of him and took to his capital and kept him in captivity. Then he was released on a request by Pulastya Rishi (Ravan's father).

Once same Sahasbahu had gone to forests with his army. On the way, they stopped at the ashram of Jamadagni Muni (Parshuram's father). Jamadagni had a Kamdhenu (कामधेनु) cow.This cow could feed any number of persons. So this cow fed the entire army of raja. The raja got a fancy for the cow and being proud as he was, he took away the cow even without asking the muni for the same. When Parshuram came to ashram and came to know of the raja having taken away the cow, he went to the raja and killed his entire army and then killed the raja Sahasbahu too. He brought back the cow. When Parshuram's father came to know of the killing of raja by his son, he was not happy and told his son that according to varna-ashram dharma, everyone had to do his job. For brahmins, battle was not their vocation. The punishment is given by the raja for the crime and if the raja himself had committed the crime, the public would take revenge and not the brahmins.

"वयं हि ब्रह्मणास्तात क्षमयार्हणतां गताः।" (9-16-39)

and "क्षमया रोचते लक्ष्मीर्ब्राह्मी सौरी यथा प्रभा।" (9-16-40)

and 'राज्ञो मूर्धाभिषिक्तस्य वधो ब्रह्मवधात गुरुः।' (9-16-41)

(1) According to varna dharma, brahmin is not to involve himself in battle. He only had to excuse the person being cruel to a brahmin. This also implies that since brahmins were made the gurus, who taught use of arms to kshatriyas, the brahmins were masters of using the arms and if they started using arms against those they had tought, it would lead to an awkward situation. Some such awkward situation had to be faced when Arjun had to fight with Daronacharya (his guru) and since the guru was rather very capable warrior, it was difficult for Arjun to defeat him in Mahabharat. So the brahmins were not allowed as per dharma to take to the arms.

(2) It was because of their dharma of excusing others even after having committed crime that the brahmins were respected by all.

(3) Killing of raja, who protected the subject against outside invasions, was a sin more so the killing of a king emperor. Sahasbahu was a king emperor. Therefore, his killing was more serious than the killing of a brahmin. Here it is evident that there were checks and balances in the exercise of authority by the persons of various varnas. Killing of brahmin by anyone was considered as a great sin. Similarly killing of a raja too was considered as a sin. This is what had been said by another rishi when his son had passed on a curse on Raja Parikshit, who had put a dead snake in the neck of the rishi, of being bitten by Takshak resulting in his death after seven days. Then

the rishi had abused his son of over-exercising his power of passing on the curse. He then had to go and begged to be excused by the raja.

(4) Similarly raja too could not do any wrong, otherwise he had to face the curse by other people in his kingdom. Raja Ram had to give up Sita as people of Awadha had not reconciled to a situation in which a person could accept his wife even after her stay at the house of a stranger for even over a night, not to speak of many days for which Sita had remained in Lanka and to redeem the public feeling, Ram had to separate Sita.

(5) Rishi Jamadagni asked his son Parshuram to repent for the killing of raja by visiting tirthas. Parshuram had to undertake tirthyatra (pilgrimage) for over an year.

Once when Parshuram had returned to his Ashram, his mother Renuka had gone to fetch water from the river to enable the rishi to perform pooja. But Renuka after seeing some Gandharvas playing there got attracted towards them and lost in seeing their play so much so that the time of pooja passed. When she returned with water, the rishi had by his tap known the reason of her overstayal and asked his sons to kill her but none obeyed except– Parshuram, who not only killed the mother but also his brothers for having not obeyed the father. The father was happy and asked Parshuram to ask for any boon. Parshuram requested his mother and brothers to be re-enlivened. This way Parushuram obeyed father and killed his mother and brothers and at the same time got them re-enlivened them; they forgetting the entire episode. Here a protocolic question arises as to whether a son could kill the mother on being asked to do so by the father. Normally a son had to obey the father but then could the father ever ask for the murder of the mother and this was to be obeyed by the son. In fact as per shastras, the position of mother is superior to that of father. That is why when Raja Dasratha had asked Ram to go to forest for 14 years and Ram reported to mother Kaushalya for her permission Kaushalya had said that if this was the order of Raja Dasratha only then she would undo it being superior to father's right over the son but if the order was that of mother Kaikayee and Raja Dasratha then she was helpless. Since the order was that of mother Kaikayee and Dasratha both, she could not do anything and asked Ram to comply with the order. So here too the position of mother is shown superior for the son compared to that of the father, how had Parshuram accepted father's order of killing the mother, the reply is contained in the next sloka itself—

पितुर्विद्वांस्तपोवीर्यं रामश्चक्रे सुहृद्वधम्। (9-16-8)

Parshuram had killed the mother and brothers knowing the tapobal (तपोबल) power of his father that he was able to re-enliven them . But the matter of re-enliving is later and the first action of Parshuram was not at all justified accept to take it that the mother had done sin in having been attracted towards the Gandharvas but then too it was not for the son to have killed the mother; the punishment was to be given by someone else viz.·husband by passing another curse on her rather than asking the son to kill her particularly when the same rishi had some time back told Parshuram, who had killed Raja Sahasbahu that brahmins were there to excuse others and not to punish them for any crime whatsoever and consequently asked Parshuram to repent for the killing. The rishi himself was not justified in having ordered the killing of the mother by the sons. There are instances of the munis having passed the curse on their wives for having committed some crime as Rishi Gautam had turned his wife Ahailya into a stone. So the rishi could also pass on any curse on his wife.

Now with the murder of Sahasbahu by Parshuram his sons were after taking revenge. Once when the sons had gone out of the Ashram, the sons of Sahasbahu came and killed Rishi Jamadagni (Parshuram's father). The mother begged to leave her husband but the rajas did not agree. She was crying on the murder of her husband. Parshuram got enraged and went to the town and killed all the sons of Sahasbahu and then having got that excuse as also seeing that the kshatriyas were indulging in all sorts of bad deeds and non-dharmaic activities, Parshuram, the incarnation of God, responsible for protecting dharma on the earth, annihilated the kshatriyas 21 times from the earth. After killing the sons of Sahasbahu, Parshuram brought the head of his father from them and by tapsya joined it with rest of the body and re-enlivened the father. This indicates that there must be so much surgical advancement in those days that even the separated head could be rejoined and the person re-enlivened. Such specialisation is yet to be achieved in modern times.

Raja Nahus had been made a crocodile as he wanted to sleep with Suchi (Indra's queen). In this way, even the rajas had been punished for indulging in undesirable activities. He had six sons. Nahus wanted to coronate his eldest son considering him capable of handling the rajya but, even being an asura, he believed in self realisation and he told that once involved in the intricacies of rajya, one could not attain self-realisation.

राज्यं नैच्छद यतिः पित्रा दत्तं तत्परिणामवित्
यत्र प्रविष्टः पुरुष आत्मानं नावबुध्यते। (9-18-2)

The next eldest Yayati succeeded the throne. He made his other four brothers rajas of countries in four directions. He married Shukracharya's (Asura's Guru) daughter Devyani and Varisparva's daughter Sharmistha. Here again the question arose how a kshatriya could marry the daughter of a brahmin. Such a matrimony was forbidden but some special circumstances led to such forbidden marriages too.

Sharmistha and Devyani had gone for a stroll in the garden. There was a lake in the garden. The girls started playing in the lake. At that time Shiva and Parvati came there and all the girls came out of the lake. In haste Sharmistha wore the clothes of Devyani. Devyani rebuked her saying brahmins are the overall Lords by virtue of their tapsya and even the gods and rajas, worshipped the brahmins and Sharmistha an asura's daughter had worn her clothes. She also said that Sharmistha's father was their disciple. Sharmistha had been listening to all this.

She got enraged and in turn told that brahmins live on the alms given by the rajas. She snatched her clothes from Devyani and threw her in the well. Sharmistha went home. During that time, Raja Yayati had reached there during hunting in search of water. He saw Devyani in the well. He gave his turban to her to wear (as she was nude) and by holding her hand, took her out of the well. Devyani thereupon fell in love with Yayati and told him that since he had held her hand, none else could hold it (in marriage) now. She told that Brihaspati's son wanted to marry her but she declined and Brihaspati's son had passed a curse on her as a result of which no brahmin was marrying her. Being against the laid dharma, Yayati did not enter into that matrimony but having been placed in such a situation, he hesitatingly agreed to the same. Yayati went to his rajya and Devyani came to her house. She told whatever had happened to her father Shukaracharya. He cursed himself being a Purohit and preferred to be a labourer rather than being a Purohit. He left the town alongwith Devyani.The Raja Vrisparva became frightened that Shukracharya would either join hands with the enemy and get him defeated or may pass some curse on him (as was usual with the brahmins in rage). The raja requested Shukracharya to return to the kingdom. He put a condition laid down by Devyani that wherever she was married, Sharmistha should go there as her maid servant. The raja accepted this condition and Sharmistha began serving Devyani. As already agreed between Devyani and Raja Yayti, they were married and Sharmistha went there as a maid. Shukarcharya forbade raja that Sharmistha should never be allowed to sleep with him. It was in these circumstances that Devyani, the daughter of a brahmin, had been married to a kshatriya raja. After sometime Devyani became pregnant and Sharmistha too requested the raja to oblige her in permitting to sleep with him. Even though the raja remembered what Shukracharya had said but allowed himself to sleep with Sharmistha leaving the result to fate. Devyani gave birth to two sons and Sharmistha gave birth to three sons, including one Puru. When Devyani came to know that Sharmistha's sons were born out of the union with her husband, she felt it and went to her father's house. Yayati tried to be excused by her but she did not agree. Shukracharya rebuked him saying that he was a liar and a womaniser and passed on a curse on him that he would become old. Yayati stated that neither he nor his daughter were so far satisfied with the matrimonial alliance and this would be bad for his daughter too as she would be starved of sex. Shukracharya then relaxed the curse to the extent that any youngman could change his youth with him, if he was agreeable to such a change unhesitatingly. He returned to his kingdom and requested his sons to exchange old age for the youth but every one declined. Puru (the youngest son), however, stated that this life was given by the father and it would be good if it could be of any use to the father. He said the best son is he, who obeys father even without askance and the second best is he, who obeys on having been asked to do some job and the third best is he, who obeys but reluctantly and the one who does not obey is not worthy of becoming a son.

उत्तमश्चिन्तितं कुर्यात प्रोक्तकारी तु मध्यमः।
अधमो अश्रध्या कुर्यादकर्तोच्चरितं पितुः। (9-18-44)

Saying this, Puru accepted the father's old age in exchange of his youth. The father again started making love. He was a Chakravarty raja. Devyani had been giving him pleasure. In this way he enjoyed the worldly life to satisfy his passions but felt that inspite of many years of matrimony, he could not satisfy his lust, rather it went on increasing day by day. He, therefore, decided to renounce the universe as all commodities, wealth, animals, and women could not satisfy the human beings' desires. On the contrary the ambitions went on increasing. One, therefore, should give up these worldly ambitions. The lust even disturb the mind of the greatest of the tapasvis. He, therefore, indicated that renouncing the grihastha, he wanted to devote the rest of the life for the cause of the almighty. This is as per the Hindu tradition of ashramas institution.

Yayati afterwards returned the youth to his son Puru in exchange of his old age and handed over the rajya of

Northern Part to him and to others the other parts of the kingdom. He, thereafter, left for forests and attained salvation. This is the speciality of Hindu Dharma that even after indulging in all worldly ambitions and sensuous satisfaction, one can attain salvation if followed by absorption in almighty God accepting the vanprastha/ sanyas. Puru became the monarch. He ruled for many years according to the tenets of dharma.

In that dynasty was born Dushyant. He had once gone to forests for hunting. He reached the ashram of Rishi Kanav. In that ashram, he saw a beautiful girl. Dushyant got attracted towards her charms. He asked her that she must be some kshatriya girl otherwise the rajkumars of Puru dynasty could not get attracted to any rishi kanya. This shows that rajas/rajkumars always remained in their limits, characterwise. On seeing Sita, Ram also said that Raghuvanis donot get attracted toward any girl's charms without any reason. So was the position of Dushyant. The Rishi Kanya was Shakuntala, the daughter of Viswamitra, who was basically a kshatriya but subsequently became Brahmrishi. Menka Apsra had left her in forest, when Indra called her back and she had been brought up by Rishi Kanav. She entertained the guest in the ashram with whatever was available there. Welcoming and entertaining a guest is prime dharma in Hindus. By mutual consent, they accepted each other as the life partner and had held Gandharva (गंधर्व) marriage (love marriage). There was a provision in Hindu Dharma to have love marriage too when both the boy and the girl agree to the same. Shakuntala became pregnant. Dushyant left for the kingdom the next day. When Shakuntala went to her husband, he refused to recognise her and denied having married her. Ultimately when Dushyant remembered having married Shakuntala in forests, he searched her and brought her back. In course of time, Shakuntala gave birth to a son, who later became the king emperor Bharat. He ruled according to tenets of dharma, to the full satisfaction of his subjects and as usual after a long reign renounced the universe and spent his last days of life in forests as a sanyasi.

Skandh – X

Krishna Avtar

Bhagwan Krishna is the creator, maintainer, annihilator and all in all of all human beings. It was because of the blessings of Shri Krishna that Pandvas had been able to defeat the mighty force of Kaurvas led by Bhishma Pitamah, who was a terror for every raja of that time. In fact Parikshit's foetus had been burnt by the curse of Aswatthama, when he was in the womb itself but Shri Krishna saved him from that evil spirit, on Parikshit's mother having sought refuge from Lord Krishna. Parikshit asked for Krishna leelas being narrated to him. As in Ramcharitmanas, which was narrated by Shiva to Parvati or by Yagyavalka Muni to Bhardwaj Muni, Krishna katha has been narrated by Muni Shukdeva to Parikshit. This had been written by Vyas Muni, who again has indicated this as a narration by Shootji to Shaunaic and other munis. Again through the media of Parikshit, this katha has been narrated by Shukdeva for the general benefit of the people at large to enable them to attain salvation.

As usual, Vishnu Bhagwan comes incarnate only when the rakshasas start destroying dharma by killing sadhus and cows; not permitting the people to live according to the dharma and extracting money/wealth from people and other rajas and spending the same lavishly on their pleasures. When Krishna was born, then too some similar situation had arisen. Thousands of rakshasas had became rajas and had been cruel to the public. The earth at that time went to Lord Brahma. As per protocol, which is applicable to even gods, the earth could not straight-away go to Lord Vishnu for help although earth knew that Vishnu only could help her as the rakshasas had mostly been acting cruelly by dint of the boon showered on them by Brahma himself. Also this too could be a reason to go to Brahma as entire environ had been spoiled because of his boons to rakshasas. For Earth, Brahma was the immediate boss. Brahma, however, took Earth to Vishnu along with Shiva and other gods. When one goes to meet the Lord for any favour, it is better to go in multiple as then their say becomes more valued. Even today the demonstrations are arranged by the crowd, who convey their feelings to the concerned authorities. Now since Brahma himself was responsible for all these evil activities of asuras, which had even frightened the gods, he himself could not redress their grievance by undoing what he had passed on as a boon because of the tapsya by the rakshasas. There was akashwani that the almighty Lord was already aware of the curelty being faced by the people on earth and to do away with this cruelty he would go as incarnate in Yadu Vansha. The gods too were advised to go and start living there incognito to help Lord in his leela of killing all rakshasas. Even Bhagwan Shesh too would go there in incarnate as Balram. Brahma advised all gods to act accordingly and went to his Loka. In those days Yadvas ruled Mathura and the area around it. Once Vasudeva was going to his house alongwith his newly wedded wife Devki along with Raja Ugrasen's son Kansa. In fact Kansa was driving the chariot of his sister Devki as Kansa loved Devki a lot. In the marriage of Devki, her father had given many golden chariots, four hundred elephants, thousands of horses, many costly clothes and ornaments along with many maids. This was the protocolic tradition existing at that time and continuing today that the bride's father gives a lot of dowry in the marriage of the daughter. This, however, was given in pleasure with a view to help organise the new house by the bride on marriage and not in consideration of the marriage as most of the dowry had inturn been passed on by the groom's father to brahmins, poors and others, as alms.

"दुहित्रे देवकः प्रादाद् याने दुहितृवत्सलः।" (10-1-32)

The dowry was given by the bride's father out of love and affection for the daughter. One more reason for giving the dowry would have been that the daughter could meet her requirements in her in-laws house (groom's house) out the things she had brought in dowry, rather than immediately having to request her in-laws to meet her requirements and in most of cases face their aspersions. Further, since all the people had both sons and daughters, the system of dowry was an accepted tradition as it involved give and take by all.

When Kansa was driving the chariot, there was an akashwani saying "O, Kansa the eighth offspring of the couple, whom he had been taking in chariot, would be his killer". Kansa was an asura and had been cruel to the people but was driving Devki's chariot out of affection for her. On hearing the akashwani,he took his sword and wanted to kill Devki. Vasudeva, however, sensing that Kansa, being very cruel, as he was, would certainly kill her, requested him that :

(1) He was quite brave and should not have any fear from the offspring of Devki, who was going in marriage in an ordinary house of Mahatma Vasudeva.

(2) Devki was a lady and killing a lady was forbidden in Hindus and that too by the Rajkumar, who was to succeed the throne of Mathura, in course of time.

(3) Such a killing would spoil his image in subjects.

(4) Then it was the time of a marriage and killing the bride in marriage itself was not good.

(5) Every one had to die one day. Who kills whom is only a pretence of death. These were in fact the facts of life then existing.

(6) Devki was like his sister and only in her teenage, it would be a sin to kill the sister in this tender age.

(7) Vasudeva in this way tried to pacify Kansa by the known policies of Sam (साम) and Dand (दंड) as the

other two policies of of Dam (दाम) and Bhed (भेद) were not applicable as Kansa was a raja and could not be influenced by wealth and again he being the sole person then, there was no question of creating any division. Even the dand (punishment) was only indirect as a sufferance on creating a sin and not direct punishment, which Vasudeva was not capable of imposing on Kansa. Kansa, however, could not be pacified. Vasudeva then thought how to save Devki's life as according to shastras one should by his intelligence and force try to evade death and even then if one is not successful, then he could not be blamed and face death.

मृत्युर्बुद्धिमतापोह्यो यावद्बुद्धि बलोदयम्,
यद्यसौ न निवर्तेत नापराधोऽस्ति देहिनः।

So Vasudeva then committed that if Kansa spared Devki's life, he would bring each of Devki's children on birth for being killed by him and in this way Kansa would, by killing all Devki's offspring, including the eighth one, be free from any fear of being killed by Devki's offspring. Saying this Vasudeva praised Kansa. Praise is the best way of pacifying a person. So Vasudeva not only gave a solution to the problem, but also praised Kansa for his generosity. Kansa had great faith in the words of Vasudeva. So he, at that time saved Devki from being killed on the assurance of handing over each of her offspring to Kansa. Vasudeva went to his house. Kansa, however, put Vasudeva and Devki in jail so that Vasudeva was not able to conceal any birth from Kansa. Keeping his word, Vasudeva had been handing over to Kansa each of the offspring born to Devki. Simultaneously, Narad Muni had told Kansa that all new born in Brij and Mathura were actually gods and they had come incognito to kill Kansa. On this, believing what Narad had said, Kansa killed all new borns in Brij and Mathura. Even to fulfil his passion of cruelty, he put his father Ugrasen too in jail. Shukdeva told that a cruel person could even kill his parents, friends, relatives or anyone else for the sake of saving his life.

मातरं पितरं भ्रातृन् सर्वांशंच सुहृदस्तथा,
घ्नन्ति ह्यसुतृपो लुब्धा राजानः प्रायशो भुविः। (10-2-67)

Kansa was himself an asura and very brave. He after succeeding to throne of Mathura, made friendship with most of the asura kings of that time like Jarasandha, Aghasura, Mustik, Aristasura, Pootna, Keshi, Banasura, Bhomasura etc. This would indicate that major part of India was ruled by asuras, who had developed inter-state relationship and had been doing all kinds of cruelties to public and themselves always indulging in satisfaction of sensuous passions. In fact, most of the people of these areas had migrated and settled in other countries (not governed by asuras), like Panchal, Vidarbha, Kaushal, Kuru etc., where there was the rule of dharma. If we see the entire ancient Indian history, we find that there had always been asura and non-asura rulers and they had been fighting with each other. Kansa had already killed six of Devki's children. The seventh was the incarnate of Sesh. God arranged for the migration of the foetus itself from Devki to another wife of Vasudeva, Rohini, who was in Brij. He later on became Balram. Now Rohini being in Brij giving birth to a child, when her husband was in jail for over 6 years, appeared insulting for Rohini but as has been confirmed by medical science in present day, the foetus could be transferred from one uterus to another. In those days too there might have been some such technology which has been named as God's creation as people could believe in the act of God, rather than in the act of human beings. The eighth child, in Devki's conception was Lord Vishnu himself. Kansa had been very anxiously waiting for this child to be killed. He also thought of killing Devki with this conception but again the same forbidding ingredients (1) a women, (2) a sister and, (3) a pregnant lady stood in way and, therefore, Kansa spared her to have the child. It might be that the Lord Vishnu had changed Kansa's mind to think it otherwise and he thus spared Devki. Kansa had now been thinking of God everytime as he knew God only could kill him and the eighth child of Devki would be God. In a way, he had become Krishna bhakta, who had always been thinking of him only although out of fear. Bhagwan has himself said that anyone thinking of him only everytime, is his best bhakta. This is the spiritual relation between the Bhagwan and human being (ब्रह्म और जीव). Bhagwan Shankar, Brahma and other gods too visited the jail and praised the almighty Vishnu. During almighty's praise, Brahma had narrated the entire vedic concept of universe which even today stands fundamentally sound. A human being has :

(1) Pleasure and worry (सुख और दुख).

(2) These two are based on three faculties—Satva, Rajas and Tamas (सत्व, रज और तम)

(3) Four ambitions relating to attainment are—dharma (धर्म), wealth (अर्थ), satisfaction of passions (काम), and salvation. (मोक्ष).

(4) Been working by five senses—eyes, nose, ears, tongue and skin.

(5) Six changes in life—to born, live, accelerate, change, decelerate and then annihilation.

The above ingredients are operated/worked by the almighty God himself even though the human beings think that these are all his creations only. This is God's 'Maya' used to maintain the universe. A human being, who rises above these weaknesses, attains salvation.

Then came the time of arrival of the almighty. It was auspicious time, Rohini Nakshatra (रोहिणी नक्षत्र), peaceful and quiet environ, clear night, full of stars, Bhadon month, eighth date, cool breeze was flowing, Jamuna was full of water. In such a situation, Lord Krishna was born. All gods were happy. Vasudeva saw a child with four hands having shell, chakra, gada and padma (शंख चक्र, गदा, पद्म) wide eyes, and handsome built body with all clothes, ornaments etc. on. He became happy to see the almighty Vishnu. He bowed before the God and started praising him. Devki too seeing God bowed and started praising him and expressed her fear also that Kansa, if comes to know that he was born out of Devki, shall kill him. The child Krishna told

Devki that in a previous life Vasudeva was Sutpa and Devki was Prisni. After a great tapsya, the two had asked a boon to have a son like God. Therefore, to fulfil that promise, God was born out of their union. This is similar to what Dasratha and Kausalya had prayed to have in previous life and they had Ram incarnate of God in there present life as their son, This confirms that :

(1) A man and his wife can become husband and wife again on subsequent transmigration of soul.

(2) The theory of transmigration of soul is established.

(3) The boons granted in one life can be fulfilled in any subsequent life.

(4) When God comes incarnation, he at first gives darshan to the mother in his full form of four arms etc. to remind the mother that he had come in fulfilment of the boon granted to her. Similar was the case with Kaushalya too when Ram had come in four arms etc. and Kaushalya requested him to now become the child. Same thing had been repeated in the case of Devki too.

Then Shri Krishna inspired Vasudeva to take him to Mathura. All gates of jail stood opened. Vasudeva took Krishna and went to Brij crossing Yamuna. There might be some electronic device in those days to open the gates, make the security men sleep by some drug and thus going out of the jail. All in Brij too had been sleeping. Vasudeva placed Krishna on the bed near Yashoda and took away the girl born of Yashoda to be handed over to Kansa, as a new born child of Devki. Then he returned to jail. Hearing the cry of the child, the security men got up and informed Kansa of the birth of the child. Kansa was anxiously waiting for the birth of this eighth child as it was supposed to be his killer. Devki requested not to kill the child as the child was a girl and it was sin to kill a girl. Kansa, however, snatched the child and threw her on a stone. The child was a goddess. She went in sky and told Kansa that his killer was already born somewhere else. Kansa on hearing this, released Vasudeva and Devki from the jail and begged to be excused for the trouble faced by them. He told him that the troubles and pleasures are all God-gifted.

मा शोचतं महाभागावात्मजान् स्वकृतम्भुजः
जन्त्वो न सदैकत्र दैवाधीनस्तदासते। (10-4-18)

This shows that although an asura, even Kansa believed in fate and was aware of all that is written in shastras. It was in fact the fear of death that had made him cruel and could not think of anything in correct perspective. Seeing Kansa repentant, Devki and Vasudeva excused him of all previous cruelties. This is what is in the core of the great men to excuse even the most guilty if he is repentant on what he had done.

Kansa narrated all that had happened to his advisors. The advisors, who too were of asura character advised Kansa to get all babies born during the last few days killed. Kansa, under fear psycho acted accordingly and even not having satisfied with that, Kansa also ordered killing of all cows, sadhus etc.

On the other side, on the birth of Krishna in Gokul, there was all jubilance. Alms were given to brahmins and beggars and others, as per tradition. The brahmins in turn gave their blessings.

Like the present day system of an emperor keeping some vassals (smaller rulers) under him, there was some such system existing in Krishna period too. Kansa was an emperor and he was keeping some small rajas under him. These vassals were considered to be :

(1) Loyal to the king emperor.

(2) Used to pay some annual tribute to the emperor's exchequer.

(3) In turn the king emperor undertook to protect such vassals from external aggression.

(4) Such vassals were otherwise autonomous in their kingdom.

Nand was one such vassal Raja. He was the raja of Gokul. He went to Mathura to confirm his loyalty to the Raja of Mathura and to pay the annual presents. There Vasudeva too met Nand. After that Nand came back to Gokul.

Having heard the akashwani, Kansa had got all newly born babies killed. He then came to know that the real killer is in Nand's house. He sent Pootna, a rakshasni, to feed her milk with poison and kill him. She became a beautiful girl, came to Nand's house, entered the house, and picked up Krishna in her lap and started feeding him. Krishna knew her and started drinking herself alongwith milk. She cried. All people collected there. Pootna came to her realself and died. The people were frightened lest Krishna would have been killed but heaved a sigh of relief on finding Krishna there. Pootna having been killed by Krishna, got salvation.

Hearing the Bhagwad leela of Pootna killing, Parikshit got interested in some more incidents of Krishna leela. These are being narrated here too to quench the thirst of readers and to enable them to understand the spiritual protocol involved in such leelas as such leelas inculcate bhakti in one's mind and absorption in the almighty.

Once Shri Krishna having become hungry, had been crying for milk but Yashoda was busy somewhere and she did not hear Krishna crying. Krishna was lying on a pram. By his legs, he turned the pram turtle. Every one was surprised how this could happen.

Kansa sent another rakshas named Trinvrat to kill Krishna. He took Krishna to space during a cyclone. Yashoda not having found Krishna in his bed, got frightened. Krishna became a heavy hillock. He caught hold of Trinvrat's neck and they both fell in Gokul. Trinvrat died whereas Krishna was all safe.

Once after Yashoda had fed Krishna, she found Krishna's mouth open and in that she saw the entire universe. She was surprised to see it. Krishna, however, made her forget this incident.

So far only Vasudeva and Devki knew that Krishna was their son and Nand and Yashoda thought Krishna was their son. Once Gargacharya, the Purohit of Yadvas, came to Gokul. Nand was happy to see him there. He paid respects bowing down and touching feet, worshipped him like a God. He requested the Purohit to perform the Christening (namkaran) ceremony of their sons. In fact, Gargacharya by his knowledge, had known that Krishna was Vasudeva's son and, he being his Purohit, it was for him only to perform the namkaran sanskar. He had, therefore, correctly gone there for this purpose to perform namkaran sanskar and have a darshan of the almighty God incarnate as Krishna. Gargacharya, however, hesitated in doing this job as the Purohit of Yadvas, as once Kansa came to know of his having performed the namkaran, he would definitely think that Devki's eighth child was not the girl, he had killed but this boy. So he had hesitation in performing the ceremony. Nand, however, insisted on quietly doing the ceremony. Gargacharya only wanted such an assurance from Nand. He named Rohini's son as Rohiney/Balram/Sankarshana and Devki's son as Krishna being of dark (कृष्ण) complexion although he is known by so many names. Namkaran sanskar is an important ceremony and as per protocol, it has necessarily to be performed by the Kul Purohit (कुल पुरोहित). Question can arise why then this ceremony was not performed by the Purohit of Nand Baba. The only explanation to this can be that Gokul being a colony of gwalas (grazers), there might not be a learned Pandit in that colony and by chance (for Nand) Gargacharya, a learned pandit, having come there, Nand requested him to perform the ceremony. The Purohit told that the boy was equivalent to God in beauty, bravery, virtues etc. The Purohit at the time of namkaran used to tell all about the past life and the characteristics of this life. He went away to his ashram after the ceremony. In this way Gargacharya could know that he was the God incarnate and also did his job of namkaran as the Purohit. Krishna had been doing his leela in Gokul and doing such actions as could not be treated to be of any ordinary person like stealing butter by many ways in his own house as well as in the houses of the neighbours.

Krishna is known for his butter theft and playing with the gopis and gwalas. In this connection allegation are held against Krishna for his being a thief and a womaniser. So far as the question of butter theft is concerned, it has to be seen in the context that Krishna was the son of Yashoda and Nand. Nand was the raja of Gokul and he had thousands of cows in his possession. So there was lot of butter in his house itself. Then why should he go to the others' houses to steal butter and eat and distribute amongst his friends. In fact when the neighbours had been complaining about Krishna stealing butter from their horses, Yashoda used to tell them why he should resort to theft when lot of butter was available in her house itself and he could eat as much as he liked. The fact, however, is that Krishna was favourite of everyone in Gokul— boys and girls and even the elders. Everyone loved Krishna according to his own thinking as in the case of Ram at Sita Swayamber it is said—

जिन्हकें रही भावना जैसी,

प्रभु मूर्ति तिन्ह देखी तैसी। (मानस)

The rishis, munis saw him as their almighty God. Raja Janak and his wife saw him as their son; Janak Puri residents saw him as their son-in-law. The asuras saw him as their death and so on. Here too the residents of Gokul saw Krishna as per their mentality. The elders saw in him the son-like affection; the boys saw in him a friend; the girls (गोपियाँ) too saw him as their playing mate and so on. Krishna had been pleasing everyone with his actions. He had already impressed everyone with his spiritual powers in having killed Pootna and other rakshasas. Being very beautiful too, he was loved and liked by all. The facts behind stealing butter can be :

(1) Krishna being favourite of everyone, he wanted to oblige everyone by his darshan. So stealing butter was an excuse to visit their houses. In fact everyone welcomed Krishna coming to their houses and might be they themselves offered him butter in their houses. The gopis complained to Yashoda because they wanted to enjoy the Krishna leela on complaining to Yashoda and on how Yashoda dealt with him.

(2) Being favourite of everyone, he had actually stolen the heart of every one. He was, therefore, a chitchor (चित्तचोर). Now heart is the most sensitive organ in human body. Therefore, the thief of hearts can also

be synonymised to stealing butter as butter too is most sensitive thing. It is clean, being the extract of milk; it is slippery like the heart and it is very mild too. Therefore, actually Krishna had not stolen butter but the heart of all gopis.

(3) Even if it was butter, Krishna had many friends in gwalas. He wanted to show to the universe the concept of eating after distribution amongst all friends. Therefore, Krishna had been visiting the houses of all people and taking butter and eating the same after distributing amongst all. Alternately he took all the friends alongwith him to see him being loved by all and so enjoying the company of all gopis too.

(4) Krishna was Bhagwan and he liked his bhaktas and bhakti. Gopis were his bhaktas and, therefore, he had been only seeing and liking the bhakti in them. Here butter can be a symbol of bhakti being the extract (तत्त्व) and all in all in the eyes of the people of Gokul, who considered butter as their best present to Krishna.

(5) Wasting some of butter would indicate that he had been coaching the people not to concentrate on collecting butter but to distribute the same to others, who needed it. So he had been eating and when it was too much in store, he had to spread it on earth indicating that the people should come up above the greed (लोभ), an ingredient of 'maya', and get absorbed in Bhagwad bhakti.

(6) Distribution of butter amongst all gwalas would also indicate the modern theory of "workers participation in management of industry" or the conept of trade union (or socialism). The gwalas had been grazing the cows and had been wandering with them throughout the day. The owner, however, milched the cows and appropriated the same to themselves. Krishna had in a way told them by taking butter and distributing amongst gwalas that the butter and milk was obtained by dint of their labour and,

therefore, they should have a share in these rather than the entire butter being appropriated by the owners of the cows.

As regard the other allegation of Krishna being a womaniser, it has to be seen :

(1) In the back ground of Krishna's age at that time. Krishna had lived in Gokul upto the age of 10-11 years only. So he started stealing butter and playing with the gopis at the age of 4-5 years only. How then can a boy of this age even know about sex and womanising. Krishna had been only playing with the gwalas and the gopis as all the children of that age do everywhere. Even in the modern age, the concept of boy friend and girl friend starts only at the teenage and prior to that they are only children playing amongst themselves to pass time. Attribution of any allegation at this tender age can, therefore, only be the strongest farce.

(2) Further, even the ladies used to come and enjoy the company of Krishna. it is only because he was so charming and attractive that everyone wanted to be with him for the maximum time. This can happen to anyone even now after seeing a charming and attractive child. Otherwise how the married ladies could indulge in sex etc. with Krishna being only equal in age to their children or grand children and in the age of upto 7-8 years. It is, therefore, only true that they enjoyed seeing Krishna; being with Krishna; playing with Krishna; and so on.

(3) The men and women of Gokul had already known Krishna as a super human being on his having killed the asuras in the childhood and in having done other actions like throwing away the pram in which he was sitting; uprooting the trees, when he had been tied with the mortar (ऊखल). So all people considered him as an incarnation of God and, therefore, had yielded before him and had become his bhaktas. It was, therefore, the affection/relation/protocol between the

Bhagwan and his bhaktas and not between a boy and a girl etc. Since bhaktas present everything before the Bhagwan, everything being his own, then why should he steal anything and how can he be called a womaniser in playing with his bhaktas and reaching upto the depth of their minds.

(4) Krishna being one (that too only 7-8 years old) amongst hundreds of gopis, how it was possible to have illicit relation with them all.

(5) Even gods and goddesses used to come to witness Krishna playing with gopis. Then how could Krishna indulge in undesirable activities before gods and goddesses.

In Krishna's leelas are the eating of earth. Once when Krishna had eaten earth, Yashoda asked him to open his mouth and show whether he had eaten earth. When Krishna opened his month, Yashoda saw the entire universe in his mouth. She was lost in herself and after sometime when she gained consciousness, she had forgotten everything she had seen in Krishna's mouth.

Once having been annoyed of listening to complaints of the neighbours that Krishna had been stealing butter from their houses, Yashoda tied him with an mortar (ऊखल) where rice is thrashed, and went to do her job. Krishna strolled along with the mortar and on the way, there were two trees. He uprooted those trees too. This astonished everyone. In fact the trees were only as a result of some curse passed on the sons of Kuber by Narad when Narad had been going somewhere and on way he found the two sons of Kuber naked. They did not even put clothes on seeing Narad, who made them trees and Krishna wanted to fulfil the curse-cum-boon by liberating them from having become trees. In this way, he liberated the two sons of Kuber and granted them salvation. Narad's passing any curse on anyone actually used to become boon for him. In this case too although Narad had passed on the curse on them to become trees, but at the same time granted them a boon that on Krishna's mercy, they would get liberated and attain salvation. So in this way, Kuber's sons not only got liberated from having become trees, but also got salvation. While passing on the curse on them, Narad had actually seen them having lost their senses after having been drunk and also in view of being the owners of all wealth (being Kuber's sons, Kuber is the treasure of God's realm), Narad wanted to teach them a lesson and releasing them from this drunkenness because anyone indulging in sensuous passions, is spoiled by the excess of wealth, which converts the incumbent in doing all kinds vices like violence, womanising, drunkenness, not respecting anyone, forgetting all protocol and indulging in gambling—

न ह्यन्यो जुषतो जोष्यान् बुद्धिभ्रंशो रजोगुणः,
श्रीमदादाभि जात्यादिर्यत्र स्त्री द्यूतमासवः। (10-10-8)

The Kuber's sons praised Shri Krishna as almighty God because they already knew that they would be liberated from the curse only when Krishna comes as the incarnation of God. They thereafter, with the blessings of Krishna, went to their respective houses.

Likewise, Krishna, when in grazing ground, saw one asura having entered his calves as a calf. Krishna could recognise him as an asura. He got hold of the hind legs of that calf and killed him. He then came to his realself of an asura. Everyone was surprised and heaved a sigh of relief on Krishna having saved them from the asura. Another asura Aghasura had also once come in the grazing ground and sat with his big mouth opened. All gwalas (including Krishna) went in his mouth. The asura thereafter closed his mouth. Every one got frightened. Then Krishna tore the asura's abdomen and killed him, thus saving all gwalas. When next day, the Brijwasis came to know of these leelas of Krishna, they were astonished and these actions confirmed their feeling that Krishna was a super human. In fact, Gargacharya, when he had come to Gokul for namkaran sanskar of Krishna and Balram, had told the Brij people about Krishna and Balram being the incarnations of God and Sesha.

On further asking for Krishna leelas by Parikshit, Shukdeva told that according to the protocol between the guru and the disciple (शिष्य) the guru does not conceal anything from the disciple and he redresses all his doubts.

श्रृणुश्वावहितो राजन्नपि गुह्यं वदामिते,
ब्रूयुः स्निग्धस्य शिष्यस्य गुरवो गुह्यप्युत। (10-13-3)

Once Shri Krishna had gone to graze cows along with all gwalas. Krishna and other gwalas left the cows grazing and they started enjoying the place and environ. They were all lost in playing. Meantime the cows went away to a distant place while grazing. When the gwalas looked out for the cows and could not find, they got frightened. Krishna, however, assured them that he would bring back the cows. Brahma wanted to enjoy Krishna leela. He, in fact, had taken the cows away and hidden the same in a cave and he himself went away. Not finding the cows, Krishna came back and found the gwalas too missing. When Krishna searched the cows and gwalas and could not find them, he could know this was the creation of Brahma only. Then to please Brahma, (There is a protocol between Brahma and almighty God too), since Brahma wanted to enjoy Krishna's leela, Krishna too thought it proper to fulfil his wish. Krishna too, thereafter became cows and gwalas equal in number and shape to the lost cows and gwalas, confirming thereby the concept of "Entire universe is almighty God himself".

सर्वं विष्णुमयं गिरोऽगंवदजः सर्वस्वरूपोबभौ। (10-13-19)

In this formation, Krishna with the cows and gwalas entered Brindavan. Nobody could know the secrecy of the incident as the cows and gwalas were completely like the actual ones. Krishna had been doing like this for many days, for about an year. Once Krishna and Balram went to the forest grazing their cows. At a distant place they saw some other cows grazing. The cows seeing their calves in Brij, ran towards them. The Brijwasis also saw their gwala children. They took them in their laps and hugged them. Balram was surprised to see all this dual number.

He came to know of Krishna's leela in it. On Balram asking the reason for all this, Krishna told it was Brahma's creation. Brahma came to Brij to see the result of what he had done and saw Krishna in the form of all cows and gwalas in Brij. He was surprised that all gwalas and cows of Brij were in his custody then how the same could be seen in Brij too. He could not make out which were the original cows and gwalas and which were duplicate. Brahma wanted to put Krishna under the influence of his maya but found himself lost in Krishna's maya himself. Then Brahma saw all cows and gwalas appearing like Krishna/Vishnu himself. He also saw another set of gods, including Brahma, rejoicing in Brij Bhumi, and worshipping almighty God. Brahma was wonder-struck and lost his senses. The almighty God's image is such that even Brahma could not make out anything of the incident. Then Vishnu brought Brahma to his senses. He found himself in ever-green Brindavan with Krishna playing there. He fell in the feet of Krishna and got up after a lot of time and started praising God apologizing for his mistake in having undertaken to put Krishna under the influence of his maya. After praising God and attaining his blessings, Brahma went back to Brahmloka. Such incidents have been narrated by the writer to show that :—

(1) Krishna is the incarnation of God.

(2) He is above the influence of any other god's maya.

(3) All gods, including Brahma, sometimes forgot the reality of Krishna being incarnate of God and tried to impress upon him his power but after realising almighty God's power bowed before him realising their mistake and also apprised the reader of the God's powers (शक्ति) and told the people of the universe that they should accept the might of the almighty which even Brahma had to accept. In a way such vindication leads and confirms the Bhagwan-bhakta relation and the way in which and the shakti, after realisation of which, the bhakta gets absorbed in almighty Bhagwan. After praising God, Brahma as per protocol, had three rounds of Krishna, bowed

before him and went to Brahmaloka. He had already released the cows and gwalas from the hideout and arranged to send the same at their respective places. The cows and gwalas were very happy to meet Krishna and in this way although they met Krishna after an year, yet this fact could not be known to Brijwasis and even the gwalas had been made to forget the incident.

Krishna had come as incarnation of God to kill the asuras and help the people live in comfort and peace. Once a senior gwala Sridama told Balram and Krishna that there were Tal trees nearby bearing lot of tal but no one could eat the fruit because of an ass type asura living there. If that asura could be killed then people could enjoy the fruit. Balram and Krishna went there and killed all the asuras. In the fighting, many trees had been uprooted too. This enabled the Brijwasis to eat the Tal fruit. It may be another case of socialistic distribution of fruits. Similarly, there was a snake family in Yamuna because of which, anyone drinking water from that part of Yamuna was killed. Once the cows and gwalas too had become unconscious after drinking water there. Krishna immediately jumped in the river and after a great fight with the snake, it was controlled. During the melee once snake bound Krishna and seeing Krishna not coming above water for a long time, all became unconscious. The Brijwasis too came there and were upset seeing Krishna not there. Ultimately snake was controlled and on his wives', request, who praised Krishna, he let the snake family go from there to the sea. In this way, Krishna saved many people from being killed on drinking water from Yamuna. In modern concept it can also be taken that this place, being near Mathura, Yamuna may be badlly contaminated and polluted because of waste of the city flowing therein and Krishna by diverting the flow of that waste, may have saved Yamuna water from the pollution and contamination, harmful for human consumption. It was an act of social protocol. The people of Brij had completely submitted themselves to Krishna and in turn Krishna too had been doing everything possible to liquidate the difficulties faced by them.

कृष्णेऽर्पितात्म सुहृदर्थ कलत्र कामा,
दुःखानुशोकभय मूढ़धियो निपेतुः। (10-16-10)

The Brijwasis had laid themselves, their wealth, their wives and children, all ambitions and passions to the cause of Lord Krishna and Krishna, as usual, helping the bhaktas, had been helping them in all difficulties. Bhagwan is kind not only to his bhaktas but anyone, who takes refuge under him. Even the snake, when got smashed under Krishna's feet, remembered Lord Krishna and then it became incumbent for Krishna not to kill the snake.

स्मृत्वा चराचरगुरुं पुरुषं पुराणं,
नारायणं तमरणं मनसा जगाम। (10-16-30)

Even the wives of the snake, while praising Krishna, seeing their husband in difficulty, said that once a person undertook his refuge, then there was no difference in the mind of Krishna between his son and enemy.

रिपो सुतानामपि तुल्यदृष्टेर्धत्से
दमं फलमेवानुशंसन्॥ (10-16-33)

In the melee, since snake had been smashed under the feet of Krishna, the snake had been enlightened having been touched by the sand of Krishna's feet and anyone having taken Krishna's feet's sand (पदरज) gets absorbed in him and does not then need even the kingdom of the entire earth.

न नाकपृष्ठं न च सार्वभौमं,
न पारमेष्ठ्यं न रसाधिपत्यम्।
न योगसिद्धीरपुनर्भवं वा,
वाछंन्ति यत्पादरजः प्रपन्नाः॥ (10-16-37)

By controlling snake, Lord Krishna had shown that :

(1) Anyone remembering him is absolved of all difficulties;
(2) gets all comforts of life; and then
(3) starts acting as per the tenets of dharma as the curtain of maya is then lifted and he realises the self and God.

(4) at the same time the purpose of God's incarnation to restore dharma on the universe is fulfilled.

(5) if even after accommodating the culprit once, he does not start behaving, then the king should punish him. Here the snake's wives had requested Krishna to once excuse the snake and then the snake would not repeat the mistake of not recognising God and oppose him. They also said that snake was temperamentally in rage and quarrelsome and it was because of adherence to the bad habits that the snake had been suffering and so the other persons in the universe.

स्वभावो दुस्त्यजो नाथ लोकानां यदसद्ग्रहः। (10-16-56)

After Krishna let the snake off on assurance that the snake with the family would go to the sea, the snake, as a symbol of lord of lot of wealth, presented costly jewels, perfumes and worshipped Lord Krishna in many ways. This is the protocol a raja has to observe when let off by another bigger/more powerful raja. Here the snake, who was a small raja of his kingdom, treated Shri Krishna as his monarch, having been defeated by him and then having been allowed to live with the family in the sea. So, the snake offered presents to him.

Then came rainy season in Brij. The trees became green; the rivers were full of water; the grazing grounds were full of grass, the field and farms could get water and ploughing had been started to sow seeds for the foodgrains, vegetables etc. The poet has mentioned here about the effects of rainy season on the people. Since India has been an agricultural country, depending mostly on rains, the rains have a special significance, particularly for the people of Brij, where the grazing grounds become full of grass enabling the cows to eat to the fill and then give more milk, which was the means of livelihood for the people of Brij. Also, this indicates a particular type of system/ protocol within the nature also. After scorching heat, rainy season comes, to give relief to the people from heat and help in the agricultural production as per laid down phenomena by the nature. It is said that the natural phenomena was always regular unless disturbed by some acts of adharma. The poet has taken extra pains in narrating in detail the on-coming of the rainy season and its effect on all beings. In Ramcharit Manas too, there is detailed description of rainy reason.

After rainy season, comes the winter, when water, which was dusty in rainy season, becomes clear. The paths become dry and walkable. There is detailed narration of Sharad Ritu (शरद ऋतु). This indicates the gift of various seasons to India by the almighty. To do away with the sufferings of summer, rainy season comes and after the people have availed all benefits of rains, this seasons comes to an end and then, comes winter to give its own charms and eliminating the sufferings of rainy season. Trade peoples' coming and going etc., which had all been stopped in rainy season (चौमासा) (even the Sadhus make a stop in these four months), is again resumed and a new wave of pleasantness is witnessed. The cows were happy to have grass. The gopis were happy to play with Krishna freely in the evenings/nights of this pleasant season. The gopis would all come out of their houses to witness the listening of Krishna's flute; his coming to Brij after grazing cows and his playing with them. Before the charm of Krishna, the gopis used to forget their house-hold jobs and would come out of their houses to see Krishna. It can he spiritual love between Bhagwan and bhakta or a social affection between so attractive and charming child Krishna and in gopis, the ladies and child Krishna, the people of Brij and their little Krishna. Krishna had been fulfilling the desires of everyone as per his wishes. In Manas too people in Sita swayamber saw Ram according their own faculties—

जिन्ह कें रही भावना जैसी प्रभु मूर्ति तिन्ह देखी तैसी। (मानस)

So in Brij too all saw and enjoyed Krishna's darshan according to their faculties. Krisan's playful evenings included all boys and girls sitting together, Krishna playing flute, others listening to the same. All singing melodious songs and enjoying the same. What to speak of the gopis enjoying the flute played by Krishna, even the peacocks and other birds and animals and even the rivers and hills used to get lost on hearing the same—

गोविन्द वेणु मनु मत्तमयूरनृत्यं,
प्रेक्ष्याद्रिसान्व परतान्य समस्त सत्त्वम्। (10-21-10)

How can then the gopis be blamed to have lost within themselves while playing with Krishna. It is these plays, full of social sanctity, that the people allege bearing evil thinking/acting by Krishna at that tender age of about 7-8 years. Even the gods and goddesses used to come to Brij to see that charming play and get lost listening to Krishna's flute.

कृष्णं निरीक्ष्य वनितोत्सवरूपशीलं,
श्रुत्वा च तत्क्वणितवेणु विचित्रगीतम।
देव्यो विमान गतयः स्मरनुन्नसारा,
भ्रश्यत्प्रस्नकबरा मुमुहुर्विनीव्य। (10-21-12)

Even cows got lost hearing Krishna's flute then how can such meetings be alleged to be full of polluted activities. It is explained that even the bhilnis (भिलनी) (in jungle) were so much attracted to Krishna that after Krishna had walked on a path, the bhilnis would go and remove the dust (Kesar) left from Krishna's feet on grass, while walking and rub the same on their cheeks, breast etc. to quench their thrust of meeting Krishna. It is, therefore, only the attraction and medodious flute, which impressed the gopis, bhilnis and others and there was no ill-feeling towards anyone.

Now again we come to a controversial subject of "theft of clothes of the gopis" (चीर हरण). People allege that an evil mind of Krishna had been behind this episode. He wanted to see the gopis nude.

(1) Here, one is the social consideration. The boys/girls should not take bath naked. In shastras naked bath is forbidden "न नग्न: स्नायात" as the naked bath arouses the animal instinct in the human being leading to wrong actions on the part of girls as well as boys.

Krishna, therefore, wanted to teach a lesson to the girls by stealing their clothes not to take bath naked.

(2) Hygienically the naked bath in the pond/river/rivulet leads to pollution of water, which is used for drinking purposes too. Therefore, Krishna wanted the girls not to spoil water by taking naked bath.

(3) Krishna was always a person of character and he wanted the gopis too to remain within the limits of good character. Naked bath is considered an evil, character-wise. Even today nude bath is resorted to only with bad instincts and not by the people of character.

(4) Shri Krishna was a God for the gopis and they had fully surrended to him. In such a situation the surrender is not complete if some veil is kept in between the Bhagwan and bhakta. He, therefore, wanted the gopis to appear before him without any veil, if they wanted to surrender fully. This carried weight and the gopis were convinced of the logic. When they were asked to come out of the water and take their clothes from him, he only wanted them to forget that there was any veil in between them and him.

(5) Here gopis had been considering Krishna as their Bhagwan/husband/friend etc. Now one does not have any veil/secrecy between himself and husband/friend or God. Everything is known to God and God is considered to be a Maryada Purushottama (मर्यादा पुरुषोत्तम). One cannot, therefore, have any veil before the Maryada Purushottama and any veil, if kept, is something that stands in the way of absolute surrender/recognition of the other party. Krishna, therefore, wanted the gopis to take their clothes coming close to him.

(6) Krishna had himself taken the clothes and he only desired the clothes to be taken from him without any hesitation. When this logic came to the gopis'

mind, they came out without any hesitation and approached Krishna to take their clothes.

(7) Krishna recognised their full devotion only after their was no veil between him and the gopis. Clothes or the veil of clothes, is only symbolic of 'maya'. Till one is down under the influence of 'maya', one cannot reach the almighty and the devotion is not complete till he attains his closeness. The 'maya' in the form of clothes, therefore, had to be taken away to enable one to attain complete absorption in him.

(8) As has already been indicated, it was not only the gopis but even the birds, animals, rivers and hills, which had been attracted by the charm of Krishna and had surrendered themselves before him. Therefore, for gopis to be attracted to Krishna was nothing unusual and having been attracted and submitted themselves before God, nothing of privacy is kept from him.

(9) To appreciate the problem, one has to take Krishna either as a God or as a human being. If he is taken as God then there is nothing, which is to be kept private/secret/under veil from God. As he is everywhere, he knows everything; he can see everything and in that case the allegation on Krishna having ill-feeling behind this episode is baseless. Alternately, if Krishna is taken as the master of Brij, then he has a right to teach the gopis a lesson and restrain them from taking bath naked as it was bad character-wise and hygienically. Thirdly, if he is to be taken as an ordinary human being then such feeling have always been in the human beings and what is there that has been done absurd by Krishna at an age of 8 years. We put this allegation on Krishna only when he did such actions being God and as already said there is nothing that can be concealed from God, there was no evil thinking or bad in character or a breach of protocol. Once there is a union of Atma and Parmatma or Jiva (Creature) and Brahma (God), there is nothing left seen or unseen in the two. Krishna had taught the gopis that there

could not be half way submission, either no submission and in that case they should not think of Krishna at all, or complete submission, in which case there should not be any hesitation in their coming naked close to Krishna.

(10) In fact it is only ones' evil/worldly thinking, which restricts one to think of the bodily relation only, and we donot think of something like spiritual relation. once we think of the spiritual relation, we would not think of any such allegations. This is amply proved from the fact that once Krishna told them the logic not to keep any veil between Krishna and themselves, if they wanted to have full satisfaction from absorption in him, they could remove their hands from the private parts. They understood, bowed before him with folded hands and begged for the grant of love from him.

(11) Now once the bhakta gets absorbed in almighty and forgets all about the worldly/bodily/sensuous feelings, it is for the almighty to save him/her from all worldly curses. So after the gopis approached him naked with full submission, Krishna himself came to them and offered their clothes to wear and go to their respective houses so that no one could raise any finger on them. And it happened too when the gopis went to their houses, nobody questioned their late coming or about what had happened when they took bath. We, therefore, have to see the entire episode in the perspective of Krishna being Bhagwan and gopis as bhaktas. Then there is nothing left to doubt the bonafides of characters. Theft of clothes (चीरहरण) is, therefore, symbolic of Krishna teaching the gopis the lesson of complete surrender before God. In this way, Krishna granted attainment to the gopis. Krishna has himself stated that although there are crores of people in the universe, yet a successful person is he, who acts for the well- being of others by assisting with his wealth, intelligence, body, speech, thinking and actions.

एतावज्जन्म साफल्यम् देहिनामिह देहिषु,
प्राणैरथैर्धिया वाचा श्रेय एवाचरेत् सदा। (10-23-35)

(12) That the gopis felt satisfied only by having Krishna's darshan and devotion to him, is fully vindicated by another episode in which, Krishna and other gwalas had been feeling hungry grazing cows in the forests. Krishna sent the gwalas to a yagyashala, where brahmins had been performing yagya, to beg for some eatables. The gawalas went there but were not attended to by the brahmins. They returned back and told Krishna accordingly. Krishna then sent them to the brahmins' wives with the same request. The brahmins' wives hearing about Krishna and Balram, immediately prepared good dishes and followed the gwalas, where Krishna was. They presented the eatables and had full attainment on having Krishna's darshan. It vindicates the position that full attainment and absorption in Krishna is not by bodily embracing each other but by having Krishna's darshan too. The gopis too at first had Krishna's darshan, then heard the flute played by him; then played with him and ultimately after chirharan, there was complete surrender and absorption in him without any physical intimacy as such. The allegation of evil thinking or bad relations of Krishna with gopis is an absolute farce when Krishna at that time was only about 7-8 years old and could not even think of any animal instincts. That is why when the brahmins' wives, after meeting Krishna, went back to their ashram on Krishna's assurance that since there was no evil thinking in anyone's mind, their husbands would accept them without any allegation, their husbands did not doubt their bonafides and loyalty to their husbands in addition to devotion to Krishna for as God. The brahmins had rather been repentant as to why they ignored the request of the gwalas for giving them the eatables when they first approached them, and were appreciative of their wives' action.

In the context of the Brij people performing Indra yagya for which lot of preparations had to be made, Krishna asked Nand the purpose, who performed, and by what the yagya was being performed, meaning thereby that Krishna had told the people that they should not have blind belief and should not perform any yagya, till they had known why and for whom the yagya was being performed. Krishna asked—

कथ्यतां मेपितः कोऽयं सम्भ्रमो व उपागतः,
किंफलं कस्य चोद्देशः केन वा साध्यते मखः। (10-24-3)

(1) What was the yagya?
(2) For whom it was performed?
(3) What was the purpose of the yagya?
(4) What was the gain from the yagya?
(5) Who had to perform the yagya?

These ingredients should be known before any religious ceremony (dharmik anusthan) is undertaken, otherwise there is no use of performing any such yagya etc. Nand Baba told Krishna that Indra was the master of rains and by performing the Yagya, Indra got pleased. He arranged proper rain, on which depended the productivity of foodgrains, grass etc. For that, purpose the yagya was performed from time immemorial. Krishna told Nand that the human being was born according to his doings and he dies too accordingly. He also attains happiness and sorrows etc. according to Karma—

कर्मणा जायते जन्तुः कर्मणैव विलीयते,
सुखं दुखं भयं क्षेमं कर्मणैव अभिपद्यते। (10-24-13)

Similar policy statement was made by Guru Vashista which consoling Bharat on the death of his father—

सुनहु भरत भावी प्रबल बिलखि कहेउ मुनिनाथ,
हानि लाभु जीवनु मरनु जसु अपजसु विधि हाथ। (मानस)

Krishna further stated that when everyone had to attain as per his doings (कर्म), then why worship Indra. One develops enmity or friendship because of karma and, therefore, karma only is guru as well as God.

शत्रुर्मित्रमुदासीनः कर्मैव गुरुरीश्वरः। (10-24-1)

Krishna told that because of rajogun mentality of the people, the clouds burst into rains necessary for production of foodgrains and foodgrains in turn used for living purposes. The gwalas, who have neither any kingdom nor much wealth but only the cows, should worship cows, Brahmains and the mountains, where the cows graze only and none else as the worship of any god, without purpose, is of no use. He, therefore, suggested that the ingredients used in yagya should be used in preparing good food for all; the Brahmains should be fed; havans performed; and all rejoicings made after giving alms to Brahmains and poors rather than wasting the same in Indra yagya. All in Brij accepted to finish the pride of Indra. The Brijwasis accordingly prepared food and worshipped Brahmains, cows and the mountains. They were all happy and content. Having heard that his yagya had been stopped, Indra got enraged on Brijwasis. He was proud of his position and considered himself as the overall Lord of the universe. He ordered the destructive clouds to attack Brij with the heavy rains so that the pride of Brijwasis was finished. It started raining cats and dogs. Hailstorms too were there to annoy the Brijwasis resulting in all animals Shivaering with cold, and the human beings facing difficulty in rain and cold. They all sought refuge under Krishna. Krishna could make out the entire creation of Indra only because of the stoppage of the Indra yagya. He, therefore, undertook to teach him a lesson. Krishna picked up Goverdhan mountain with one hand and asked all to take refuge under the mountain with all their cows, households etc. All acted accordingly. Krishna held the mountain on his hand for seven days without eating anything. Indra was shocked to see his design not getting fulfilled. He stopped rains. Then Krishna requested all to come out of the mountain. All came out with their belongings and Krishna placed mountain at its place. All respected Krishna and blessed him. All gods too worshipped Krishna. In this way, Krishna finished the pride of Indra. This shows that even among the gods, the checks and balances theory is applied to keep everyone of the gods within his limits. All in Brij were surprised to see the force and strength of Krishna. So far they had seen some of his super human actions but this action of holding mountain was superb and everyone now considered him the incarnation of God after linking all his previous deeds too. At this time Krishna was only seven years old.

"क्व सप्तहायनो बालः क्व महाद्रिविधारणम" (10-26-14)

When all Brijwasis asked, who this child was, Nand Baba told what Gangacharya had narrated that this child was with all gunas and had been coming as incarnate of God in various formations. Now he had come as Krishna and he would do all good jobs for the people of Brij and others. All then started treating him as incarnation of God.

Having been put to his place, Indra came to Krishna, bowed before him, praised him and begged to be excused as whatever had happened had happened because of his 'maya' only, which put a veil on anyone's mind and he is not able to think of good or bad. It is good that Krishna, the almighty, had annihilated Indra's pride. Krishna told Indra that he had to take this step as Indra had lost in his wealth and position and to make him realise his position, Krishna had to do this action. Krishna told that one should not get lost under the influence of wealth as Krishna snatches such richness from the persons to set them right and in this way checking them from going on a wrong path.

मामैश्वर्य श्रीमदान्धो दण्डपाणिं न पश्यति,
तं भ्रंशयामि सम्पद्भ्यो यस्य चेच्छाम्यनुग्रह्म्। (10-27-16)

He then advised Indra to go back to his place and never to feel proud in future. Indra worshipped Krishna before all gods and named him "Govind". All gods, rishis etc. also came there and paid respects to Krishna as per protocol. Thereafter the Brijwasis too lived very happily.

Once while taking bath in Yamuna, Varuna's people took Nand Baba to Varuna. Krishna went in search of Nand Baba and found him with Varuna. Varuna and other gods worshipped Krishna there as the almighty God and sent Nand Baba back. Nand was surprised to see everyone in Varuna Loka worshipping Krishna as their God and he narrated all what he had seen to Brijwasis, who had already been thinking him as the incarnation of God only. Krishna then took all Brijwasis to his Dham and made them visit Brahma Loka, Shiva Loka and other gods' residences. All were surprised and got involved in Krishna pooja.

Now comes the context of Krishna's Raslila (रासलीला) with the gopis. These gopis included married ladies, unmarried girls as also the gwalas of Brij. It is said even goddesses, gods, (including Shiva) had come there incognito to enjoy Krishna Raslila. In the evening, when Krishna blew the flute, all gopis left whatever they had been doing—some were milching the cows, some were cooking, some were offering food to their husbands and children and so on. They left the engagement in hand and left to see Krishna because Krishna's flute was so charming and melodious and his company too was so appeasing that the ladies could not afford to miss the same inspite of their husbands and fathers/brothers checking them. This may appear to be unprotocolic but for a person lost in Bhagwan, it is natural. Even the husbands etc. knew of the greatness of Krishna and his being incarnate of God. So they would have been checking them only outwardly otherwise how could it be possible for an Indian lady of those days to leave without the consent of the husband/father etc. When they went at the Yamuna bank, where Krishna was playing flute, Krishna told them that they should not have come like that ignoring their husbands'/fathers' orders. He, therefore, asked them to return to Brij as :

(1) It was not advisable for ladies to stay out during the nights.

(2) Their husbands/parents would be searching for them and feeling uncomfortable.

(3) They being from good respectable families, their job was to attend to the comforts of their husbands/parents.

(4) Although there was nothing bad in their having love/affection for Shri Krishna, as even the animals/birds/rivers/mountains and trees had the same feeling for Krishna, yet the primary duty of the women was to serve their husbands/parents.

(5) It was bad for the married ladies to be with other persons.

(6) His bhakti/love could be attained by listening to his lilas, doing kirtan and getting absorbed in him through concentration on him and it was not necessary to be close to him.

(7) Some of the ladies, who could not leave their houses in view of strictness of their husbands etc., had been remembering Krishna in their houses and getting lost in their thoughts about Krishna. They, in this way, had the full attainment. Therefore, all others should also go back to their respective houses, Krishna advised. The gopis, however, had their own story to narrate.They stated that they had come to him leaving all their belongings and it was too rude for him to ask them to go back. They only loved to be always in his feet. Also they stated that according to Krishna himself, their dharma was to serve their husbands/parents etc. but Krishna being almighty God, was swami/father of their husbands/parents. Therefore, they should aptly serve him and this was what they were doing.

अस्त्वेवमेतदुपदेशपदे त्वयीशे,
प्रेष्ठो भवां स्तनुभृताँ किल बन्धुरात्मा। (10-29-32)

The gopis insisted on remaining there to serve Krishna and get absorbed in him for self attainment. He being the almighty God, there was no sin in remaining and loving him. Like other bhaktas, the gopis too had come to take refuge under him and to remain embedded to his feet and when Krishna had no objection to the bhaktas remaining close to him, why should he have any objection in gopis staying with him. This indicated the instinct of full devotion to Krishna of the gopis and Krishna had to accept their plea and allowed to have contentment in having his darshan and remaining with him during the night. Afterwards Krishna asked them to return to their husbands'/parents' houses and Krishna undertook that they would not object to the gopis having stayed away with him. The gopis went back and had been welcomed in their houses. They had since become fully Krishnamay (कृष्णमय) and started acting like Krishna. The gopis asked a very pertinent question to Krishna—

(1) There are people, who love those who love them;
(2) There are people, who love even those who donot love them; and
(3) Those, who donot love even after being loved by others.

They asked which of the three he liked. Krishna told them that the persons of first category are only selfish. They love only after having been loved. The persons of second category are actually selfless lovers like parents and in category three, there are 4 kinds of people :

(1) Who are lost within themselves and donot see others loving them;
(2) Those, who are already contented and donot have much to do with others;
(3) Those, who donot know if they are loved by anyone; and
(4) Those, who intentionally ignore their well wishers like guru etc.

Krishna told that he did not reciprocate the love extended by others so that the others continue to have more and more love whereas if it is reciprocated then they will stop at that. Krishna had performed Raslila (रासलीला) with the gopis by just playing with them. There were thousands of gopis and one Krishna. Also the Raslila was being witnessed by all gods and their wives. Krishna being only 7-8 years old and the gopis too would be either middle aged (married) or of the same age 7-8 years (unmarried). In such a situation how could there be any passionate love or anything of that sort. Krishna being a man of character could not have indulged in such practices as has been clearly indicated that Bhagwan had come to establish dharma and annihilate adharma then how could he indulge in these adharmik/unprotocolic activities—

संस्थापनाय धर्मस्य प्रशमायेतरस्य च,
अवतीर्णो हि भगवानंशेन जगदीश्वरः। (10-33-27)

Also there is a mention that the married gopis' husbands had been feeling during the night that their wives were with them. It would then appear that either the number that thousands of gopis took part in the Raslila is imaginary or exaggeration or the gopis were creation of Krishna himself by his maya or also there might be only a few girls, who had been playing with Krishna as any boy and girls would be playing in that age. Further, when Krishna himself had been educating the gopis to religiously serve their husbands/parents and that only was their dharma then how could same Krishna indulge in adharmik activities with the same ladies—married and unmarried. It is also possible that on Krishna's telling them so, the married ladies and most of the unmarried gopis would have gone back and a few only remained there with whom Krishna continued playing. Also on Krishna's above preaching, some had even said that they loved Krishna, who was the master of their husbands/parents and such a love was accepted as dharmik according to Krishna himself. Then the love with Krishna as God would be only the internal instinct of love and absorption in God and not physical relation as such. Such absorption was achieved even by the ladies, who continued to stay back at their houses only due to some limitation/fear/reservation etc. Therefore, the milan of Krishna and gopis was only like the absorption of a bhakta in Bhagwan through love/bhakti etc. Krishna in Geeta had told Arjun to leave all dharmas and come to his refuge and that is the best accomplishment of dharma—

"सर्वधर्मान् परित्यज्य मामेकं शरणं व्रज" (गीता—18-66)

Since the gopis had come to take refuge under Krishna, there was nothing adharmik about it.

Consequently there can be two things—one to accept Krishna as an ordinary human being. In that case Krishna being of 7-8 years of age at that time, would not have known anything about sex and so the gopis of that age and they would have just been playing like any other children of that age and their parents would be having full confidence in Krishna that nothing untoward would happen in Krishna's company. Alternatively, if Krishna is taken as God, then nothing is secret/concealed or private from God and as God, he would have been only loved/ worshipped/by the gopis as such and by his yogmaya Krishna gave a feeling to the husbands/parents as if their wives/daughters were with them only. Either way, any allegation on Krishna is untenable.

Krishna and Balram had been going in the morning for grazing cows alongwith other gwalas. On the other side Kansa had been trying to get Krishna killed by sending one asura after another. In the chain, he sent Aristasura, who came as an ox and mixed up with the cows herd. Krishna, however, recognised him and after giving a fighting, killed him. After this Narad thought it was now time to get Kansa killed. He went to him and told him that Vasudeva-Devki's eighth child was a boy, who was being brought up by Nand and the girl killed was Nand's daughter taken in exchange and as such Krishna and Balram would kill him. Kansa got infuriated. He called in some Pehalwans (wrestlers) and advised them that he would be inviting Krishna and Balram to Mathura on the pretext of showing them wrestles but as soon as they entered Mathura, they should be got killed by elephants. He, at the same time called in Akroor and told him to go to Brij and bring Krishna and Balram on the pretext of showing them wrestles in Mathura. He also told him his designs of killing Krishna as he was the eighth offspring of Vasudeva and Devki. They, therefore, should be killed before they grow up. Here he tempted Akroor of making him a raja after Krishna/ Balram were killed, after killing Vasudeva, Ugrasen etc. For the purpose of bringing Krishna and Balram, he told Akroor to present lot of wealth to Nand so that he agreed. Giving position and wealth have always been the policies of the kings to tempt the smaller Rajas/Chieftains for getting their jobs done.

तावानय समं गोपैर्नन्दाद्यैः साभ्युपायनैः । (10-36-31)

And ततश्चैषा मही मित्र भवित्री नष्टकण्टका। (10-36-35)

Akroor was Kansa's Minister. He too agreed to the proposal saying that efforts should be made to see that the evil is annihilated and leave the result to God. This is same as Krishna had told in Gita that a person should do his job leaving the result on God.

राजन् मनीषितं सम्यक् तच स्वावद्यमार्जनम्,

सिद्धयासिद्धयोः समं कुर्याद् दैवं हि फलसाधनम्। (10-36-38)

Meantime Kansa also sent Keshi and Vyomasura asuras to kill Krishna. Keshi came as a terrible horse. He jumped over Krishna seeing him. Krishna caught hold of his legs and threw him. He again got up and attacked on Krishna and Krishna killed him.

After having told Kansa about Krishna, Narad came to Krishna and praised him as God and reminded him that he had come to annihilate the rakshasas. He narrated the design of Kansa for him. Narad was a person, who had been acting (like a God's spy) between God, other gods, rajas and rishis etc. and had always been thinking of doing good to the people at large. He was believed and confided by all. Narad also apprised Krishna of what was to happen in next some days—Krishna's going to Mathura, killing Chanura and Mustic wrestlers and then killing Kansa and subsequently killing/defeating many other rajas and arranging several marriages etc. and then establishing a kingdom in Dwarka. Narad was happy to see Krishna. He paid his respects and went back and Krishna continued to play with his friend gwalas as usual. At that time Vyomasura had come there, whom too Krishna killed. Akroor left for Brij next day. He was happy that he would have a darshan of Shri Krishna, the God almighty. He had been appreciating his luck to have the darshan. Akroor was in fact Krishna's man, who had become the confidant of Kansa and had been living in Mathura to take care of

Krishna's interest there. He was, therefore, happy to have been entrusted with the job of bringing Krishna to Mathura. He had his doubts whether Krishna would take him as his enemy, who had come to Brij to take Krishna for being killed by Kansa. But the fact is, as he thought, Krishna being almighty God, would understand his position and take him as his bhakta, and make him attain salvation by taking pity on him in the situation he was placed and still having love for Krishna. Akroor reached Brij and entered the village in the evening. He saw both Balram and Krishna there and became happy. He bowed before them. Krishna picked him up and embraced him followed by Balram embracing him. They went to their house where Akroor was welcomed and treated as an honourable guest and was made all comfortable in Brij. Nand asked about his well-being, as per protocol, and all about Kansa's rajya in Mathura. Kansa's rajya in Mathura was like a butcher in his realm of killing animals etc. After meals etc. when Akroor sat in peace, Krishna asked him about the future programme in Mathura. Akroor too was a Yadava's man living in Mathura as the confidant of Kansa too. Krishna also checked up about Kansa's behaviour with Yadavas and other people of the kingdom. Akroor told about the cruelty Kansa had been causing to Yadavas and other people and that he had now called Krishna and Balram to Mathura. Krishna told Nand about their going to Mathura. Nand ordered the ghee and butter to be collected for being presented to Kansa on their visit to Mathura. Nand was a small raja within the territory of Kansa. Therefore, he had to go with some presents only to see his king. This is the normal protocolic requirement for a vassal, when he meets the king. The gopis. as usual, felt very bad on hearing that Krishna and Balram were going to Mathura. Many thinking of Krishna got absorbed in him. They had been cursing God for this separation, as they could think that once Krishna went to Mathura, he might get involved in the ladies of that place and might not then return to Brij.

Next day chariots were loaded with butter etc. and Krishna/Balram and Nand Baba, with some others, left for Mathura. Gopis and gwalas met Krishna and Balram to have their last darshan. Krishna assured them of his return and departed for Mathura. On the way, Akroor, while taking bath in a tank, saw Krishna and Balram being worshipped by various gods under the water. He was surprised since he had left them on the chariot. He again checked up and found them on the chariot and again in water too. He was shocked to see all this. In this way, Krishna obliged Akroor as his bhakta and Akroor was very happy and started praising him. He saw Krishna in everything and everywhere. He told Krishna too accordingly—

अद्भुतानीह यावन्ति भूमौ वियति वा जले,
त्वयि विश्वात्मके तानि किं मेऽदृष्टं विपश्यतः। (10-41-4)

This is the normal feeling a bhakta could be having after getting absorbed in Bhagwan. On the way many people from villages came to see Shri Krishna and became happy. Nand and others had already reached Mathura with presents for Kansa and were waiting for Krishna to come. Krishna told Akroor to go to his house and he and others would be reaching after seeing the town. As per protocol, Akroor invited Krishna etc. to his house. Krishna, however, assured that he would visit his house after killing Kansa. Akroor went to town and apprised Kansa of Krishna and Balram's arrival and went to his house. Krishna and Balram entered Mathura and saw it very beautiful and decorated. The men and women had gathered to see Krishna. As per local tradition, the ladies saw Krishna from the top of their houses whereas men gathered in streets. They had been listening to Krishna's lila but now saw Krishna himself and felt contented. All citizens welcomed Krishna and Balram in Mathura in the traditional way. On the way, he met a dhobi (washerman). Krishna asked him to give him clothes for the city. Dhobi, who was Kansa's man, refused. Krishna, however, beat him and snatched clothes. He then met a tailor, who gave to Krishna decorative clothes. Then he obliged Sudama, a gardener, who paid his respects. He gave Krishna good-smell flowers for decoration. Now Krishna and Balram and other gwalas were fully dressed up to enter Mathura. On the way further,

Krishna saw lady Kubja. She was also a Krishna bhakta, having sandal in her hands for being used by Krishna. She used to supply sandal to Kansa too. But applied the same on Krishna and Balram's bodies. Krishna, in turn, straightened Kubja, who was curved at several places, in body. She then wished to embrace Krishna, having become very beautiful and attractive and invited Krishna to her house. Krishna promised to meet her in her house in due course. Krishna had not been missing any chance of obliging his devotees even on way to Mathura. On the way, the traders paid respects in their own way by worshipping them. They, then reached the Rangshala (the place of show). A bow (dhanush) had been placed there. Krishna easily picked it up and by stretching broke it in no time like Ram had broken dhanush in Sita swayamber. The security men challenged Krishna for having broken the dhanush without permission. Krishna and Balram, however, killed them all. Such a show of bravery is strategically necessary to demoralise Kansa, whom they had to face and other men of Kansa, deputed to kill Krishna and Balram. Then they started visiting various parts of Mathura without being checked by anyone. Kansa, as expected, got frightened after knowing that Krishna had broken dhanush and killed the scuritymen. He had been witnessing all bad omens. Next day, the wrestling started. All had been made to sit as per their position. Kansa had occupied the topmost seat surrounded by his small rajas (vassals). He was, of course, still frightened.

तेषु पौरा जानपदा ब्रह्मक्षत्रपुरोगमाः,
यथोपजोषं विविशू राजानश्च कृतासनाः। (10-42-34)

There were separate places for seating of Brahmains, kshatriyas, people from villages, small rajas and then Kansa. In the case of Sita swayamber too people were made to sit according to their position—

उत्तम मध्यम नीच लघु निज निज थल अनुहारि। (मानस)

This would show that there was a particular system according to which all people had been made to sit. King Kansa, being at the top, then smaller rajas under him, then Brahmains, kshatriyas, people from town, people from villages and so on. This system would have been prescribed for such formal occasions like the present system of 'Order of Precedence' according to which, president, Vice President, Prime Minister, other Ministers, beaurocrats and others are made to sit on formal occasions like Republic Day ceremony etc. Some such order of precedence must be available in those days too as also in Ram Kal. The wrestling started with due pomp and show. Then Kansa called for Nand and others. They offered the presents brought by them and sat at their allotted seats. Krishna and Balram too came. Krishna found a horrible elephant standing on way. Krishna requested the elephant owner to give way but he did not. Then Krishna shouted on him. On that, the elephant was directed to attack on Krishna. Fight with elephant ensued and Krishna killed the elephant. This was the first line of attack by Kansa. Like the present strategy of war in phases, Kansa too had arranged some such series of fighting with Krishna; the aim being to kill him. Krishna and Balram entered the Rangshala. Like Ram entering Sita swayamber, everyone present there saw Ram as per his faculties viz rishis and sants saw him as the God; the asuras saw him as their enemy; the people of Janakpuri as their affectionate son-in-laws; and so on. So Krishna too was seen by everyone according to his faculties. To the wrestlers he was a person with steel body; to ordinary persons, a super power, to asuras their enemy; to Kansa his death itself; to yogis the absolute truth and so on. All, at the Manch, were happy to see Krishna and Balram.

At that time, Chanura, who was the administrator of the show, addressed Shri Krishna and Balram to tell that they, being good at wrestling, had been invited by Kansa to take part in the wrestling. He also told that those, who work for the raja are gainers and those who work against the interest of raja are punished. Like the present day tradition, where one protocol authority is appointed to arrange the entire formal ceremony, in Krishna period too, some such protocolic authority was engaged to announce the functions; the conditions of taking part in the functions and then to declare the result of such a participation.

Chanura was appointed by Kansa keeping his purpose in view, as an overall administrator of the show. He also made it clear that everyone had to work keeping raja's interest in view meaning thereby that Krishna had not been obedient to raja and so he might be punished here. He did not know that Krishna was an overall Lord. In Sita swayamber too Shatananda had been appointed as overall incharge of the swayamber. He too did not know the strength of Ram. Krishna accepted the challenge and wanted to have a chance to please Kansa in the wrestling. But he said that the wrestling should be between equals. He being a child, the other competitor should be of the same age otherwise even the audience would feel it unjust.

बाला वयं तुल्यबलैः क्रीडिष्यामो यथोचितम्.,
भवेन्नियुद्धं माधर्मः स्पृशेन्मल्ल सभासदः। (10-44-38)

But Chanura, who had been entrusted by Kansa with the job of killing Krishna did not accept Krishna's plea and said that he shall have to fight with the best wrestlers. Then wrestling started between Chanura and Krishna and Mustic and Balram. The wrestling was by adopting all the tactics of the game. It appears there were some rules for the game as at present and the wrestling was being conducted according to those rules. The ladies witnessing the wrestling thought that Krishna and Balram, being young boys, were not fit matches for Chanura and Mustic, who were professional wrestlers as was the case when Ram came to break the dhanush in Sita swayamber. They accused Kansa of arranging fight between the unequals, which was against the rules and even all, who witnessed the wrestling, would be responsible for abeting this non-dharmic action. The wrestling was on with all tactics on either side, each attacking the other. Krishna and Balram killed both Chanura and Mustic respectively. Then Kootshal and Toshal appeared for wrestling against them. They too had been killed. The remaining fled away from the scene having seen their masters killed. All in audience were happy and surprised and Kansa got frightened to see the wrestling. He ordered Nand to be arrested; his wealth snatched and Krishna and Balram being expelled and Vasudeva, Devki and Ugrasen being killed. Krishna climbed on Kansa's munch. Kansa got up and took sword and dhal in his hands. He tried to attack on Krishna but Krishna got hold of him and threw him down from the munch and sat on his chest. He was killed. Since Kansa had all the time been thinking of Krishna only due to fear and out of rage, Krishna granted him paramgati (परमगति). Any one, who always remembers Krishna, even as enemy, is awarded such a position. Kansa's eight younger brothers, who came forward to take revenge of Kansa's death, had also been killed by Krishna and Balram. As usual, out of protocol, gods showered flowers on Krishna and Balram and Brahma, Shankar etc. came to praise them treating them as their Gods almighty. The wives of Kansa etc. came crying on their husband's death and realised that they had met this destiny as they had been cruel to the innocent people.

अनागसां त्वं भूतानां कृतवान् द्रोहमुल्बणम्,
तेनेमां भो दशां नीतो भूतध्रुक् को लभेत शम्। (10-44-47)

A man, who is cruel to others cannot have peace in life. Krishna, however, consoled the ladies and ordered the last rites of the dead being performed. Then Vasudeva, Devki, Ugrasen etc. had been released from the jail and Krishna and Balram paid their respects. Vasudeva and Devki, were in doubt whether they could consider Balram and Krishna, as Gods, or as their sons and deal with them accordingly. This happened as they had not brought them up and had only listened to their super-human activities and also seen Krishna as God before his birth. They, therefore, could not develop son's affection for them. Krishna then, through his yogmaya made Vasudeva and Devki accept them as their sons. They paid respects to the parents and Ugrasen and were repentant that they had to pass tough time in jails. Vasudeva and Devki in turn picked them up and embraced as sons. Ugrasen was coronated as king of Mathura although he had said that the throne belonged to Krishna as he had conquered it by killing Kansa. But Krishna persuaded him to accept it. This is all protocolic accomplishment. The king is he, who conquers the kingdom, is the general theory but since

Ugrasen was the real owner of the throne, he having been dethroned by Kansa and thrown in jail, Ugrasen was, therefore, recognised as the dynastical owner of throne. Krishna distributed wealth amongst rishis, Brahmains and others, who had suffered at the hands of Kansa. They then came to Nand and told that Nand and Yashoda were the real parents as it is they who brought them up, when their parents had abondoned them since birth itself.

सपिता सा च जननी यौ पुष्णीतां स्वपुत्रवत्,

शिशून् बन्धुभिरुत्सृष्टान कल्पै पोषरक्षणे। (10-45-22)

He requested them to go to Brij and he too would come to Brij after settling the matters in Mathura. They were given a lot of costly clothes, ornaments etc in respect and bade farewell.

Then Vasudeva, through his Purohit Gangacharya, arranged for Balram and Krishna's thread ceremony (यज्ञोपवीत) and gave cows and other alms to Brahmains and beggars and other deserving persons. Balram and Krishna then went to Sandipni Muni for their education. They had so far been busy in killing asuras and grazing cows. So officially they had to undergo studies too. In those days the students had to go and stay in Gurukul for studies irrespective of their position in society. Even Ram and other brothers had to go to Muni Vashista's Ashram for studies and live there like other students. This only put in the pupil the habit of—

(1) sacrifice;
(2) leading a simple life;
(3) complete submission to guru;
(4) forgetting their identity as rajkumar etc. and even begging for the livelihood;
(5) being used to democratic way of life in which everyone in the ashram was equal.; and

By this time Krishna had already established himself as God but he served the guru as a pupil only. The muni coached them all vedas, shastras, fighting skills, politics, administration, management, financial rules etc. as were necessary for a king to know. They learnt everything within a short time (64 days as per Bhagwat). There was a tradition to offer anything, the guru wished to have, in Dakshina after the studies were over. Krishna too offered for anything. The Guru told that their son had died drowning in the sea and he could bring him back. The guru knew Krishna could do it. So gurus were quite considerate in asking for such Guru Dakshina. Only bad example is that of Guru Daronacharya, who asked the thumb in guru dakshina from Eklovya, so that there was no equal to Arjun. This was a selfish action, not behoving of a guru. Krishna went to Yamraj and asked for the Muni's son. Yamraj paid all protocolic respects to the overall Lord Krishna. Yamraj then brought guru's son to Krishna, who handed him over to guru in fulfilment of guru's wish. The guru blessed them to be prosperous in universe and to be the overall Lords of the universe.

Thereafter having settled in Mathura, Krishna had been remembering Nand, Yashoda, gwalas and gopis. He sent Udhava, his friend to go to Brij and console them all as they were very much feeling the separation. Udhava went there in the evening and during the night stayed with Nand and Yashoda. They had been upset at the separation of Krishna and remembered before Udhava all Krishna's activities in Brij and became sentimental. Udhava then told them that Krishna was in fact incarnate of God, who have no father, mother, friend etc. and all were equal before him.

न ह्यस्यास्ति प्रियः कश्चिन्नाप्रियो वास्त्यमानिनः,
नोत्तमो नाधमो नापि समानास्यास्मोऽपिवा।
And न माता न पितातस्य न भार्या न सुतादयः
नात्मीयो न परश्चापि न देहो जन्म एव च। (10-46-37/38)

Krishna, as God, have none affectionate, nor any unaffectionate; neither superior nor inferior, even those with biased mentality are same for him. He has no father, no mother, no wife,, no sons, none his own nor any other's. He has no body nor is he born. It was all his lila only. The night passed in such dialogue and next morning, the gopis seeing the chariot before Nand's house started surmising, who had come from Mathura. They then saw Udhava, who was similar to Krishna in figure, shape, dress etc. They gathered around Udhava and came to know that he had come with a message from Krishna. They told Udhava that he had been sent by Krishna to console the gopis and their parents but Krishna is one, who could not be forgotten. They told Udhava so many things of relation between guru and disciple, raja and praja, parents and son, and so on but said that their relation with Krishna was different, which could not be broken by any words of consolation. They started enumerating all Krishna's lilas before Udhava. Gopis being down with shame while explaining their relation with Krishna, directly to Udhava, they selected one big black bee (मधुप) as the medium of telling all about their innersole. They asked the bee (symbolising him as Krishna) not to touch them as he is now not pious having been in contact with girls of Mathura. They also said so many things attributing to Krishna's cunningness in having left them in Brij and enjoying with others in Mathura. They also said how in various incarnations, he had cheated many people. As Baman, he cheated Bali (बली). Again as Ram he killed Bali (बाली) from a hideout and so on. The gopis were very anxious to see Krishna. Udhava told the gopis that he had great affection/love for the gopis and that he would once come there to meet there also. They were the best in devotion and submission to Krishna better than the bhakti attained by jap, tap, alms giving, yagya, havan etc., Krishna had told that he was always with them and, therefore, there was no question of separation. Udhava in this way told the gopis the spiritual love of Krishna with them but the gopis had reached the spiritual love by seeing Krishna; meeting Krishna; listening to Krishna and thinking of Krishna. They could not follow the ethical spirituality. They were, however, happy to listen to what Krishna had conveyed. They were also glad that Krishna was living with his people, happily. They only wanted to know if Krishna ever remembered them. Then they narrated how they passed time with Krishna. They told that although the greatest happiness lies in not expecting anything from anyone yet they were unable to get rid of the hope of Krishna coming to Brij as they lived only for his darshan on his visit to Brij—

परं सौख्यं हि नैराश्यं स्वैरिण्यप्याह पिङ्गला,
तज्जानतीनँ नः कृष्णे तथाप्याशा दुरत्यया। (10-47-47)

This was the instance of spiritual as well as physical love of gopis for Krishna and the protocolic relation between the two, which only they could feel and none else befailing all worldly protocols in the bargain as in raslilas etc. The gopis then paid their respects to Udhava. He lived there for several months listening to the incidents of Krishna lila in Brij. Udhava never expected gopis so much absorbed in Krishna that they could not think of anything other than Krishna. In fact anyone absorbed in Krishna cannot think of any worldly thing or relation or job. Udhava was in all praise for the gopis and wished he too had lost himself in Krishna's love as much. Udhava then left for Mathura and, as per protocol, Nand, Yashoda and gopis came out of Brij to see him off and offered many presents to him. They told they were not interested in salvation but wanted to live in Krishna bhakti in as many lives as they are born hereafter. On reaching Mathura, Udhava paid respects to Krishna, Ugrasen, Vasudeva, Devki etc. and gave them all the presents he had brought from Brij.

As promised, Krishna went to the houses of Kubja and Akroor and granted them the attainment of salvation. On seeing Krishna at her house, Kubja paid all respects and worshipped him. She also honoured Udhava, who had accompanied Krishna. Following the worldly protocol, Krishna sat on the stage meant for him whereas Udhava sat on earth. Krishna called Kubja also close to him. Kubja felt satisfied. Krishna then returned home along with Udhava. Likewise at Akroor's house, Akroor welcomed, respected, honoured and worshipped Krishna and Udhava. Krishna also in turn granted him his bhakti and ultimate salvation. Krishna then asked Akroor to go to Hastinapur as after Pandava's death, Yudhisthra and others were not happy although Dharitrastra had brought them to Hastinapur. His son is quite mischievous and Dharitrastra, being under his son's control, was not able to do justice to the Pandvas. So he was to go as Krishna's man and find out the correct position. Like present time, there was the system of one king sending his spies and representatives to other kingdom to check up particular position and apprise him of the same.

Akroor, as per protocol, first reported to king Dharitrastra, Bhishma, Vidur, Daronacharya, Kripacharya, Duryodhan, Yudhisthra and other brothers and then to Kunti. Kunti asked about the well-being of her parents etc. and whether Krishna ever remembered his cousins. She told that she had been living like a lamb amongst the wolves and expected only Krishna to take care of her children. Saying this, she started crying :

सापत्नमध्ये शोचन्तीं वृकाणां हरिणीमिव,
सान्त्वयिष्यति मां वाक्यैः पितृहीनांश्च बालकान्। (10-49-10)

Akroor and Vidur consoled Kunti saying that his sons are the offspring of gods/dharma and would establish dharmaraj in Bharat. On his departure back for Mathura, Akroor again met Dharitrastra and requested him to take care of Pandava's children too and not to indulge in partiality for his children against Pandava's children.

Dharitrastra accepted his partial behaviour in favour of his children because of partial affection for them and he could not help it. Akroor after knowing the position, returned to Mathura and reported the position to Krishna.

After Kansa's death, his two wives, the daughters of Jarasandha, an asura king, went to the father's house and narrated about Kansa's death. He got enraged and undertook to annihilate yadvas. He invaded Mathura with 13 kshoni (lakh) soldiers belonging to all his vassals. Here, the writer has indicated about the vassal Rajas under the king. Also being an asura, he had done an unprotocolic work in suddenly invading Mathura. Krishna, who had come to kill all the asuras, was happy to face all the asuras and their army in one stroke. As a long term strategy, however, he decided not to kill Jarasandha as in case he was alive he would again invade Mathura with another set of army and so on and in that case Krishna would be able to kill them all whereas in case Jarasandha was killed, all vassals under him, would also surrender to Mathura and in this way the asuras would be able to keep themselves alive, who in course of time could again invade Mathura. Krishna had himself indicated the purpose of his incarnation as—

एतदर्थोऽवतारोऽयं भूभारहरणाय मे,
संरक्षणाय साधुनाम् कृतोऽन्येषां वधाय च। (10-50-9)

(1) Killing the asuras so that the earth gets relief;
(2) Protection of sadhus, who were being crushed by the asuras;
(3) Establishment of dharma and checking adharma.

Krishna then got the godly chariots and his armaments. Krishna and Balram boarded the chariots with their arms and left to face the enemy with the small army, he could collect at short notice. Krishna blew his shell. Jarasandha asked Krishna to get away as he did not want to fight with a child. Krishna, however, challenged him in battle field. Jarasandha surrounded the small army of Krishna by his large army. Krishna showered arrows on the army killing them. Balram too attacked the army from another side. The two brothers killed the entire army of Jarasandha. Balram arrested Jarasandha. Shri Krishna, however, asked Balram to let him be off (thinking that alive he would bring more army to be killed by him). Jarasandha, however, felt ashamed in having been let off. Jarasandha wished to resort to sanyas but his vassals somehow consoled him to continue and again give fight to Krishna. This time Krishna had luckily escaped but such victory might not be repeated. As usual, gods came to praise Krishna and Balram. They were welcomed in Mathura with great honour as a victorious raja is received in his kingdom. Jarasandha again repeated similar attacks with large army and was defeated. 17 times he tried his luck but lost the battle and this way crores of asuras in his army had been killed.

Meantime Narad also sent Kalyavana, a great warrior to go and fight with Krishna. As already indicated, Narad used to act in a dual strategy. He knew Krishna was able to defeat any army. So with a view to annihilate this great asura warrior with his army, Narad inspired him to attack on Krishna, who was becoming stronger and stronger having defeated Jarasandha. Simultaneously, Jarasandha too attacked Mathura. Krishna, therefore, arranged to construct a fort for the people of Mathura to live in. It was inaccessible by anyone. The fort was constructed under the sea with all requirements for living. This became Dwarka, the kingdom of Krishna. He kept Balram to protect Mathura and himself came out of the town alone. Kalyavana could recognise Krishna, as told by Narad. Krishna was without any arms. Kalyavana also, therefore, decided to fight with him without arms. This indicates that there were laws of war according to which the fight was (1) one to one (2) with similar arms (3) in case of no arms with one party, the other was obliged to fight without arms. Kalyavana ran towards Krishna. Krishna took a turn and ran. Kalyavana had been following him. Krishna took him in a cave. Running from the battle field is known as Ranchhod Bhagwan (रणछोड़ भगवान). This was only a strategy adopted by Krishna to make him tired in running after him. In the cave, Kalyavana saw one man sleeping. He thought it was Krishna only. He kicked him by his feet. The man got up and was in rage for having been awakened. He saw towards Kalyavana in rage and in the fear of rage, he was burnt alive. Krishna then met that man. He was Raja Muchukunda, who had helped gods in the battles and gods as per obligation, requested him to take rest. He had been given a boon that anyone disturbing him while asleep would get burnt. So now Krishna met him. Muchukunda gave his introduction and enquired who he was in that hilly area. Krishna told him that he was known by many names but at present he was Krishna, an incarnation of Vishnu. He had come to protect dharma and annihilate rakshasas. He had already killed Kansa and another asur Kalyavana, has been burnt now. He asked Muchukunda to ask for any boon. Muchukunda could then remember of Krishna as incarnation of Vishnu and praised him. He mentioned about the people, who after attaining the form of human being waste it in worldly ambitions and satisfaction of passions etc., and do not devote to Bhagwad bhakti.

लब्धवा जनो दुर्लभमत्र मानुषम्
कथंचिदव्यगंम यत्नतोऽनघ।
पादारविन्दं न भजत्यसन्मति-
गृहान्ध कूपे पतितो यथा पशुः॥ (10-51-47)

Further Raja Muchukunda indicated the end of human body as :

(1) Throwing away and thus submitting the body to be eaten away by birds

(2) Burrying under the earth and thus making it the food for insects to be eaten away; or

(3) By burning in which case it becomes all ash.

The book had been written by Vyas Muni thousands of years back, when there was only Hinduism in India and according to Hindus the dead body was only burnt. But the writer could either anticipate that in course of time dead bodies would be disposed off in one of the above three methods or possibly these systems were even then available in some other countries and the indication in the book reveals the knowledge of the writer of the entire universe. These three systems are being adopted these days too. Throwing to birds is used by the Parsis; burrying under earth is adopted by Muslims and Christians and cremation by burning is done by Hindus and Budhists.

"कलेवरो विट्कृमि भस्म संज्ञितः"
(10-51-51)

Leaving aside all worldly ambitions, raja asked for refuge under God only. God granted the wish saying that he only wanted to test his involvement or otherwise in the universe, otherwise normally his bhaktas are always bereft of worldly wishes. Krishna told him that on next birth he would be a Brahmain and after worshipping him, he would get absorbed in him. Here the writer has made Krishna himself to tell that there is the institution of transmigration of soul according to which a being after death comes in another form and continues so till he attains salvation.

Krishna came back to Mathura and annihilated Kalyavana's army, which had still surrounded Mathura. He took the entire booty to Dwarka. On the way, Jarasandha again attacked him with large army. Balram and Krishna, however, went away from the place indicating that although Krishna could, as in the past, defeat Jarasandha with his entire army but he wanted to tell to the world that one should act intelligently in war and sometimes it becomes necessary to go away from the battle, particularly when one is suddenly attacked and in that case rather than harping on the principle of not to flee from the battle field, and give up one's life, one should try to escape and such an action is not adharmik or unmoral but is only diplomacy or mere strategy. Such a diplomacy has always been adopted during the war even today. Jarasandha, however, followed Krishna. Krishna and Balram climbed on a hill. Not able to find them, Jarasandha put the entire forest in flames. Krishna and Balram, however, escaped and went to Dwarka. Jarasandha thinking that they had been burnt, returned with his army to Magadha.

Krishna and Balram having settled in their kingdom in Dwarka, the next course of action was getting married. The rajkumars were generally married in those days either through swayamber in which the bride used to select a groom for herself out of the gathering as in the case of Sita-Ram marriage. Another way was that one raja invaded another and on either's defeat, the daughter of the defeated was taken in marriage. Still one more method was that the girl would make up her mind for marriage with a particular person and on the parents arranging marriage with another person, she would invite the man of his dreams for marriage. He would come and take away the bride forcefully or by kidnapping etc. These were the systems apart from the arranged marriage by the parents of the girl.

Balram was married with Revti, the daughter of Raja Revat, at the instance of Brahmaa. For Krishna, Rukmani, the daughter of Raja Bhismak had vowed to marry. Raja and his elder son, Rukma wanted to marry her to Sishupal. Krishna too had heard of the beauty and desire of Rukmani and had made up his mind to marry with Rukmani. She sent a message to Krishna indicting her wish to marry with him but her father and brother desired her marriage with Shisupal. A Brahmain had come with the message. He was escorted to Shri Krishna, who received him with due respects, and worshipped him being a Brahmain. He gave the message. Shri Krishna told that he wanted to marry Rukmani. Only two days were left for the marriage. Krishna immediately started for Rukmani's place.

On the other side, Rukmani's father, Bhismak had made all arrangements for the marriage of Rukmani with Shishupal. All the roads, streets and highways had been decorated and perfumes/sandal sprinkled. The people had dressed themselves to suit the occasion. The Brahmains had been worshipped and alms had been given. Rukmani too had been properly adorned for the marriage. Raja Bhishmak was well-versed with religious, political and social protocol for the occasion. He had made proper arrangements for the stay of the rajas from various places. Bhishmak received every raja as per protocol. Even according to present day protocol, the head of a state is received by the Head of the other state and the incumbent is treated as state guest for the period of his stay. Similarly in those days too, raja Bhismak had received every raja with full protocol, made them stay in comfortable suites, appropriately decorated for the occasion, according to the importance of each raja. Bhismak and Shishupal surmised that Krishna might come up and marry Rukmani against the will of her father. They had, therefore, invited Raja Salva, Jarasandha, Dantvactra, Viduratha, Paundrika etc. and they had all vowed to fight with Krishna, if he created any disturbance in marriage of Rukmani with Shishupal. These rajas had come with their chaturangani (army comprising of chariots, elephants, horses and on foot is chaturangani army). Balram had known the presence of these rajas at Bhismak's place and having known that Krishna had alone gone there, and there was a chance of a battle taking place, Balram as an extra precaution also started with his chaturangani army.

Only one day was left in marriage and Krishna had not so far arrived. This created tension in the mind of Rukmani. Even the brahmin had not returned. She was, however, confident of Krishna's arrival. She had then witnessed good omens. The brahmin reached and apprised Rukmani of Krishna's plan. As per protocol, Rukmani had to give some presents to the brahmin for such a service and also news of Krishna's arrival . But she could not locate any suitable present. She, therefore, only bowed before him and thus symbolically gave everything to him, being the incarnate of Lakshmi.

When raja Bhismak came to know that Krishna and Balram had been coming to witness the marriage, he received them as per protocol, gave them appropriate presents and worshipped them as per tradition. He arranged for the proper stay of Krishna, Balram and their army. The other rajas, asuras, other than those, who had been invited by Raja Bhismak also paid their respects and gave many presents knowing their bravery and position. They were Krishna bhaktas and had his darshan. They all wished Krishna's marriage with Rukmani.

Rukmani left for the pooja along with her friends and escort. Many brahmin ladies, and other ladies duly adorned had also accompanied with the materials required for pooja etc. Before pooja she washed her hands etc. and made herself clean as per rule. After that she entered the temple and bowed and worshipped Shiva and Parvati. They are considered to be good at fulfilling the wish of the brides for attaining suitable groom. She requested for fulfilling her wish of having Krishna in marriage. The brahmin women blessed her. Rukmani was properly adorned. She had her walking as if she was going to garland Krishna as she had already known Krishna's plan. On her return after pooja, she found Krishna standing there. He picked Rukmani up and boarded her on his chariot even amidst the other rajas and their armies. Raja Jarasandha, Shishupal etc. felt much ashamed over the incident. They along with Rukma, the brother of Rukmani, followed Krishna and Balram for a fight. Jarasandha's army by a shower of arrows, covered the entire army of Krishna. Rukmani got fightened. Krishna, however, consoled her.

Then Krishna's army attacked the enemy's army and killed most of them. Jarasandha fled from the battle field. Shishupal was quite upset on not having been able to get married with Rukmani. Jarasandha consoled him saying luck is with them and when they would have luck on their side, they too would defeat Krishna. Here the writer has emphasised that all beings (even asuras) believed in fate and the effect of time.

रिपवो जिग्युरधुना काल आत्मानुसारिणि,
तदा वयं विजेष्यामो यदा कालप्रदक्षिणः। (10-54-16)

Thereafter Shishupal went to his kingdom with whatever army was left. Rukma too was unhappy over the incident as he wanted Rukmani to be married with Shishupal.He too with a large army, followed Krishna with the undertaking that in case he was not able to kill Krishna and bring Rukmani back, he would not return to his kingdom. He challenged Krishna either to face him in battle or leave Rukmani and go back. He attacked with sword, arrow, and other arms but Krishna made them all ineffective. Then Krishna took a sword but Rukmani did not want her brother to be killed and requested Krishna to take pity and spare her brother from being killed. Rukmani had been shivering out of fear. Krishna did not kill Rukma and only arrested him and spared him after shaving his head, moustache etc The entire army had also by that time been crushed. Balram further took pity on Rukma and released him from the arrest. He, however, asked Rukmani not to mind her brother having been shaved, as all punishments are granted not by human beings but by virtue of one's deeds—

सुख दुःखदो न च अन्योस्ति यतःस्वकृतभुक्पुमान (10-54-38)

Then again adressing Rukmani, Balram stated that kshatriya dharma was such that in the battle field even a brother may kill his own brother.

क्षत्रियाणामयं धर्मः प्रजापतिविनिर्मितः,
भ्रातापि भ्रातरं हन्याद् येन घोरतरस्ततः। (10-54-40)

This shows that in the battlefield one cannot care for one's relations and one has even to kill one's own closet relation. Such was the dharma of kshatriyas. The tenets of dharma for each varna had been written in detail in our shastras so that there is no ambiguity in the compliance/following of the same and such tenets of dharma have to be followed strictly so much so that in the battle field a brother had even to kill his brother. In Mahabharat, Krishna had advised Arjun to fight as per his dharma even with his Guru Daronacharya, grand father Bhishma and all cousin brothers Duryodhan etc. and Arjun had to kill them all including Karan, who was his brother.

Balram also told Rukmani that in the battle field, Rukma could have been killed justifiably but on her request he had been spared. At the same time, some punishment had to be inflicted upon him for his having indulged in battle. Shaving head etc. is not a corporal punishment but only symbolic to make him feel his mistake in—

(1) having stood in the way of a bride and groom, who liked each other; and

(2) having developed fighting with Krishna.

Rukmani got consoled. Rukma left and since, as per undertaking, he could not go back to his kingdom, he created a new town named Bhojkut and started living there.

Krishna returned to Dwarka and married with Rukmani with all traditional rites and pomp and show. Entire Dwarka was decorated. People wore good dresses. Alms were given to brahmins, beggars etc. All relations, gods, rishis, and friends attended the marriage. The marriage is attended by so many people with a view to have proper and adequate evidence of the marriage having taken place. Same evidence of marriage holds good even today as per evidence law.

People allege as illegal Krishna's kidnapping and marriage with Rukmani. But this is not so as—

(1) Krishna and Rukmani were both adults and could marry as per their will.

(2) They wished to marry each other.

(3) It word have been rather cruelty to have married Rukmani with Shishupal against her will.

(4) Krishna had faced and fought with all rajas, who opposed such a marriage including Rukma, the brother of Rukmani.

(5) After having taken Rukmani, defeating all rajas, who opposed her marriage with Krishna, Krishna married with her according to vedic rites before a large gathering.

(6) Although the asura rajas Jarasandha, Shishupal etc. were in the know of Krishna's intention of marriage with Rukmani as they had come with their armies to give him a fight, if chance be, Rukmani's father Bhishmak had welcomed the arrival of Krishna and Balram at the time of marriage, indicating thereby that even Rukmani's father was not averse to her marriage with Krishna and it was only her brother Rukma, who opposed such a marriage.

Rukmani, in course of time, gave birth to a child but he was kidnapped by an asura Shambrasura, when he was only ten days old. The asura threw him in ocean, where a big fish swallowed him. The fish was caught in a net and when the fish was cut, the child appeared. The maid servant Mayawati took him and brought him up. The boy was named Praduman. He was none else but Kamdev, who had been burnt by Shiva and as per his boon was now born and Mayawati was his wife Rati. Narad came, as usual, and told the entire history to Mayawati, who started taking him as her husband . In course of time, she told him the entire historical background and the two were married. Praduman then killed Shambrasura. Shambrasura knew many tactics of illusive (मायावी) battle and Mayawati too had coached Praduman about all those. A fierce battle took place, in which many illusive arms had been used. The illusive arms were nothing but like the rockets/missiles of present day. As ordinary people could not understand the technique, they termed these arms as illusive (मायावी). Technology would have been so much developed in those days that all kinds of rockets had been made in those days. Similar arms were also available in Ram period and used in Ram-Ravan battle.

Then Praduman and Mayawati came to Dwarka through sky way again confirming the availability of rockets/ aeroplanes in those days. In Dwarka again Narad came and told the entire history of Praduman and Mayawati. There was great rejoicing in Dwarkapuri on coming back of Krishna's son.

Krishna subsequently married Jambvati the daughter of Jamvant, a bear king after fighting with him. When Jamvant was defeated, he married Jambvanti with Krishna. Similarly Satrajit, a bhakta of sun, who had got a mani (Jewel) from sun in lieu of his bhakti, married his daughter Satyabhama with Krishna and gave the mani in dowry. That mani used to produce 8 maunds of gold every day. Krishna told Satrajit that he had obtained the mani by virtue of his bhakti of sun. Therefore, he was the owner but since he had given it in dowry to his daughter, married with Krishna, Krishna was entitled to the gold produced by it only. The principle told by Krishna to Satrajit was like a king conquering another king and returning to him his kingdom accepting wealth and other presents from him and treating him as his vassal. Thereafter Krishna married Jambvati and Satyabhama according to all vedic rites

भगवानाह न मणिं प्रतीच्छामो वयं नृप,
तवास्तां देव भक्तस्य वयं च फल भागिनः। (10-57-45)

Krishna had married many girls. This only confirms the fact that the king was allowed as per law to have as many queens as he desired although it was desirable to have only one living wife. This is evident from the fact that Raja Dasratha had several queens but Ram refused even to have a second wife even when Sita had been separated. In Duapur again the kings had started having several wives. All Pandavas—Yudhisthra etc. had Daropadi as common wife plus other wives each of the brother was having—Bhima having Hudamba, Arjun having Sabhadra and so on.

Having known that Pandvas had not been killed in Lakshagriha (लक्षागृह), Krishna went to meet them in

Indraprastha. He was welcomed by Pandvas. Krishna bowed before Yudhisthra and Bhim and embraced Arjun and Nakul and Sehdeva bowed before Krishna. This is the social protocol having been observed here. Yudhisthra and Bhim were older cousins to Krishna. Therefore, he bowed before them. Arjun being treated as a friend, was embraced and Nakul and Sehdeva being younger to Krishna, they bowed before Krishna. As per protocol, Pandvas offered sinhasan to Krishna. Daropadi, a newly wedded came and paid respects to Shri Krishna. Pandvas respected other Yaduvanshis too, who had accompanied Krishna. Kunti met and embraced Krishna and asked about the well-being of the family members. The Pandvas praised Krishna. Krishna stayed there for a few months. Shri Krishna got a beautiful town created there. After some time, Krishna returned to Dwarka.

Krishna married Kalindi, the daughter of Sun as she had performed prolonged tapsya to have Krishna as her husband, as per vedic rites. Similarly, Mitravinda, the daughter of Raja of Avanti also wished to have Krishna in marriage. Krishna took her away from swayamber although her brother did not like her marriage with Krishna. Krishna also married Satya, the daughter of Raja of Awadh. For Satya, one had to fight with seven ferocious oxen. None was able to fulfil the condition, which Krishna did. Satya too wanted marriage with Krishna and had worshipped god for this purpose. Krishna was welcomed by the Raja of Awadh, as per international protocol, first by receiving him outside the town and then making him sit on proper stage (आसन) and treating him as a royal guest. Krishna mentioned that he wanted to marry his daughter with a view to establish good relations with the Raja of Awadh. The raja mentioned about his condition of marriage, to control the seven oxen. Shri Krishna fulfilled the condition. Satya was then married with Krishna with great pomp and show. Krishna also married Bhadra, the daughter of the Raja of Kaikaye.

Bhomasura, a rakshas had by virtue of his force snatched the umbrella (छत्र) of God Varuna, kundal of Aditi and Maniparvat, an abode of gods. Indra had requested Krishna for help. Krishna proceeded to that place. The kingdom was like a fortress and no one could dare enter the same. There were hills alround, then there was an escort by armed men all around, then there was a water trench and then an electric/fire currented wall and then another wall between which gas had been filled; then nets had been spread to entrap anyone passing through all these obstacles and then there were the warriors with elephants, horses etc. This indicates that there was full knowledge of providing forts in those day. The fort was fortified by

(1) hilly wall
(2) armed personnel
(3) water trenches
(4) electric currented wall
(5) gas filled walls
(6) nets
(7) protection by army

This indicates the strategic knowledge of the people as also the technological development in as much as people were aware of the electricity and its power as also the gas filled between two walls, which could choke if anyone entered there. Krishna, however, broke all these obstacles with his gada (गदा) and killed all escorting armed men. Knowing all this, Mura rakshas, the owner of the forest came out. Fierce fighting took place and Krishna killed him. Then his seven sons came to fight but they were also killed. Then Bhomasura came and after fierce battle he too was killed by Krishna. The earth then came to Krishna and offered the umbrella, kundal etc. to Krishna as presents and praised him. She said God was acting with all his gunas for different purposes. Rajoguna for creation, satvagun for bringing up and maintaining the creation and tamogun for annihilation of the creation. Krishna then entered the Mahal of Bhomasura. He found that Bhomasura had by force snatched 16000 girls from various rajas and kept them in his captivity. They all felt attracted towards Krishna and wished him to be their husband. Krishna accepted them all, sent them to Dwarka, properly dressed and sent all wealth of Bhomasura too to Dwarka. Then Krishna with Satyabhama went to Indrapuri (Amravati). Indra worshipped them. Satyabhama expressed desire to have Kalpavriksa (कल्पवृक्ष) from swarag to her mahal. This was objected to by Indra and other gods. Krishna fought with them, defeated them and then brought Kalpivriksa to Dwarka. The writer has indicated here that like human beings, even gods too are very assuming because of the wealth available with them as also selfish in as much as in case of difficulty, they want everyone's help but at other times they do not recognise the person at all. For killing Bhomasura and other rakshasas, Indra and other gods were completely prostrated before Krishna but after they had been killed and Satyabhama desired to have Kalpvriksha, they developed fighting with Krishna and could not even afford to present the small thing desired by Krishna's queen. This indicates that at this even the gods do not act as per protocol and they had to suffer for the same, whenever they acted otherwise. On reaching Dwarka, Krishna married all the 16000 with as many of his forms and settled them in individual mahals. Krishna had been doing justice as a husband to all his queens by converting himself in as many forms and each thinking that Krishna was with her during the night. Krishna visited each queen's mahal, where he was respected and served by the queens.

Regarding Krishna marrying above 16000 girls and keeping them as his queens in mahals it is observed that—

(1) Krishna had married them all as per vedic rites meaning thereby that the king was allowed to have as many queens as he desired to have.

(2) Krishna had done justice to them as he was able to convert himself in as many forms, being a God indicating that one should have more than one wives if he is able to satisfy and do justice and treat them equally, otherwise one should have only one wife.

(3) Krishna had married the girls, who were fully aware that Krishna was already married and had more than one wife, but still wished to have Krishna as their

husband. So Krishna married as per their wishes and not by force.

(4) Krishna had married a number of girls after defeating their fathers who were rajas of various kingdoms.

(5) By killing the asura rajas as Krishna had incarnated to annihilate the rakshasas from the earth.

(6) In other cases to make friendship with various rajas, as a matter of diplomacy. Even today such diplomatic tactics are adopted by various states to woo the states in their favour or in their group like NATO/SEATO etc. Krishna had, therefore, married various girls to develop diplomatic relations with other kings or to oblige girls, who had devoted themselves to be the queens of Krishna only.

(7) Krishna had married many girls as he wanted to have many sons to fight and kill the rakshasas in battle fields.

But what was there in Krishna that was not in other rajas has been discussed by Krishna and Rukmani themselves, when Krishna asked Rukmani why she had been for marriage with him inspite of the fact that compared to other rajas. He did not :

(1) have a beautiful figure being black in complexion;
(2) have much wealth compared to many other rajas;
(3) have any kingdom/region to rule;
(4) have that much strength as many others had; so much so that he had fled from battle field while fighting with Jarasandha;
(5) have the stature to the liking of many rajas viz. inspite of Rukma's opposition to him and favouring Shishupal, Rukmani desired to be married with Krishna only;
(6) have a sinhasan like other rajas.
(7) have a large army as owned by other rajas.
(8) have friendship with many rajas. Had rather enmity with them.
(9) have any fixed religion.

(10) have the label of being an kshatriya as he was only a yadava (an ingredient of vaish varna).
(11) have any principles in life; sometimes grazing cows and other times playing with the gopis and gwalas.
(12) have any belonging—neither relations nor friends nor well wishers—rather always risking his life in battles and otherwise.
(13) have wealthy people close to him as they were afraid lest Krishna might snatch their wealth.
(14) make an equal match as is required for a marriage; equal matches are equal in richness, status, position dynasty, varna, luxury and should not be either from inferior or superior family.

ययोरात्मसमं वित्तं जन्मैश्वर्या कृतिर्भव:,
तयोर्विवाहो मैत्री च नोत्तमाधमयो: क्वचित्। (10-60-14)

Hearing all this from Krishna, Rukmani got frightened; was in tears and was very upset and later became unconscious. Krishna felt that Rukmani could not make out that it was only out of humour. He picked her up, wiped the tears and embraced her and consoled her. He told her that it was the advantage in grihast that after remaining busy day and night, some time is taken for mutual amusement, humour etc. to please oneself. Rukmani could then realise it was only a joke. She then praised him being almighty God and so none equalled him. She also told that whatever deficiencies he had told in himself were actually his merits like even though dark in complexion he was very attractive and charming; having no earth but was the owner of the wealth of entire universe; having no kingdom, he was the overall Lord of not only entire universe but entire galaxy (ब्रह्माण्ड); not having any sinhasan or kingdom but was the king of entire universe; not having army or force but was most forceful in universe; not having any friend or relations as all human beings were his own and he had same consideration for all; not have any religion or varna/caste but was the one worshipped by people of all religions/varnas etc.; not having any principles in life but was the creator of all vedas/shastras; the wealthy people do not come close to him as they are under the influence of maya for which they repent after death and so always remain away for him and so on. Krishna admired her sense of understanding. He was also able to judge her devotion for husband (पतिव्रत धर्म) in which she surpassed all and was fully his only.

Krishna got ten sons from each of his queens. They were equal in beauty, charm and strength to their father. Krishna had married so many girls as he wanted to have many sons equal in strength to him to help him in annihilation of rakshasas from the universe in battle fields. To please her sister Rukmani, Rukma had married his daughter to Rukmani's grand son and Praduman's son Anirudha as Rukma's daughter had selected him in her sawayamber. Even though they knew such a marriage was not permissible as per law but in view of their love for each other, the marriage had been performed.

दौहित्राय अनिरुद्धाय पौत्रीं रुक्म्यददाद्धरेः,
रोचनां बद्धवैरो स्वसुः प्रियचिकीर्षया,
जानन्नधर्म तद् यौनं स्नेहपाशानु बन्धनः। (10-61-25)

After the marriage, Rukma's asura friends prompted him to play gambling with Balram and since Balram did not know playing gambling, he would be embarrassed. On such invitation, Balram agreed. At first Rukma won in 3-4 chances but then Balram won but Rukma told that only he had won. Again a bigger stake was put and Balram won but again Rukma said he had won. Then there was Akashwani that Balram had won but ignoring that Rukma and his other friends taunted and passed bad remarks against Balram saying that he was a gwala and did not know playing gamble etc. Balram got enraged and killed Rukma in the Sabha itself. The friends fled away from the scene and those who opposed were also injured or killed. Krishna, Balram etc. returned to Dwarka with Anirudha and the bride.

As already indicated, Shri Krishna had come as incarnate of Vishnu to annihilate the rakshasas from the earth. Shri Krishna had either killed them or made his vassals. Most of the rakshasas had been killed with their armies too. One Banasura was a great warrior king. He was the eldest son of raja Bali (बली), who had given the entire earth to Baman avatar Vishnu and Vishnu had assured that his sons would not be killed. Banasura had a daughter Usha. She once saw in her dream Anirudha, the grandson of Shri Krishna. She liked him and became upset to find who he was. She had a friend Chitralekha. She drew the pictures of all gods, rishis, great rajas, Krishna, Vasdev, Praduman and Anirudha. Seeing Anirudha's picture, she stated that he was the person of her dream. Chitralekha could go anywhere flying. (There must be some aeroplane in the kingdom of the great king Banasura and Chitralekha might have used the same). She brought Anirudha in the night itself to Usha. Usha was in a mahal where no person could even enter. Usha and Anirudha lived and loved there for a long period. Usha developed some signs on the body to indicate that she had been in love with some person. The security men were surprised and reported the matter to Banasura. Banasura arrested Anirudha and kept him in his captivity. In Dwarka, everyone was upset over the disappearance of Anirudha. As usual Narad came and told the whereabouts of Anirudha. Narad was a link between God and human beings. He had access everywhere. Being Krishna bhakta, it was for him to keep a watch on each movement in Dwarka. Krishna, Balram and Praduman etc. attacked Banasura. Banasura's kingdom was guarded by Shiva as a result of some boon granted by Shiva to Banasura on his having pleased Shiva with his tapsya. So Shiva came to fight with Krishna. Shiva and Krishna were the bhakta and swamis of each other but here each, as per his dharma, had to fight with the other. Fierce fighting took place. Ultimately Krishna with his arrow made Shiva sleepy. He, therefore, went away from the field. In his place Banasura came to fight with Krishna. Again fierce fighting took place. Krishna cut all his arms except four. Meantime Banasura's Dharma-mata Kotra, seeing her son would be killed by Krishna, came naked in between Banasura and Krishna. A kshatriya, as per dharma, could neither see a naked woman nor attack on her. Krishna turned his head from her side, giving a chance to Banasura to run away. Shiva came and to save Banasura's life, requested Krishna to save him after praising Krishna as his swami. Krishna excused Banasura but was left with only 4 arms instead of 1000.

During the battle between Krishna and Shiva, Shiva had sent his Jawra (an arm) to fight with Krishna. So since the fight had to be amongst the equivalents as per rule, Krishna also sent his Jawra. Both Jawras fought and ultimately Shiva's Jawar surrendered. He came and praised Krishna and begged to be pardoned. He said the human beings have to suffer till they are entrapped in one ambition or the other and do not take refuge under Krishna.

तावत्तापो देहिनां तेऽङ्घ्रिमूलं ०
नो सेवेरन् यावद् आशानुबद्धा। (10-63-28)

Krishna took pity on him and excused him. Then Banasura had come and Shiva came seeing Banasura on the verge of being killed by Krishna. Shiva praised Krishna. The writer, through Shiva, has said that God has no religion, or caste or shape and is above all these. There cannot be a greater assimilation of all dharmas than in Hindu Dharma, which does not recognise different religions, castes etc and as per their philosophy all lead to same almighty God, who by virtue of his maya appears in various forms as human being, bird, animal, god etc. and the human beings under the influence of his maya only get indulged in wife, offspring, wealth, property and even gets proud of his bodily force etc. resulting in various kinds of sufferings.

Krishna excused Banasura, who praised him and brought Anirudha and Usha duly decorated to be married. He also gave lot of dowry as per tradition. Krishna came back to Dwarka, where he was received with all protocol by the public, mantris etc. in the town duly decorated for the occasion when the raja returned after victory over the enemy.

After leaving Brij, Balram had always been thinking of visiting Brij. He once came there. He bowed before Nand and Yashoda and after they asked mutual well-being, sat there. All gopis came there. As per protocol, Balram bowed before the elders amongst them and the younger bowed before Balram. There was a session of gossips with gopes. Then came the turn of gopis. They, as expected, enquired about the well-being of Krishna and got lost remembering his deeds in Brij. After being amongst them for sometime, Balram desired to take bath in Yamuna. But Yamuna was at a distance from there. He, by his plough, brought Yamuna there. Possibly he during his stay in Brij, would have seen Yamuna having gone away changing the path and the people of Brij would have been facing difficulty. So Balram would have diverted Yamuna from the changed path and would have brought it back near Brij. This shows the civil engineering fete of that time, Balram, doing such actions of welfare for the people of Brij, stayed there for several months.

In the series of killing asuras, next came the turn of Raja Pundrik and the Kasi Naresh. Pundrik had declared himself as Krishna and challenged Krishna that he was not the real Krishna. Since there cannot be anyone equivalent to God, Krishna invaded Kashi, where Pundrik had been staying. He killed Pundrik, and the raja of Kashi. Kashi Naresh had several sons. They got enraged on the death of their father. They held a Shiva yagya. Shiva was pleased and asked for the boon. They asked for a method to kill Krishna. Shiva advised for holding a yagya. Out of the yagya, one Kritya appeared and proceeded to Dwarka. Dwarka people got frightened and came to Krishna for help. Krishna sent his chakra. The chakra annihilated the effect of Kritya and killed the sons of Kasi Naresh and came back to Krishna. In this way, Kashi came under the rule of Krishna.

Once Duryodhan had held a swayamber for the marriage of his daughter Lakshmana. Krishna's son Samba took her away from the swayamber. Kaurvas felt it and proceeded to bring Lakshmana back. Fierce fighting took place. But when Samba could not be won over, six of Kaurvas attacked on him. This was against the laws of war but Kaurvas had been repeatedly resorting to such actions that is why they had been killed because of their adharmik thinking. When Yaduvanshis came to know of the arrest of Samba, they prepared to attack on Hastinapur but in view of the good relations with them, Balram decided to first go to them for a compromise. This is the faculty of Indians that they try to avoid war to the extent possible and resort to peaceful manners to sort out the differences, particularly with the friendly kings.

Balram sent Udhav to inform the Kaurvas of his arrival and to check up the thinking of Kaurvas. This was the theme of protocolic conduct by one raja with other to apprise the arrival through a messenger. This served two purposes—one if the other raja cared to keep good relations, he would welcome and come to receive the incumbent raja and if he had thinking otherwise then he may not behave well with the messenger. On hearing the arrival of Balram, the Kaurvas at first honoured Udhava and then proceeded to receive Balram in the traditional way as a raja is accorded by another raja. Even today such a reception is organised when the head of one state (The raja of present day) visits the other state. The Kaurvas met and paid respects to Balram according to their position/age as per protocol—i.e. the youngers bowing to Balram and Balram bowing to elders. They presented cows and other things in honour. Then they asked mutual well-being of each other. Then Balram, who had come as a royal representative of Raja Ugrasen told them of the message of Ugrasen telling them that they had by a non-dharmik action, arrested Samba collectively by six persons. This was not digestible and, therefore, if they cared to have friendly relations with Mathura, they should leave Samba and Lakshmana. Kaurvas, however, got enraged and said that Mathura was a vassal of Hastinapur and still they could pass threats to Hastinapur. This was not tolerable. They had been granted kingship by Hastinapur only. This confirms the institution of vassalage in those days, where a king awarded the Rajaship to his vassal and the vassal in turn accepted him as their king. So the Kaurvas told Balram that whatever Ugrasen had said was not apt for a vassal raja to say. They were so much proud of their strength and wealth that they forgot to even observe the normal protocolic behaviour with another raja and came back to Hastinapur.

जन्म बन्धुश्रियोन्नद्धमदास्ते भरतर्षभ,

आश्राव्यम रामं दुर्वाच्यमसभ्याः पुरमाविशन्। (10-69-29)

Balram got enraged and thought that the persons proud of their strength and wealth could not understand the language of peace and had to be dealt with likewise by punishing them. He did not accept Mathura being a vassal of Hastinapur and whatever Kaurvas had said was factually incorrect. He, therefore, took his arm, the plough and with it attracted Hastinapur to be sunk in Ganga. When Kaurvas saw Hastinapur being moved towards Ganga, they got frightened and came to Balram to be pardoned as they did not realise his position. Balram excused them for the sake of keeping good relations. Samba and Lakshmana were then got wedded. Duryodhan gave away many elephants, horses, wealth in dowry. The institution of giving away dowry by the bride's father to groom's father had been there in Duapur too as also in Treta, when Janak had given a lot of dowry in Sita's marriage to Dasratha. But such dowry was not in consideration of marriage but was given willingly by the girl's father unlike today when dowry is extracted by the groom's father from the father of the bride. Balram accepted the dowry. Acceptance of dowry indicated that the groom's men were happy with the marriage and that the bride would now live happily in the house of the groom. Balram then came back to Mathura, where he, Samba and Lakshmana had been welcomed in traditional way.

Even today Hastinapur is elevated on southside and is tilled toward Ganga as a result of the movement of Hastinapur to be sunk in Ganga by Balram.

अद्यापि च पुरं ह्येतत् सूचयद् रामविक्रमम,

समुन्नतं दक्षिणतो गंगायामनुदृश्यते। (10-69-54)

Once Narad Muni thought of seeing how Krishna had been doing justice to all his over sixteen thousand queens. he went to Dwarka and saw gardens, parks, mahals etc. The town was very well planned and all the mahals had been suitably decorated. They are stated to have been constructed by Architect god Viswakarma. There would have been high class architectural technology and civil engineering but with a view to make people believe of such town planning and construction, the writer, as usual, has attributed this to have been constructed by Viswakarma for Shri Krishna. Today we see a railway line constructed under the sea as an engineering fete whereas in those days the entire Dwarka was constructed by reclaiming land from the sea. For Krishna, it may be said to have been constructed by Viswakarma but what about Indraprastha and other palaces and towns of various rajas. In Indraprastha, the passage of canal had been provided which had put Duryodhan into doubt as to whether it was water or dry place. This was constructed by Indian architects only. It, therefore, goes to prove the prime achievement of architecture and town planning in those days that even gods wished to be born in India.

Seeing Narad, Krishna got up from the bed where he was sitting with his queen Rukmani. He bowed in the feet of Narad and made him sit on his sinhasan (सिघासन). This was the protocol in those days that guru, rishis etc. when they visited the rajas, they shared the sinhasan as a mark of respect for them, showing that they had the first right over the sinhasan as also that because of their blessings only they had been occupying the sinhasan. Although Narad had come to Shri Krishna, the almighty God and he should have bowed before Krishna but since here Krishna had incarnated only as a human being for whom the rishis were respectable. So Krishna honoured Narad as he always respected/worshipped brahmins and rishis. He washed Narad's feet and took the charnamrit (चरणामृत); then worshipped him; gave eatables and then asked what he could do for him. Narad then praised Shri Krishna as God and requested his bhakti being granted for ever. Narad then went to another queen's mahal. There again Narad found Krishna playing chauser (चौसर) with his queen and Udhav. Krishna again welcomed and worshipped Narad as he did in Rukmani's mahal and asked him as a stranger as to when did he come. Narad then went to third mahal and again found Krishna there too and again Krishna respected and worshipped Narad here too. He went to next mahal where Shri Krishna was taking bath. In another mahal, he was playing with children. Like that Narad saw Krishna in different jobs in different mahals. Somewhere he had been consulting his advisers/mantris on serious problems and at other places, he had been playing with his queens, and still at other places he was found managing his finances. He was talking of battle with someone and peace treaties with others. There were, it shows, proper policies on battle and peace treaties executed between various rajas like what is done these days. It also shows the jobs of a raja—

(1) Dealing with other rajas—battles and peace treaties execution.
(2) Managing finances and treasuries.
(3) Discharging religions duties.
(4) Respecting rishis/guru etc.
(5) Arranging meals for brahmins and respecting them.
(6) Worshipping (God Krishna worshipped Shiva as his God and Shiva worshipped Krishna as his swami.)
(7) Enjoying the grihastha (गृहस्थ) life with his queens.
(8) Caring for the bringing up of his children. etc.

Shri Krishna told Narad that since he had to coach the religion to the universe, he himself had to act on that first. Narad was surprised to see all this but Krishna told him not to fall under the influence of Maya seeing the living of Krishna in Dwarka otherwise Krishna would have to redress the same as he had done when Narad felt proud of winning over kama.

Krishna used to get up early in the moving and leaving the queens got out of bed. Then remembered his three powers (शक्ति) Brahma, Vishnu and Rudra. Then took bath, performed pooja, yagya, hawan and Gayatri jap, paid respects to his elders and gods, arranged for the meals for brahmins, gave alms to them and then took his meals and started doing the Rajya jobs (राज्य कार्य), where he heard the difficulties of people of all varnas/his residents; discussed the matters with his advisers/mantris and prepared for battles etc., when necessary. Although there was strict security arrangement at the mahal but it seems everyone was allowed to get in and see Krishna after the gate keeper had obtained Krishna's permission. That is how even Sudama, an ordinary brahmin, was allowed to get in unlike present time where it is not only difficult but impossible to see the high authorities, ministers etc. This shows that protocolic formalities, although entirely observed, were not quite cumbersome. Krishna not only permitted the citizens to see him but he used to redress their grievances too.

Once one person came and complained that Jarasandha had been annoying the public, extracting money from them and harassing them. As already indicated, Jarasandha had attacked Krishna 18 times—each time raising a huge army which costed the exchequer a lot and, therefore, he had to raise money for that purpose. Jarasandha had also been harassing his vassals, to spare army to fight for him and pay for the expenses too. All such rajas, therefore, requested Krishna through this person to help them. At that, Narad too came there and Krishna after worshipping him as per normal protocol and making him sit comfortably, asked him about Pandvas. Narad told him that despite knowing everything, Krishna had asked him like an ordinary man. This shows that Krishna, as a king, had a vast net of spies, who kept him well informed about what was happening at various places. Likewise, Narad was his spy to give him the news of entire Brahmand (ब्रह्माण्ड). Narad told Krishna that Yudhisthra wanted to perform Ashwamedha yagya and, therefore, wished Krishna to be there in person. Krishna was in dual mind whether first to help Yudhisthra in performing Ashwamedha yagya or to fight with Jarasandha as per the request of many rajas. Krishna consulted his advisers to advise him as to which job should be done first. This shows that even the kings in those days were not autocrats but used to consult their advisors/mantries and all kings had such sabhas of mantris/ elders etc. with them. Even Raja Ravan had been frequently consulting his sabha people on the question of war with Ram. Dasratha had been consulting his sabha for all major decisions like Ram's coronation etc. Krishna's advisors had neither any biased opinion nor selfish interest to influence Krishna's views. Udhava, the great advisor, told Krishna that Yudhisthra had requested for Krishna's assistance in holding Ashwamedha yagya and so many rajas had requested him for subduing Jarasandha. Both purposes would be served if Yudhisthra is helped as, for Ashwamedha yagya, one has to administer his authority on all rajas, and Jarasandha would not accept such an authority, so a battle would take place in which only Bhima could defeat him as he is very brave. In this way helping Yudhisthra would serve both the purposes.

Such was the logical advice given by the mantries to Krishna. Krishna, Narad and all others consented to Udhava's advice, Krishna proceeded to Inderprastha along with his army. Since Krishna was going to join the Ashwamedha Yagya, his queens and sons too accompanied him. Narad was happy with Krishna's decision and went to his home. Krishna told the representatives of various rajas to tell them not to get frightened and Jarasandha would be eliminated soon. Yudhisthra was happy to know about Krishna's arrival. He, as per protocol, proceeded to receive him along with his brothers and other elders. Krishna was received with all honours—as a friend, a cousin and a raja. Both embraced each other and then similar embracing was followed by other brothers. On his side Krishna paid respects to gurus, brahmins etc,. who had come to receive him. The streets and roads of Inderprastha had been duly decorated for the occasion and people were standing on both sides of roads/streets and ladies were at the top of their homes to welcome Krishna. Many persons presented costly things to Krishna on the high way. Kunti embraced Krishna; Daropadi paid her respects etc. Krishna was honoured, and worshipped in raj mahal and was made comfortable in the appropriate suite in the mahal along with all his queens, and their attendants. Yudhisthra expressed his desire to perform Ashwamedha yagya. Ashwamedha yagya was performed by Chakarvarty Raja with a view to establish his sovereignty over other rajas. A horse was sent around all countries. If any one caught the horse, he was to be given a fighting and after defeating the holder the horse resumed further journey. If the holder was not defeated, then the yagya was not performed. One, therefore, had to properly assess his strength before resorting to such yagya. Krishna agreed to the suggestion given by Yudhisthra. All brothers thereafter set off for conquering various rajas. The brothers, besides conquering and making all rajas so conquered as their vassals, brought a lot of wealth from them as presents as per vassalage laws for incurring expenditure on the yagya. There was, however, one king Jarasandha, who did not submit to Yudhisthra. Yudhisthra, therefore, was upset over it. Krishna knew that Jarasandha could be defeated by Bhima only in dual battle (wrestling). So Krishna along with Arjun and Bhima went to Jarasandha as brahmins and begged for something. These asur kings too had their principles, one being that they could give anything in donation to a beggar :

किं दुर्मर्ष तितिक्षूणां किमकार्यमसाधुभिः,
किं न देयं वदान्यानां कः परः समदर्शिनाम्। (10-72-19)

The brahmins told Jarasandha that there was nothing. which a donor could not give. Jarasandha recognised them as kshatriyas and not brahmins from their voice, and the signs of operating arrow and bow on their hands. He however, did not question it since the beggars were brahmins so far as he was concerned. He, being in the dynasty of Raja Bali, could give anything to the beggars. He told Krishna etc. to ask for anything including his head. Such were the donors in India at that time and such was the hospitability of the guests even as strangers. Then Krishna disclosed that they were not brahmins but kshatriyas and had come to ask for dual fight with him. Being a brave man Jarasandha told that dual battle could be amongst the equals as per laws of war indicating that there were such detailed laws of war in those days and these were complied with even by rakshasas. He said Krishna had already fled from the battlefield, so he was out from the fight and Arjun being very weak was not a match for him. So only Bhima could fight. The fighting started and continued for several days as neither was prepared to yield. Ultimately Bhima got discouraged and wanted to yield when Krishna tempted him to continue fighting. Krishna picked up a branch of the tree and tore it through and through meaning thereby that Bhima should tear off Jarasandha through legs as otherwise he could not be killed because of some boon he had earned. Now such a thing could not be openly said as per laws of war but Krishna made Bhima understand symbolically. Bhima acted accordingly and so killed Jarasandha. As per tradition/protocol at that time after conquering a raja, the kingdom was not taken over by the conquerer but handed over to the defeated raja's successor and (1) he was made a vassal and (2) he paid a lot of wealth and other things like elephants, horses etc. as compensation/present to the conquering raja. It was only during the late Hindu rulers and in Muslims and English period that the conqueror started ruling the conquered kingdom himself or through his viceroy/ lieutenant. Krishna coronated Jarasundha's son Sehdeva on the throne and all the rajas in his captivity, were released; their kingdoms returned to them and they were bade farewel to take over their kingdoms with many presents. Of course they all became vassals of Yudhisthra as per law. The released rajas praised Krishna as the almighty and requested for his bhakti. Krishna acceded to their request. Krishna then returned to Indraprastha. Yudhisthra was happy that now he would be able to accomplish the yagya. They were received in Indraprastha with all honours designed to receive a conqueror king.

After consulting Krishna, Yudhisthra invited great rishis like Vashista, Vyas, Gautam, Kunava, Maitreya, Parsuram, Shukracharya, Daronacharya, Kripacharya, Bhishma, Dharitrashtra, Duryodhan, all rajas of the country, their mantries, and all brahmins, kshatriyas, vaishyas and shudras of his kingdom to perform/take part in the yagya:

ब्रह्मणाः क्षत्रिया वैश्याः शूद्रा यज्ञदिदृक्षवः,
तत्रेयुः सर्वराजानो राज्ञां प्रकृतयो नृप। (10-74-11)

This shows that such yagyas were not restricted to the invitation of rajas to establish one's sovereignty over others but also a rejoicing for the people of the kingdom or in other words democracy/will of the people/well-wishes of the people were always in play in the kingdom, although it was a monarchical regime. Even the gods (including Brahma and Shankar) attended the yagya. Since in the yagya, all gods were worshipped and their part of the hawan taken out, possibly all gods had come to take their respective part of the hawan/yagya. The yagya was got conducted by the rishis with proper pooja etc. A question arose as to who should be worshipped first and a unanimous decision was not possible. Then Sehdeva, suggested Krishna, who was the overall lord of all gods, be worshipped first. This suggestion was accepted by all as all gods and infact the entire universe was part of Krishna himself; he being the incarnate of Vishnu. Yudhisthra, along with his brothers, wife (Daropadi), minsters, and other family members then worshipped Krishna as per vedic system, presenting him valuable dresses, ornaments etc. Shishupal too was there. He had been listening to the praise of Krishna. He could not tolerate it and started abusing Krishna. He also condemned the decision taken to worship Krishna first as Krishna was from a mean dynasty without any varan or ashram or kingdom as such. Krishna continued listening to all abuses as Krishna had given an undertaking to Shishupal's mother that he would excuse him upto one hundred abuses and nothing more. The others present there were feeling embarrassed to listen Krishna being abused and requested Krishna to annihilate him but still Krishna kept quiet and went on counting the abuses and also checked Pandvas and other kings from attacking Shishupal as Krishna only wanted to kill him after he had abused Krishna hundred times. Krishna then killed Shishupal with his chakra. His followers ran away from there. Shishupal, having been killed by Krishna, attained Paramgati. The yagya was thereafter finished with all vedic rites and Krishna, with permission of Yudhisthra, left for Dwarka alongwith his queens and others. All gods too went to their respective lokas. All rajas were happy on the accomplishment of the yagya, except Duryodhan, who, because of his jealous nature and being, full of vices, could not tolerate Pandavas performing Ashwamedh yagya.

दुर्योधनमृते पापं कलिं कुरुकुलामयम,
यो न सेहेश्रियं स्फीतां दृष्टवा पाण्डुसुतस्य ताम्। (10-75-53)

In fact it is this family jealousy which ultimately led to the Mahabharat and killing of lakhs of people, including all Kaurvas.

In the yagya, all family members, including Pandavas, Kaurvas and others, had been entrusted with different jobs viz Bhima was looking after food, Duryodhan was treasurer, Sehdeva received all guests, Arjun served all rishis, gurus etc and so on. This shows the systematic division of various jobs in the kingdom existing at that time like the present day distribution in various ministries/departments etc. Donations and alms were given to all brahmins, beggars and others as per their wishes. Yudhisthra honoured all present in the yagya, including all brahmins, kshatriyas, vaishyas and shudras. Here the equality of people of all varnas has been established by indicating participation of persons of all varnas in all important state functions and equality in honouring them.

During the course of the function, as already stated, Duryodhan was very jealous of Pandavas' escalating image, and the beautiful and luxurious mahal constructed by Pandavas in Indraprastha where all Pandavas with Daropadi and Krishna with his queens stayed. One day when Yudhisthra was on the sinhasan, Duryodhan came there with his brothers. He was so much enraged because of jealousy that he had been rebuking all security men etc. The construction in the mahal was such that there seemed water on dry places and dry where water was flowing. Duryodhan, blind in rage, could not differentiate the factual position. He became wet and fell in water where he thought there was dry place and arranged his clothes to pass through dry places where he thought there was water. All rajas laughed although Yudhisthra checked them. Duryodhan felt insulted and leaving the Sabha, he went to Hastinapur in rage. This further created the differences and Duryodhan's rage against Pandavas. Here the Pandavas had also acted in an unprotoclic way as Duryodhan, being their honoured guest, should have been escorted at all such places comfortally and not allowed to become a matter of laughter. Having failed here, they should not have laughed on Duryodhan's folly as Yudhisthra knowing all protocol rightly checked them from doing so. The Pandavas, therefore, had to pay for it having had to face Daropadi's insult in Kaurvas' Sabha and Pandavas having to live in forests for many years due to their having been defeated by Kaurvas in gambling.

When Krishna had gone to Indraprastha in the Ashwamedha yagya and had killed Shishupal there, Shishupal's friend Shalva attacked Dwarka after obtaining in boon a plane which could be carried anywhere as per wish and which could accommodate the entire army. Although the writer has attributed this plane having been given in boon by Shiva but it indicates the technological development in that period. Such planes/rockets were available in those days confirms that in Krishna period too such planes would have been in existence, which operated electronically through remote control. Krishna's son Pradyuman came to face Shalva, along with his brothers and army. Fierce fighting took place and Pradyuman annihilated most of Shalva's army but Shalva, knowing the art of appearing and disappearing, could not be traced. Then one of the commanders of Shalva attacked Pradyuman, who fell unconscious. His sarthy brought him out of the battle field. When Pradyuman became conscious, he found himself away from the battle field. He rebuked his sarthy as to why he brought him from the battle field as running away from the battle field was a curse for an kshatriya and he had no face to show to Balram and Shri Krishna. But the sarthy told him the dharma of the sarthy, according to which he had to save the life of the raja. As per law, in time of difficulty, the raja should protect sarthy and vice versa. So he had done nothing wrong in having brought him away from the battle field. Our shastras had laid down even the dharma of sarthi and others in the battle field.

धर्मं विजानताऽऽयुष्मन् कृतमेतन्मया विभो,
सूतः कृच्छ्रगतं रक्षेद् रथिनं सारथिं रथी।

Pradyumen then went back to battle field and started fighting with same commander and killed him. Meantime Krishna returned from Inderprastha and went straight to the battle field. Fierce fighting took place with Shalva, particularly because of his illusive (मायावी) tactics. These tactics, as also a rumour was spread by him that Krishna's father Vasudeva had been kidnapped by Shalva. Although Krishna knew the fact that it was only a rumour but acted and expressed sadness like an ordinary man. Then Shalva brought an artificial Vasudeva and killed him before Krishna. Krishna again expressed sadness like an ordinary human being and then removed the influence of maya resulting in the artificial Vasudeva vanishing. Krishna then, in the fierce fighting, killed Shalva. After Shishupal and Shalva had been killed, their friend Dantvaktara attacked on Krishna with a gada (गदा) in his hands. Krishna too climbed down from the chariot as Dantvaktara was on foot and as per laws of war, the battle had to be on equal footing. At first Dantvaktara attacked but Krishna was not effected. Then Krishna attacked on Dantvaktara and he died. Having been killed by Krishna, he got salvation. Here too the writer has emphasised on the fulfilment of laws of war by all the warrior kings/rajas.

Krishna and Balram had come incarnate in the universe to establish dharma, protect rishis, sadhus etc. and annihilate rakshasas. After many rakshasas had been killed, Balram once went out of Dwarka to meet the rishis. He visited many Tiratha places and met many rishis. The rishis knew Balram was the incarnate of Sesha. Therefore, as per protocol, Balram worshipped the rishis and rishis in turn gave blessings as also they respected Balram as the incarnate of Sesha. In Vyas Muni's ashram, Balram saw Romharshan, a person of mean varan sitting on muni's stage (आसन). Seeing Balram, who was a raja, Romharshan neither got up from the asan nor respected him. Balram felt it as insult as also the person of mean varan sitting on Muni Vyas's asan was considered wrong. Although having come for tirathayatra, he should not have got enraged and resorted to killing anyone as per tenets of tiratha-yatras, Balram could not tolerate this wrong action by a mean person because if a person assuming to be preaching dharma does not himself observe the tenets of dharma, he is apt to be killed by the raja.

एतदर्थो हि लोकेऽस्मिन्नवतारो मया कृतः,
वध्या मे धर्मध्वजिनस्ते हि पातकिनोऽधिकाः। (10-78-27)

He therefore killed him. Subsequently the rishis came and told Balram that Romharshan did not occupy Vyas Muni's asan of his own but by approval of all rishis as he had been a disciple of Vyas Muni and had learnt all dharma shastras, vedas etc. Having read all these shastras, he had attained brahminship with the approval of other rishis and as such had to be considered as such and his having been killed is a sin for which Balram should resort to repentence. This proves (1) Although there was the institution of varan dharma and everyone was supposed to be complying with the tenets of his dharma, yet there could be exceptions, where even a person of mean varan could improve his varan by virtue of his actions and capability as in Ram period Nishad (a shudra) had become Ram's friend and again Sabri had attained salvation being Rambhakta. Vishwamitra, a kshatriya had become brahmrishi by virtue of his tapasya. So Romharsan too had improved his varna (2) Once a person had improved his varan and recognised as such within persons of the improved varan, he had to be treated as such by others. Romharsan having attained capability of brahmin dharma and having been recognised as such by the rishis, Balram was bound to treat him as a brahmin and his killing was treated as brahamhatya (ब्रह्महत्या) (3) Accordingly, Balram was obliged to resort to repentence for the brahmhatya. As a repentence, Balram created Romharsan's son with the same capability and ability to preach amongst the rishis. The rishis accepted this repentence. (4) So even the rajas had to face the punishment inflicted by rishis on a wrong done by them. Such was the 'Rule of Law' in those days.

During his tiratha yatra, Balram also killed another rakshas Balwal, who had been harrassing the rishis. The rishis were very happy on his killing and blessed Balram with their ashirwad. In this way worshipping rishis and worshipped by rishis, as suited to each occasion, Balram met many rishis and completed his tiratha yatra. The writer has mentioned various rivers of India and various tiratha-places, which stand geographically confirmed even today indicative of full geographical knowledge in those days. In this way Balram passed all his time of Mahabharat in tiratha yatra as he did not want to fight in favour or against either Pandavas or Kauravas in Mahabharat. Balram came to Kurukshetra the battle field of Mahabharat, on the day when Bhima and Duryodhan were to have their fighting. All Pandavas and Krishna bowed before Balram, honoured and respected him. Without interfering in the battle, Balram returned to Dwarka. In a situation where a raja is not able to decide in favour or against any one, then it is better not to take part in such a battle. Even today in the voting in Parliament on a 'no confidence motion', a party which does not want to vote in favour or against the government, abstains, although indirectly it is a help to the government as government has to obtain majority of the members present and voting. Balram too being absent from the battle field, helped each party as anyone of the two parties on whose side, he would have fought, the other would have been a loser. So this was like the Non-alignment strategy of the present day.

Krishna was great brahmin bhakta and a sincere friend. This is evident from his meeting with Sudama. The meeting has been an instance of protocol between friends and a brahmin and kshatriya. Sudama was a brahmin. He was quite poor and was not able to afford even meals for himself and his family. Having suffered because of poverty, Sudama's wife once requested him to go and see Krishna, his friend, as he was the king to Dwarka and his small kindness could better their life. Sudama was a man of ego. He did not want to go to beg for something from Krishna. But ultimately he yielded. Now, as per protocol, some present had to be offered to a friend or a raja, when one meets him. Sudama's wife brought some rice (चिउड़ा) from a neighbour and gave it to him. When Sudama reached Dwarka, he found it to be a great town flourishing with all luxuries. He reached Krishna's mahal and the gate keeper informed Krishna of Sudama's arrival. Sudama was a very poor man and when he went to Krishna, he was not properly clad and was quite in a mess. Today none will permit such a person to reach nearer to the residence of President/Prime Minister, what to speak of his meeting him. But it appears in those days even an ordinary person could meet the raja for the redressal of his grivence. Krishna immediately went to receive Sudama. He embraced him and made him sit on his sinhasan. He himself worshipped Sudama, made him take bath, washed his feet and took the charnamrit (च्रणामृत), decorated him, dressed him well and made him comfortable after serving meals etc. Then they started talking of their student days. Krishna praised Sudama saying that he was one, who did not indulge in worldly luxuries and was free from all passions. Krishna remembered their past days in Gurukul. He said father is the first guru for any person, then the teacher is second guru and the third guru is one who coaches the person to attain salvation. Krishna even told that he is present in the last guru. Therefore, whatever he coaches is as per his inspiration as a guru. One, who, even passing through the institution of varna-ashramas, is able to know him, he is the real bhakta.

नन्वर्थकोविदा ब्रह्मन् वर्णाश्रमवतामिह,
ये मया गुरुणा वाचातरन्त्यंजो भवार्णवम्। (10-80-33)

Guru makes the person a learned man. Therefore, one should not feel shy in submission of his complete self to his cause. After a day's stay, Krishna asked Sudama if he had brought some present for him (Krishna knew Sudama had brought something but was hesitant in offering the small present to such a great raja). Krishna, therefore, reassured him that even a small thing, offered with affection, was more valued than a valuable thing offered without any affection, Krishna then took the pack of rice and ate with enjoyment. Krishna also thought that Sudama was his friend and then he had never expected wealth in consideration of his pooja.He therefore, deserved to be helped. Krishna, without telling him, sent a lot at his residence. Sudama after a few days left Dwarka. On the way he had been praising Krishna's character, his behaviour in meeting him so warmly and so on. He had, however, been thinking that Krishna had not given him anything and as such the purpose of his visit to Dwarka was not fulfilled, except that he could meet the almighty God, Krishna. He reached his place and found a big mahal constructed there. He saw his wife duly decorated with valuable clothes and ornaments and a big fully furnished mahal. He and his wife were full of praise for Krishna. This is how Krishna gave so much to a friend without even mentioning about what he had given.

Once at the time of a solar eclipse, all rajas, Brijwasi and other people had gathered in Kurukshetra to take bath at the time of eclipse. Krishna too went there with his queens. There Krishna met all rajas, who were surprised to see Krishna in such a luxurious way with his queens. This was a tradition in India that at tiratha places, one used to forget all friendship and enmity and treated everyone as equal. Krishna met all rajas, his friends as well as enemies, and was received well by all. Then Krishna came to know that Nand and Yashoda had also come. He went to meet them with Devki and Vasudeva. Nand, Yashoda, Devki and Vasudeva met with respect for each other and embraced each other. Then Devki and Vasudeva praised Nand and Yashoda in having helped them at the time, when Krishna was born and they were in jail. Bringing up a child is a tremendous task and one could not evaluate it in monetary terms. Krishna and Balram too bowed before Nand and Yashoda. They took them in their lap and embraced them as usual for a father and a mother. Krishna came to know that gopis had also come there. Krishna met them in isolation and preached them all about Brahmgyan (ब्रह्मज्ञान). They out of deep love for Krishna, got themselves fully absorbed in Krishna and only requested to be given a boon that they always remained so absorbed in Krishna.

As already indicated, all rajas, their queens and rishis etc. had collected at Kurushetra on the occasion of the solar eclipse, and all had been meeting each other. Such occasions have been created in Hindus to enable all people to meet their relations, friends and foes forgeting all their enmities etc. as at such places, all are treated equally. Ladies had been meeting ladies. Daropadi met the wives of Krishna and enquired from each of them how she had been married with Krishna. Basically all stated that they had wished to have Krishna as their husband and Krishna fulfilled that desire. On that occasion all rishis (Vashist, Valmiki, Atri, Gautam, Narad etc., also came to meet Krishna as inspite of Krishna's human being character, they knew he was overall Lord incarnate of Vishnu. Krishna welcomed them as rishis, washed their feet, gave them cows etc. in donation and fed them properly and then made them sit comfortably. Shri Krishna appreciated/praised the rishis. He said that the water places were not the only tiratha places, and the idols were not the only gods, it is the saints, who infact are the actual tirathaas, because one have to go to tirthas at various places to earn some virtues (पुण्य) and the same virtues can be had by darshan of sadhus/rishis/saints :

न ह्यम्मयानि तीर्थानि न देवा मृच्छिलामयाः,

ते पुनन्त्युरुकालेन दर्सादेव साधवः। (10-84-11)

All the rishis heard Krishna quietly and thought that although Krishna is incarnate of almighty God yet he had been acting as an ordinary man for the consumption of the people at large as huge gathering had accumulated at that place. Then rishis too praised Krishna as God. They too in their turn bowed before Krishna as God. This is the reciprocal protocol followed by rishis and Krishna (as an ordinary man and as God).

"नमस्तस्मै भवगते कृष्णायाकुण्ठमेधसे।" (10-84-22)

They appreciated their luck to have been able to meet Krishna, the God. They said they were his bhaktas and requested for being kind to them, as such kindness can be attained only by complete submission towards Krishna.

Then Krishna's father Vasudeva came to the rishis and requested for telling a way through which salvation could be attained. Rishis were surprised over Krishna's father asking them for such advice but then they realised that he had been considering Krishna as his son (child only) and such advice had to be sought from a guru only and not from the child even though he might be incarnate of God. As such Vasudeva had first followed the normal protocol of requesting the rishis for an advice. The rishi too took it in that stride and advised him that the best way for a grihastha (गृहस्थ) of brahmin, kshatriya and vaish varnas is worshipping the God by using his hard earned (न्यायजित) wealth. The man should leave the worldly attractions by utilising the wealth in alms and donations and the fulfilment of ambition of wife and sons by following grihastha dharma. In this way after one has got absolved of the worldly passions, even while living in the universe, one should proceed to forest for tapasya and in this way one could attain salvation. The man is born with some obligation and this obligation is discharged by at first studies in brahmcharya ashram, producing children in grihastha ashram and by resorting to yagya etc. in vanprastha and sanyas ashramas. Vasudeva having already finished the obligations of brahamcharya and grihastha ashramas held several yagyas to discharge the obligations of sanyas ashram. He gave alms/donations to rishis, brahmins and beggars and devoted to Vishnu bhakti. Subsequently the Pandavas, Dharitrastra, Guru Daron, Kunti, Vyas muni etc. met the Yadvas and embraced each other. Then Krishna, Balram and Ugarsen honoured and gave many costly presents to Nand, and other gopis and gwalas. Then presents were given to all the Brijwasis separately by Vasudeva, Ugrasen, Krishna, Balram etc. With these presents, the Brijwasis departed for Brij. It is a protocol for the wealthy persons to give costly presents to the poorer relatives as a mark of respect/honour (may be to help them financially).

Since Vasudeva had learnt from the rishis that Krishna and Balram were incarnations of God, one day he addressed them as such and praised them. There is nothing new in it. Even Dashratha could not attain salvation on death as he had died having in his mind the affection of his sons and a biased mind against Kaikayee. A person does not attain salvation unless he is absolved of all attachments. So for fulfilling that purpose, he came and worshipped Ram as God after Ram had killed Ravan. After that only he got absorbed in Ram bhakti and attained salvation. Here too Vasudeva had to recognise Krishna and Balram as incarnations of God with a view to attain the finality. He, therefore, praised them saying they were the over all lords of the universe and were omnipresent.

All the human beings are influenced by his maya only and they attain salvation only after they get rid of the influence of maya and get absorbed in God. Devki was also there. She had learnt that Krishna had brought back the late son of the guru. Devki too after praising him asked him to bring her dead sons. Krishna and Balram went to Yamraj Lok. Yamraj honoured them; worshipped them; fed them properly and made them sit on sinhasan and praised them. Krishna then told Yamraj that Devki wanted to see her children, who were killed by Kansa. Yamraj gave them the children. Krishna and Balram came to Dwarka with the children. Devki was happy to see them. She loved them and hugged them immensely. The children paid respects to Devki and Vasudeva and then went to their lokas. The writer has mentioned such incidents with a view to emphasise on the fact that (1) There was freely coming and going to all stars in those days. Such visits were possible, is proved by having sent rockets to several stars today. (2) It is confirmed that the atma never dies and it rests at its place after death either in Yamloka or in the form/specie awarded, as per deeds. (3) It was possible to even bring the atmas (आत्मा) from Yamloka (यमलोक) to earth and vice-versa (4) means of transport were such as could traverse between various stars.

Kidnapping of the girls (brides) was very common amongst the rajas in those days. This would indicate and confirm the theory of 'might is right.' But apart from the might part of it, such kidnapping was generally with the consent of the brides—either bride would send a message to the groom of the liking as Rukmani had sent to Krishna or somehow express her feelings for marrying a particular boy. Therefore, when the kidnapping is through consent, it is strictly not kidnapping but getting away with the groom. Similar had been the case of Sabhadra's marriage with Arjun. They loved each other but Sabhadra's one brother Balram wanted her to be married to Duryodhan whereas Krishna wanted the marriage with Arjun. Arjun came to Dwarka as a yogi and Vasudeva as usual worshipped and entertained him as such. He saw Sabhadra there and fell in love. Sabhadra too fell in love with the yogi and expressed her desire for marriage. Once when Sabhadra had gone to worship in the temple, Arjun took her away defeating the escorts. Since it was with the consent of Krishna, he somehow managed to pacify Balram too. After that Balram sent a lot of dowry in marriage in token of his acceptance of the union of Sabhadra and Arjun.

As already stated, Krishna had come as incarnation of God to annihilate the rakshasas and as a matter of spiritual protocol with persons of this universe help sadhus/ rishis attaining salvation after his darshan. Krishna's battles with various asur rajas has already been described. In the extent of visit to bhaktas once Krishna proceeded to visit various places of his bhaktas along with several rishis including Narad. Ved Vyas, Vamdeva, Atri, Maitreya, etc. In this voyage, Krishna covered Anart, Dhanava, Kurukshetra, Matasya, Panchal, Madhu, Kaikeye, Kaushal, Arna etc i.e. almost all countries of Southern, Eastern and Northern India. Wherever they went, they were immensely entertained and worshipped. They reached Mithila, the kingdom of raja Videh (विदेह). All the residents were very happy. They had heard of the visit of Ram to that town in Tretayug and now a repeat visit by Krishna was very much enjoyed by them. The raja of Mithila, Bahulasva and Shrutdeva, a brahmin bowed before Krishna as incarnate of God and other rishis accompanying him. They both invited them to their houses. Krishna made his dual forms and went to both the places to please them both but they could not know this mystry. Each thought Krishna had come to his house as was the case with his queens too. They honoured and entertained Krishna in the best possible way by washing the feet and taking the charnamirat, giving him costly presents, and making him comfortable. They, after that, praised Krishna. They were both lost and absorbed in his thoughts and said that the people get rid of all their worries with Krishna's darshan :

एतदन्तो नृणां क्लेशो यद् भवानक्षिगोचरः। (10-86-49)

Krishna told them that he and the rishis were happy with their bhakti and had, therefore, to comply with their part of job in visiting them in their houses. Krishna told Shrutdeva, a brahmin that brahmin was superior to all beings from birth itself and if he resorts to studies, tapasya, pooja and is content, then he is at the top. Krishna loved the brahmins even more than his ownself. Therefore, brahmins are the God's formations in a way and are to be respected as such. This shows that like the bhaktas worshipping and honouring Bhagwan, Bhagwan too is under the control of the bhaktas. To please his bhaktas, Krishna stayed in Mithila for several days and then returned to Dwarka.

Brahma (God) is above all deeds and doings. One can neither explain him with speech or by indications. On the other hand, the vedas explain the abstract, including the formation, doings and traditions. Then how can vedas be said to be explaining Nirguna (निर्गुण) Brahma. God is almighty and have all objects and the vedas narrate this form only but while one goes deep into the narration, one finds god as Nirguna (without any form). God has blessed the human beings with intelligence, heart, senses and the life. By these only he attains dharma (धर्म), wealth (अर्थ), satisfaction of senses (काम) and salvation (मोक्ष). By using the senses and intellegence in earning satoguna (सत्वगुण) rajoguna (रजोगुण) and tamoguna (तमोगुण). With satoguna, he attains dharma and salvation; with rajoguna the wealth and with tamoguna, he indulges in the satisfaction of worldly desires and of senses. Once the person absorbs himself in God by satoguna, he crosses the limit of God in form (सगुण) and reaches the Nirguna Bhagwan. This is what is preached by vedas too. This is like the raja after having slept for the night is awakened by a group of bards by singing songs in appreciation of raja. God too sleeps after assimilating the entire universe within himself and the vedas through appreciative slokas awaken him saying that the entire universe is influenced by his 'Maya' and without his mercy cannot get rid of the same. Even the vedas, which are able to explain Indra, Varuna, Kuber etc. as per their forms are not able to explain God as he does not have a particular form and after explaining some of the forms have to say "There is no end," "There is no end" (नेति, नेति) and that makes the Saguna God as a Nirguna one and whatever one thinks of, hears of, sees or speaks of, is God in one form of the other. The human beings, therefore, can only devote themselves to the cause of almighty, remember him and act according to their dharma to attain salvation. For this purpose, the persons of different thinking, remember the God of their belief but ultimately all reach him only. This perpetuates the theory that God is one and all beliefs lead to that one. He can only be had by jap, tap, yagya, havan, kirtan etc. as per one's way, and once one gets absorbed in him, he is away from the influence of his maya and accordingly gets rid of the love/ affection of wife, children, wealth and worldly attachments.

भजतां हि भवान साक्षात्परमानन्दचिद्धनः
आत्मैव किमतः कृत्यं तुच्छदारसुतादिभिः । (10-87-14)

One, who has known God, is above any influence of good or bad deeds, happiness and sadness and remains steady in either and always thinks of God only. The writer has made the Brahma's son Sanad say all this in appreciation of God with a view to see that the people believe it and start thinking of getting absorbed in him. He can then realise the self and the God (आत्मा और परमात्मा). All the rishis felt obliged to Narayan to have awakened them. They bowed before Narayan and went to their respective places.

Worship of each of the gods, Shiva, Brahma and Vishnu, gives their own rewards such as Shiva, who is above all luxuries, rewards his worshipper with wealth and other wordly luxuries, while Vishnu, who is the husband of Laxmi herself, does not bestow wealth and other luxuries. He rather snatches the same wherever one is owing them. This appears self contradictory. The possible reason for this is that Shiva and other gods are always with their powers and by virute of having those powers, bestow the desired wealth etc. on the bhakta, when pleased on him, whereas the almighty God is above all these powers, and virtues and anyone worshipping almighty God, becomes part of him and hence should not require any such virtues/ wealth etc. Further, God considers that his bhakta should not be influenced by his maya once absorbed in him and since God sees that the bhakta is not influenced by 'maya', he withdraws all such attachments and bestows on him the attainment of salvation. Since there can possibly be one attainment only—either the attainment of worldly belongings or the salvation—the other gods and Shiva bestow on their bhaktas the worldly attainments, whereas the almighty God bestows the attainment of salvation. Hence the difference in the rewards by all gods, by Shiva and Vishnu.

For this purpose, Krishna told that he withdraws the wealth from his bhaktas and then all his relatives leave him. He again tries to have wealth but again fails. Ultimately he becomes averse to having wealth and then gets attracted to his bhakti and it is then that the almighty God bestows his mercy on him and consequently he attains the ownership of all wealths i.e. salvation. Attainment of wealth has no limits but after attainment of salvation, wealth has no meaning, even in a limited way. Brahma, Vishnu and Mahadeva, all are capable of sanctioning boons. Brahma and Mahadeva gets pleased easily as also gets displeased easily and so sanctions boons or curses too easily, whereas Vishnu is hard to be pleased and once pleased, the incumbent becomes his part perpetually. That is how Shiva and Brahma, without thinking of long term repurcussions of granting any boon, sanction the same and when the incumbent tries to exploit the same and harrasses the mankind then only Vishnu comes to rescue by undoing the effect of the boon. Hirnakashyap, Ravan, Banasura Vrikasura etc are the examples, who got boons from Brahma and Shiva and those had to be undone by Vishnu as Narsingha, Ram and Krishna or Vishnu himself. Also once a question arose amongst rishis as to who of the Brahma, Vishnu and Mahesh was the greatest. Bhrigu Rishi was entrusted with this job. He went to Brahma first and rebuked him. He got enraged but, subsequently finding Bhrigu his son got pacified. Then he went to Shiva and rebuked him. He also got enraged and ran to kill Bhrigu but then Parvati checked and pacified him. Bhrigu then went to Vishnu and kicked him. Vishnu got hold of Bhrigu's feet and massaged them lest the same had been injured. So Bhrigu could decide Vishnu as the greatest, having the maximum patience and respect for brahmins.

In this way, the order of precedence was established by the sabha of rishis even amongst the Gods. Krishna was the incarnation of Vishnu. He also performed many lilas (लीला) in the universe in the discharge of his aims of annihilation of rakshasas and protection of sadhus. One such act was taking Arjun to Vishnu Lok to find the dead children of a Brahmin, who had held Krishna responsible for the same as it was in his kingdom that such deaths had taken palce. In a dharma established rajya,the children donot die when parents are alive; rains take place in time, harvests never fail; no one falls chronically sick etc. Krishna lived in the universe like ordinary persons as Ram too had lived, enjoyed all luxuries of worldly life and performed many yagyas and killed all asuras.

इतीदृशान्यनेकानि वीर्याणीह प्रदर्शयन्,
बुभुजे विषयान् ग्राम्यानीजे चात्यूर्जितैर्मखैः। (10-89-64)

Shri Krishna had adopted grihastha life to show other people in the universe that even as a grihastha one could lead a life as per dharma deciphered by vedas for a grihastha and in this way one could attain dharma, wealth and satisfaction of senses (धर्म, अर्थ और काम). Only one achievement left is salvation (मोक्ष), which could he achieved by following sanyas.

Krishna had been living with his 16,108 queens and doing justice to all so far as the matrimony was concerned. Krishna had been doing it by converting himself in as many forms but for the ordinary grihastha of the universe, one should have only such number of wives, as one can do justice to, that is why Ram had established the rule of one wife after seeing that his father Dasratha had to suffer and give up his life because of multiplicity oif wives. Krishna got ten sons from each queen. As already indicated, the need for Krishna to have so many queens was also in view of the fact that to enable him to annihilate so many rakshas rajas and their armies, Krishna required a force of brave worriors. So Krishna could achieve this objective with the help of his over one lakh sons, who constituted his army. In fact the sons of Krishna were all gods, who, after Krishna's jobs were accomplished, vanished fighting amongst themselves and went to their respective places as they had come to assist Krishna in the fulfilment of his job of annihilation of rakshasas. Gods had come as vanaras to assist Ram in fighting aginst rakshasas of Lanka.

Skandh – XI

As already indicated, Krishna with the help of his sons and grandsons had been able to annihilate all rakshas rajas and their armies. They had fetched lot of wealth from the kingdoms of defeated rajas and had dumped the same in Dwarka. As a natural phenomina, the sons and grandsons of Krishna, because of excess of wealth, started leading very luxurious life and had started indulging in several misdeeds. Krishna started feeling anxious about them. They were so brave that they could not be conquered by any king or god. Therefore, only possible way found out by Krishna was that they should fight within themselves and kill each other. Krishna, being almighty God is above all love and affection for the children and is, therefore, above the influence of maya, which is his own creation otherwise he would not have been able to kill any being as all were his creation only and were his sons only. He could, therefore, take such a drastic decision. He thought he could peacefully go to his Dham after they all had been killed too and with their remaining alive, Krishna's full task would not have been over.

One day a few of the sons of Krishna had gone out of the town. There they saw many rishis sitting. They made one of Shri Krishna's sons Samba, a lady and went to the rishis to ask whether that pregnant lady would give birth to a male or a female child. The rishis, after knowing the correct position, told that she would give birth to a stone, which shall annihilate the dynasty. Krishna's sons got frightened. On coming to Dwarka, they told whatever had happened, to Ugrasen, the raja. Ugrasen thought the curse passed by brahmins would not go waste. He got hold of the stone, which came out from Samba's abdomen and broke it into pieces and threw them in the sea. One piece was eaten by a fish and the others came at sea shore and some grass grew out of the pieces. The pieces recovered from the fish was put by a hunter on his arrow. Same arrow subsequently killed Shri Krishna.

Once Narad told Vasudeva that Bhagwat dharma was such that grants salvation to a person, who listens, speaks, or remembers and follows :

श्रुतोऽनुपठितो ध्यात आदृतो वानुमोदितः,
सद्यः पुनाति सद्धर्मो देव विश्वद्रुहोऽपि हि। (11-2-12)

Bhagwad bhakti is best attained by satsang.

संसारेऽस्मिन् क्षणार्धोऽपि सत्संगः शेवधिर्नृणाम्। (11-2-30)

However, no method of Bhagwad bhagti can precisely be narrated, except to speak/think/listen to God's leelas through satsang or otherwise. Then a person rises above the worldly passions and gets lost in the memory of God, who is available in all mortal and immortal substances. Such a person is not happy on getting the ambitions fulfilled and also not very distressed on the results being against. Such a person can only be above the influence of Bhagwad maya, otherwise his maya does not leave even the great yogis from its influence. The form of maya is inexplicable. It is the power of the almighty, through which he monitors the deeds of all the beings performed by the senses existing in the gods, human beings and other creatures. The being acts as per the senses within himself and then starts depending on the ingredients of his body and considers the body only as all in all for him. This is Bhagwad maya. The being remains indulged in the worldly performances thinking this as the aim of his life. It is only when the senses donot help the being in getting the desired deeds done, that the being looks towards the power controlling these senses *i.e.*. The 'atma' and realisation of atma leads to belief in almighty and subsequent absorption in God. But the human being tied with his worldly relations—wife, children, wealth etc,—tries to find happiness within these but gets contrary results. He gets cornered by distress and then realises their relation as farce and turns in search of real happiness. He has to find a guru for this purpose and on enlightenment by the guru, starts absorbing himself in God by listening to his lilas, (लीला) and his action as Brahma for creation; as Vishnu for bringing up and maintenance and ultimately as Shiva for the annihilation of the creatures. Once one has realised the three powers, one is able to submit to the cause of the almighty.

As already indicated, God comes as incarnation in the universe to annihilate rakshasas and establish dharma. He has come many times but a few of the important incarnations may be mentioned as the incarnations are a protocolic link between the human beings and God. The formations and virtues of God cannot be enumerated. Even vedas end up in saying 'नेति' 'नेति', 'There is no end'. He at first created the universe by five elements, earth (पृथ्वी), water (जल) air (वायु) fire (अग्नि) and space (आकाश). Then he created human beings and other creatures with the help of these elements. Man is made of these elements and on his death, each element gets assimilated in the respective parent element. Apart from these five elements, which go into the making of the body, the immortal part in it is life (आत्मा). This is part of God (परमात्मा) himself and on death, it reports back to him. God on the basis of his karmas (कर्म), decides, which next form be allotted to that life and so on. This cycle goes on till the man attains salvation.

Now if one starts misusing the body and harrasses other human beings, the parent atma (परमात्मा) has to come incarnation and annihilate and absorb within himself that 'atma.' At first Brahma was born out of rajoguna to create the universe; then for maintenance and upkeep of the universe, Vishnu came up by satvaguna and then with a view to complete the cycle by arranging annihilation, Shiva came up out of tamoguna. This cycle, therefore, goes on. The incarnation of God are :

(1) Sanak, Sanandan, Sanatan, Sanat Kumar and Rishabha to teach the ways of self-realisation.

(2) Haigrieve to kill Madhu and Kaitabh rakshasas to release vedas.,

(3) Matsyavtar to protect Manu, Satyavrat earth and medicines.

(4) Varahavtar to kill Hirnakshya rakshas.

(5) Koormavtar to accomplish amritmanthan.

(6) Incarnated to protect Gajendra from the crocodile.

(7) Incarnated to protect Valkhilya Rishi.

(8) Incarnated to kill Varitrasura Rakshas.

(9) Incarnated to get the gods' wives released from captivity.

(10) Narsingha avtar to kill Hirnakashyap rakshas and protect Prahlad.

(11) Incarnated to kill rakshas rajas in gods and asuras battle.

(12) Vamanavtar to defeat/kill Bali.

(13) Parshuram to annihilate Kshatriyas, who had started indulging in worldly passions by misusing public money.

(14) Ram avtar to kill Ravan and other rakshasas.

(15) Krishna avtar to kill Kansa, Shishupal etc. rakshas rajas and their armies culminating in Mahabharat.

(16) Budha yet to born when Bhagwat was written.

(17) Kali Avtar to come at the end of Kalyug.

The writer in the context of Bhagwan and human being relation, indicates that the human beings are influenced by his maya. He, therefore,discusses how a person influenced by maya, indulges in worldly passions, and having no control on his senses, could still attain salvation. For this purpose, we will have to go into the genesis of varna and ashram institutions. The four varnas were created by God himself—brahmins from his mouth, kshatriyas from hands, vaishas from middle part of the body and shudras from legs. Accordingly, brahmins are satva influenced, kshatriya satva and rajo, Vaishas are rajo influenced and shudras are influenced by tamoguna. Similarly ,brahmchrya ashram is born out of heart, grihastha from middle part of body, vanprastha from chest and sanyas from forehead. Then Bhagwan fixed up the dharma for people of each varna and ashram. Anyone not following his dharma is considered as fallen from dharma and a man complying with the tenets of his varna and ashram attains salvation. The writer has mentioned that most of ladies and shudras have strayed from Bhagwad name and Hari katha. It is, therefore, for the saints to bring them up.

दूरे हरि कथाः केचिद् दूरे च अच्युतकीर्तनाः,

स्त्रियः शुद्रादयश्चैव ते अनुकम्प्या भवादृशाम्। (11-5-4)

The ladies and shudras had strayed from Bhagwad katha because there was a thinking that some of the people responsible for bestowing dharma on people had spread that ladies and shudras were not eligible to listen to Hari katha etc. In this way, most of the ladies and shudras had been deprived of such katha. But without designating the ladies and shudras as ineligible for listening to Harikatha, Vyas Muni has thrown an obligation on the rishis etc. to coach them and bring them at par with men and people of other castes. Also the word केचिद (some) would indicate that even amongst ladies and shudras, some had attained the bhakti of their own like Nishadraj and Sabri in Ram period and gopis and other gwalas in Krishna period. Even Ram/ Krishna had recognised them as eligible of their bhakti. Thus the spread of the word of their ineligibility is without any base and farce otherwise how could Ved Vyas, a learned rishi worry for bringing them up at par with others. Ved Vyas had accordingly elevated Romharsan, a shudra, as his disciple. The writer further states that by virtue of having born in the upper castes—brahmin, kshatriya and vaish—people are eligible to reach the almighty but having indulged in worldly attachments, they have strayed away. They too, therefore, have to be brought in mainstream of following the tenets of varnashram institution. This would show that basically vedic dharma provides equal chances of resorting to Hari katha/dharam but it is only some interested persons had evolved the proposition otherwise. Such persons indulged themselves in all vices of womansing, telling lies, snatching others' riches, eating non-vegitarian meals, becoming proud of their positions etc. Infact they are the biggest sinners of society and should be deprived of dharmic appreciations. Vedas clearly state that God is equally available in all beings and he treats all equal. Then why this man-made difference? Although the institutions of varna and ashram were introduced with a view to divide the jobs (Division of labour amongst all and all to smoothly lead the life in society as also in this way one could specialise in the vocation he gets in succession and come out a better worker in society) but there was nothing forbidding any person from improving his varna. Viswamitra being a kshatriya had become Brahmrishi by dint of his tapsya and was recognised and worshipped as such in the sabhas. Parshuram, a brahmin by birth, had become fighter and annihilated kshatriyas 21 times from the universe. Even Ravan was the son of a rishi (Pulstya). Those who love themselves and hate others are the greatest sinners as Bhagwan is equally existing in others too. They too, therefore, have to be respected as per their positions. Those, who keep indulged in making up of their bodies, restricting themselves to their wives,children and wealth and have no time for Bhagwad bhakti, have to repent in the end, when they have to leave everything here on their death.

In Satya yug, the people were truth loving, well- wishers of all and treated every one equally. They could control their senses and used to please God by tapasya. In Tretayug, the people were by and large learned and they knew the tenets of vedas/dharmas etc. The people of this yug pleased the God by worshipping him, listening to Harikatha etc. In Duapuryug, the people used to please the God as per tenets of vedas and in tantric way they bowed before God and pleased him. In Kalyug, people would neither be truth-loving, nor learned to know vedic tenets. They also would not know the tantrik way in the form, it was known in Duapur. Such people, therefore, would be able to please God by remembering him, listening to his katha (lilas etc.) and praising him as per their prevalent traditions. Since the way to achieve Brahm bhakti and attain salvation is easiest in Kalyug, even gods wish to be born in Kalyug to enable them to please God and attain salvation..

In this way Vasudeva and others heard the Bhagwat dharma from these rishis and were very happy. Pleasing the rishis, bhaktas/sadhus etc. in this way, Krishna returned to Dwarka after having the round of all countries then existing.

As already indicated, even gods wished to come to this universe to see for themselves the Krishna leela. They, therefore, once came to Dwarka along with Brahma. They saw Krishna there; paid their respects and praised him. They told that they all were involved in satva, rajo and tamo gunas and above all were under the influence of God's maya, whereas Krishna was not effected even by the charm of over sixteen thousand queens, he had. So Krishna (God) is only one, who only influenced others by his maya but was himself not influenced by it inspite of of having been involved in worldly passions. Brahma and others then indicated that on their request, he had come as incarnate in this universe to kill the asuras and please the sadhus. He had accomplished that job. Now they themselves were of the opinion that he could now return to his abode. His life stories were enough to be memorised by the people and by dint of the same, to achieve salvation. Krishna told them that he himself had been thinking of leaving the universe. He told that only one job remained to be done and that was finishing his sons/grandsons etc., who, were all indulged in leisures and pleasures because of the extra resources at their disposal. He had created all these off-springs with a view to accomplish his job of annihilating the rakshasas and now with that job having been done, they were only creating nuisance in the universe. They, had to be finished. Therefore,if he returned to his abode without finishing them, they would be another clan of undesirable people and his purpose of incarnation would be defeated. Their annihilation, because of the curse of the brahmins, had already started and after they are finished and Dwarka sinks in ocean, he could go to his abode. Gods and Brahma paid their respects and went to their respective lokas.

Here the writer has tried to impress upon the people by presenting the annihilation of the Yadvas' family by Krishna himself, that one may indulge in untold passions, create wealth, offspring and lead a grihastha life, enjoying it fully, but should not involve himself in it so that he does not feel the separation. He should be able to say 'good bye' to such a life, anytime, without any murmur. That is why, there is the provision of vanprastha after grihastha ashram in which people leave the family and home and live in forests detaching themselves fully from the worldly involvements. Even Krishna having created a very leisurely place Dwarka and a big family, himself got it annihilated. The only difference in a person leaving grihastha and adopting vanprastha is that he leaves his wife, offspring etc. alive whereas Krishna completely finished them before leaving the universe as he thought that they would resort to unprotocolc methods and devastate the universe :

यद्य सहंत्य दृप्तानां यदूनां विपुलं कुलम्,
गन्तास्म्यनेन लोकोऽयमुद्वेलेन विनंक्ष्यति। (11-6-30)

Krishna thereafter advised the seniors in Dwarka to leave Dwarka and settle in Prabhas khetra, which was considered a sacred place to pass last days of life. All the people set to leave Dwarka as per Krishna's advice. Udhava, who was closest friend and bhakta of Krishna, could see the game and requested Krishna that he would not be able to live without him and would, therefore, request his being taken with him.

Krishna advised him that after a few days when he would have left the universe, Kalyug would start and all people would be non-religious. He should, therefore,control his senses and get absorbed in the almighty. Udhava, however, told that the people, who were indulged in universal materialism were not able to leave the same, particularly those who were atheists. He himself stated to be one of those. Although Udhava was not like that but he was speaking for the people of the universe in general and wanted to have a reply from Krishna himself for such a querry.

Krishna told that a person, who is able to analyse what this universe is and what is happening here, can save himself from the involvement in universal passions and for this purpose one's atma is the sole adviser of the good and bad actions, if properly followed. Of all the beings in the universe, human being is supreme. He can, therefore, by his brain, feel the existence of almighty God and learn from the nature all that is existing and what is required to be done in the universe *e.g.* courage from people do all sorts of nuisances on land but the land does not get raged and tolerates all such nuisances. From air (वायु) one should learn to do what is necessarily required as air can be taken by beings to the extent required only and cannot be stored so the human beings should not try to accumulate much more than what is required. Also as air does not get effected by pollution and is self curing, so human beings too should, living amidst all worldly pleasures, keep themselves aloof from indulgence and addiction. Similarly, space (आकाश) too watches and maintains all good and bad elements but is still above all these. So human beings should also keep themselves above all good and bad elements and remain non-involved (सम). Also, as water (जल) is the greatest purifier, the human beings too should purify all others by their touch and should not get effected by their impurities. The fire (अग्नि) teaches us that inspite of all things dumped in her, she assimilates everything by herself and is again pure and powerful as ever.From the moon one can learn that inspite of its increase and decrease in size, the moon is quite steady. Similarly, the good and bad days or the change in the formation (योनी) is always there but it does not effect the atma, which is constant. The sun dries up water and again it falls as rain, like the yogis, who sometimes involve themselves in worldly vices but again leave these as if they were never involved in these. Further, one should not be very intimate and indulgent in anyone so that in case of separation, he is able to stand it. Likewise the person should be able to adopt vanprastha renouncing the universe at the appropriate time and should not get so much involved that he is not able to leave the family and the worldly environ. One should do within what one gets to eat, wear or live upon and be content on what one gets. If one goes on thinking of more and more, then there is no end.

From the ocean, one can learn to be deep and happy always. The ocean absorbs the water of flooded rivers, tolerates the evaporation of water in clouds and is still calm and peaceful. From the moth (पतंगा), one should learn to sacrifice oneself for the sake of one; he loves and this love should be for the almighty God. From elephant, one should learn to be away from getting indulged in woman as he elephant gets into the trap of the she elephant and then suffers. Similarly a person indulging in women also have sufference only at the time of renouncing the universe. From the honey bee, one can learn not to accumulate wealth and should also donate or spend or use it otherwise one day on falling prey to death, he shall have to leave it all here or robbers would take it away giving only agony to the accumulator. From deer one can learn not to get entraped in worldly vices or amusements as these will spoil him. Similarly, a fish gets caught with the greed of the bait in the angle. One should, therefore,learn never to fall prey to such baits of worldly vices. One can even learn from a prostitute. A prostitute once waited for the rich man to visit her and pay her for the pleasure, he got from her but inspite of long wait, he did not come. She got vairagya out of that itself. So, vairagya can be attained after one does not get the wanted thing and after the disappointment. In other words, disappointment too can yield to another better way of life:

आशा हि परमं दुखं नैराश्यं परमं सुखम,
यथा संछिद्य कान्ताशां सुखं सुष्वाप पिगंला। (11-9-44)

The collection of the things one likes most is the root cause of all ailments and renouncing the same leads to attainment. One should, therefore, live without caring to accumulate any thing like a child. Also one gets all vices and disturbances in living amongst many. One should therefore, live alone to attain vairagya, like a snake,who sits alone in his mood.

God creates the universe, maintains it and ultimately annihilates it. After annihilating, he feels loneliness and so again starts creating universe. One learns from it that one should not get involved in one's own creations and should be able to destroy it all when need be or when its purpose has been served. Shri Krishna created Dwarka and a big family of lakhs of sons, grandsons etc for the purpose of fighting with the asuras and when this purpose had been served, he himself made them all killed and Dwarka to sink in ocean. Similar is the position of a spider, who creates the net and also eats it away. So it is the thinking and setting one's mind in anything and one would be able to attain vairagya out of the same, even without any guru as such.

Under the guise of the spiritual protocol, Krishna told Udhava to take refuge under him and act as directed by the institution of varnashram and vedas. This shall lead him to 'Mukti' (The ultimate attainment). By following it, one can realise the self and the realisation of self only is the first step in getting absorbed in the almighty because he only is the innerself of the beings. Krishna even told that the pleasures in this universe ultimately lead to discomfort as one cannot go on satisfying the same. The pleasures after death are also terrifying as the rivalry and jealousy emerges there too amongst the inhabitants of swarga etc. This leads to the lessening of the good deeds day in and day out, and reach a stage of zero after which the effect of the bad deeds only starts and in this way he gets into the rut of the cycle of transmigration of soul. What to speak of gods, even Brahma or Indra has always got the fear of descendence. This shows that there is a proper system and protocol in Brahmloka too, where God is at the top followed by Brahma, Shiva and then Indra and others of his rank and then the other gods. They all obey the tenets of the almighty God and have a discipline to be followed. Similar is the situation in the universe. Here the people have to follow their environmental dharma and dharma prescribed by the almighty. By doing this, when one gets absorbed in the almighty then the fear of reincarnation vanishes and one becomes part of the almighty. That is the real salvation. One is subject to transmigration into various forms if one continues to be involved in wordly vices which have been created by God or in other word the God's 'maya'.

When one gets above the effects of 'maya', one attains mukti or self-realisation or absorption in the almighty. This position is better than the position available to gods even, as when one reaches this position, one does not have any fear of anyone or any ambition or jealousy etc., which influence the gods (including Brahma) too and after absorption in the almighty, one does not have any fear from anyone or any ambition etc. as one is already above these ambitions. Such a man, therefore, prefers to remain absorbed in God rather than even becoming god or attaining swarga. Even having the knowledge and following of vedic tenets is of no use unless one falls in love of the Bhagwad leela. It is the absorption in Bhagwad lila, which leads to absorption in almighty God. Therefore, Bhagwad lila and one's absorption in the same should be the real aim of life as other things follow them only.

श्रद्धालुर्मे कथाः श्रृण्वन् सुभद्रा लोक पावनीः,
गायन्ननुस्मरन् कर्म जन्म चाभिनयन् मुहुः। (11-11-23)

Udhava, then asked to be told the secret of bhakti and bhakta. As already indicated, it is not that Udhava did not know all this but he wanted all these to be narrated by Krishna himself for the benefit of the people at large. Krishna told that a bhakta is :

(1) One, who is kind to all.
(2) One, who does not have enmity with anyone.
(3) One, who can stand by all bad times.
(4) One, who remains same in good and bad times.
(5) One, who does not indulge in worldly vices.
(6) One, who does not resort to accumulation.
(7) One, who does not have any pride.
(8) One, who have confidence in the almighty God only.
(9) One, who does not have any greed nor get enraged.

(10) One, who has known the innerself.

(11) One, who keeps absorbed in God and for its sake even forgets the attainment of godly life in swarga.

(12) One, who keeps busy in Bhagwad Kirtan, lila etc.

Krishna further told that satsang vanishes the vices of the man and a satsangi can even control the almighty God. Such an attainment is not possible even by yagya, tap etc. Satva, rajo and tamo are the three faculties of brain. One should control rajo and tamo by satva. With the increase of satvaguna, one get closer to the almighty. A religion, which leads to escalation of satvaguna is the real religion. Satsang leads to increase of satvaguna in the being and the annihilation of the other two rajo and tamo gunas. One considers the body as his own and is prepared to do any service to the body in the shape of satisfying the various kinds of lusts (which actually never get satisfied) and keep the body in comfort but one day this body leaves the being and then only one comes to know that he had been after a wrong thing viz he had been trying to satisfy a mortal thing which never gets satisfied. One, therefore, should consider the only one e.g. atma as his own and try to have the realisation of the same. Till such realisation, one keeps indulged in the worldly vices and one cannot explain how one should get out of these. This can be only by self-realisation and not by anyone else's narration . This can be attained by seeing God in everything, including one's body and all in the environ. Then one shall forget the worldly vices or indulgence in the same as in every indulgence, he shall see the God existing there and shall then avoid to resort to that vice.

The religious leaders (rishis and munis etc.) are the creations of the Prajapatis. The Prajapatis were created by Brahma and Brahma by almighty God. All such leaders interpreted the vedic tenets in their own ways and each claimed his method to be better than that of the others. They got their own followers. The followers of each of them became a caste or creed and gave birth to multi-religions/ multi castes etc., each claiming to be leading to salvation.

याभिर्भूतानि भिद्यन्ते भूतानां मतयस्तथा,

यथाप्रकृति सर्वेषां चित्रा वाचः स्रवन्ति हि। (11-14-7)

This, however, created confusion. Manu,therefore created four varnas after consolidating the people with these beliefs and other mankind into four—brahmin, kshatriya, vaish and shudra. They also had to follow the four ashrams so that by following these ashramas, each one could attain salvation as ultimately all get combined in vanprastha and sanyas forgetting the different varnas, they belonged to. In sanyas, they are above all worldly vices and get absorbed in the almighty God. This is the real aim/attainment/ salvation of life. After getting absorbed in God, he forgets all about the universe; sometimes he laughs, sometimes cries, sometime sings etc; all in the taste of absorption, which he only can feel and none else. Such a situation cannot be attained by a person involved in worldly passions. Absorption in God can be by first controlling all senses and then thinking only of the God's idol and then getting absorbed in him. After such an absorption, one reaches the state of absorption in Nirguna Brahma as well.

God too had advocated the following of the varnashram dharma by the people to attain salvation. But with the passage of time, the essence of varnashram dharma had started diminishing during Krishna period itself that is why there is an occasion now for finding an alternative to this dharma :

यस्त्वयाभिहितः पूर्वं धर्मस्त्वद्भक्ति लक्षणः

वर्णाश्रमचारवतां सर्वेषां द्विपदामपि। (11-17-1)

Krishna appreciated the question, which was for the benefit of the people at large. In fact this seems to be in fulfilment of the requirement of the position of dharma forecast to be available in Kalyug, when varnashram dharma would not be followed as varnashram dharma had served its purpose in Satya yug, Treta and Duapur. This is the social protocol, which had been propounded by the writer through Krishna himself for the benefit of the people in Kalyug. Krishna told that in early Satya yug, there was only one varna and everyone of that varna could attain salvation by worshipping one almighty God. Then the vedas had come into being followed by the creation of four varnas—brahmin, kshatriya, vaish and shudra and four ashramas—brahmcharya, grihastha, vanprastha and sanyas. The persons following the dharma prescribed as per varnashram institution could attain salvation. Brahmins were pure, tapasvi, content and followers of truth, Bhagwad bhakti etc.; The kshatriyas were brahmin bhaktas, strong and forceful warriors. Trade, brahmin bhakti, agriculture, industry were the jobs of vaishas and serving the above three varnas and be content with that was the dharma of shudras. The people of these varnas then had to follow the four ashrams as per vedic tenets and attain salvation by virtue of Bhagwad bhakti in vanprastha and sanyas ashramas. Here too there was some flexibility for improving the varna e.g. an kshatriya could become brahmin as Vishwamitra had become Braham-rishi although he was kshatriya; Parshuram had become kshatriya although a brahmin; Nishadraj had become Rambhakta although from a mean caste, and so on. Such a change could be to any of the varnas by a person of any varna. Similarly, in Brahmcharya ashram, one could, after studies, continue further studies or adopt the grihastha ashram. A grihastha too could proceed to vanprastha or resort to Bhagwad bhakti, while remaining in grihastha ashram itself but it was very difficult to do so and while living in grihastha, one could not be above the influence of 'maya' and hence no salvation. That is why the concept of vanprastha and sanyas had been provided so that one could after renouncing the worldly involvements, resort to Bhagwad bhakti in vanprastha and sanyas.

A grihastha person adopting vanprastha could take his wife along or leave her with the offspring but in either case, he had to live like a hermit in forests after adopting vanprastha ashram. He was to do tapsya, eating what was available in forest and renouncing all sensual lusts etc. Subsequently with this tapasya, either one could attain salvation or resort to sanyas thereafter. In sanyas ashram again, he had to live as per tenets of vedic dharma, sacrificing his life to the benefit of others and doing tapasya etc. without any consideration. The life as a sanyasi was still more tough after which one could attain salvation. For a vanprastha, the primary dharma was tapasya and Bhagwad bhakti and for a sanyasi the dharma was peace, purity and ahimsa. Bhagwat bhakti, however, continues to be performed in all the ashramas and by people of all varnas.

The bhakta, on self realisation, gets absorbed in God. Such an absorption cannot he attained by jap, tap, tiratha, donation etc. Therefore, the best thing to be done is to know oneself and then get absorbed in God by bhakti. The body which suffers from the three sufferings—spritual, ordained by nature, or worldly sufferings—is actually under the control of the human being and it should be treated as such and not get into the trap of bodily senses' satisfaction. Once a man has control over his body, he would be able to cross the effect of 'maya'. Once this is achieved, then one can think of Bhagwad bhakti by remembering his name; his lilas; kirtan etc.; have faith in his bhaktas; have satsang and surrender everything he does to the cause of almighty. Once this is done and bhakti is aroused, then one is one with God (आत्मा-परमात्मा-मिलन).

Krishna told that for controlling oneself, one has to exercise the controls (यम और नियम) of 24 kinds like truth, ahimsa, excusing others, brahmcharya, belief in God, fearlessness, jap, tap, hawan, hospitability, tirathyatra, worship etc. This should be performed without any consideration because one gets everything one needs even without askance as God knows best one's requirements. Sudama did not ask for anything but still Krishna gave him everything. Bhagwan further mentioned of three kinds of yogas— karma, gyan and bhakti. Those, who have already performed karma and have known its effects, which only take one to discontentment, can resort to gyan and those, who have so far not known the effects of karma have still to keep themselves engaged in karma; and those who are neither very much involved in worldly passions nor are completely above these passions, but have somewhat of inkling of God's lilas, they should resort to the yoga of bhakti.Reaching at the climax of either of these two, bhakti or gyan, is vairagya, which can take one to salvation. One can continue doing these yogas while living in the universe and thinking of the God almighty always. Such a person does not have to think of swarga or naraka but his ultimate destination is God almighty. In swarga or nakaka too, one again have to suffer and, therefore, these are not the ultimate attainments for a person. Krishna has even covered the persons, who have known the result of karma; have faith in Bhagwad lilas and have also known that all passions lead to annoyance only but is still not able to rise above these passions. Such persons should resort to satisfying their passions but at the same time treat them as bad. Such a person shall also, in course of time, get rid of such passions, if he continues Bhagwad bhakti and then rise above the effect of "maya" and become one with God. To conclude, there are only the above three ways—vairagya, gyan and bhakti, to reach the almighty and if one cannot resort to any of these, he would have to suffer in this universe, have transmigration from one form of specie to another till at last he is able to resort to one of these three yogas. Now to enable resorting to these, there is a sequence and that sequence has to be dismantled from the root itself. When one sees some satisfation in having a particular thing, one makes up his mind to have it and with a view to have it, one has to snatch it from others, acquire it by at first having money for it, money being had by fair or foul means. Such an action leads to rage, greed, selfishness and absence of the right thinking. Therefore, one has to attack the root cause of possessing a thing for pleasure, comfort or satisfaction unless it is a must to keep living in the universe. The moment this proposition is understood and one is able to uproot such passion of acquisition, one rises above maya and gets absorbed in God, otherwise one continues to lead the worldly life of an animal.

A man is made to perform various jobs in life and to enjoy the result of these jobs, he has five senses. The body, with five senses is the human being but this body is distinct from the 'atma'. Whereas the body on death gets changed as per karma, the 'atma' is static. It neither dies/nor changeth. But when the 'atma' synchronises itself with body, it feels as if it also dies and changes form. It starts guiding the body to perform actions to satisfy the senses only and thus gets lost in such satisfaction only, which is momentary. He loses the closeness of almighty God and always thinks of 'me', 'mine', 'You', and 'yours'. After sometime, however, when he is not able to satisfy the senses (such a non-satisfaction is a must as the requirement of senses keeps on rising and then comes an end to such satisfaction), he stops the actions and achieves vairagya. It is, therefore, the mind (मन), which controls the body and its senses but starts feeling satisfaction in the satisfaction of senses and annoyance and pleasure as per verdict of the senses as the mind starts synchronising itself with the senses.

नायं जनो मे सुखदुख हेतुर्न,
देवताऽऽत्मा ग्रहकर्मकाला।
मनः परम् कारणमामनन्ति,
संसारचक्रं परिवर्तयेद् यत्। (11-23-43)

Therefore, if one is able to control the mind and diverts it from satisfaction of senses to the Bhagwad bhakti, one would have the attainment, leaving aside the concept of 'me' or 'mine'. If, therefore, one starts to have no feeling of annoyance or pleasure, one would not have got rage, greed, enmity, pride, passion etc. and when these vices are not there, one would be above the effect of 'maya' and get absorbed in God.

'सुख दुख प्रदो नान्यः पुरुषस्यात्मविभ्रमः', (11-24-60)

मानस में भी कहा गया है—

कोउ न काहु सुख-दुख कर दाता,
निज कृत करम भोग सब भ्राता। (मानस)

Krishna further told that a person leads his life involved in three kinds of nature. One is with satoguna ,if one performs tapasya, truth, kind-heartedness, tolerance, contentment, mercy, vairagya, non-passionate, donor, simple and pure; with rajoguna, if involved in ambitions, pride, non-contentment, passionate, hardworking, earning, spending, satisfaction of passions etc; with tamoguna, if involved in rage, greed, telling lies, himsa, quarrels, frightening, etc. One can, therefore, be recognised by virtue of one's involvement in one or more of the above ingredients. Now all these ingredients arise out of one's thinking and one's conclusions towards life only. One should, therefore, have control over one's thinking and should not allow it to be involved in tamoguna or rajoguna and should be maximum involved in satoguna ingredient only if one wants salvation. The involvement in the ingredients, tamoguna and rajoguna, is complete involvement in worldly passions and even one passion of worldly life viz. the weakness for women, demars all achievements, then what to speak of so many ingredients of tamoguna and rajoguna.

किं विद्यया किं तपस्या किं त्यागेन श्रुतेन वा,

किं विविक्तेन मौनेन स्त्रीभिर्यस्य मनो हृतम्। (11-26-12)

If one is involved in women, there is no use of education, tapsya, tyag, vivek etc., and, therefore, the involvement in woman and in other ingredients would completely destroy one's thinking and consequently the life. There are three kinds of worships vedic, tantric and mixed. (वैदिक, तांत्रिक और मिश्रित) and one can adopt any one of these methods. The bhakta has first to finish his daily routine and then make up his mind to resort to vedic (वैदिक) or tantrick (तांत्रिक) worship. Here Krishna himself has prescribed the idol worship. The idol can be of earth, stone, metal, jewel etc.

शैली दारुमयी लौही लेप्या लेख्या च सैकती,

मनोमयी मणिमयी प्रतिमाष्टविधा स्मृता। (11-27-12)

In the case of fixed idol, the daily invocation or dispersal is not necessary whereas in the case of others it is optional—may be on daily basis or otherwise. Either way the idol is got bathed, made to wear clothes, ornaments etc. and then workshipped by smells, flowers, fruits etc. The fruits put before the deity are treated as 'Prasad ' and taken by all present. The worship also includes hawan, water sprinkling etc. Such a method of pooja helps in cleansing the environ and self. Such a worship leads to inculcation in the mind of the bhakta of gyan, vairagya, religion and ultimately absorption in the almighty. Such a worship is performed to purify soul and environ and to attain the ultimate. Although, Krishna told, the universe is constituted by the beings but in fact there is no universe. It seems in existence so far as the atma appears to be tied down to the body and life. The moment such assumption disappears *i.e.* the atma leaves this body on so called death, there is no universe for such a person. Till the body and soul are together, one is bound to fall prey to pride, pleasures, sorrows, greed, passion, etc. Although atma has nothing to do with these yet being with the body, it is considered that these vices are exercised by both—body and atma. It is only after one attains gyan that one starts feeling that the two— body and atma are distinct and whereas body is mortal, the atma is immortal. One can get rid of the various ingredients of maya, as indicated above by remembering God and essentially passion and rage disappear when one thinks of God. Also pride and greed can be finished by satsang. Some people also propagate redressal of these ingredients by yoga but infact yoga can undo the effect of rage or greed etc. but not the rage and greed perse. This can be finished by remembering God and once these are finished, the institution of yoga does not come in exercise.

After hearing all the sadhna etc. from Krishna, Udhava was not satisfied as any layman would still need some easier way to get over this universe. As already told, Udhava had been asking all these for the sake of benefitting the people at large and not for himself. He was already a man capable of all bhakti and sadhna and this he wanted Krishna himself to narrate, so that it becomes believable by all. Krishna then told the easier and simpler way of attaining salvation :

(1) The bhakta should dedicate all his doings to God, and keep remembering him.

(2) Try to get absorbed in God by thinking of him and remembering him.

(3) Live with the bhaktas and follow them.

(4) Recall and sing God's lilas by dance, speech, or even heartily.

(5) Try not to allow the heart and brain to wander about and whenever it goes out, to bring it back to Bhagwad bhakti.

(6) Seeing God in all mortals and immortals.

By above exercise, one shall attain gyan followed by absorption in God himself. There cannot be any other method simpler than this to attain salvation. To conclude Krishna had himself stated that anyone, who ponders over the questions asked by Udhava and replies given by Krishna, shall easily get absorbed in God:.

सुविविक्तं तव प्रश्नं मयैतदपि धारयेत्,
सनातनं ब्रह्मगुह्यं परं ब्रह्माधिगच्छति। (11-29-25)

Krishna had made it clear here that only those are eligible for bhakti as are not atheists,non-believers in him, proud and without dedication. He has,however,made shudras and women eligible for such bhakti.

"साधवे शुचये बूयाद्र भक्तिः स्याच्छूद्रयोषिताम्।" (11-29-31)

Krishna had been made to say so by the writer as in those days, people at large, and brahmins in particular, did not consider women and shudras eligible for Bhagwad bhakti although in Ram period too, Ram had himself propounded the eligibility of his bhakti to them by specially giving recognition to Nishadraj, a shudra and Sabri, a women so much so that Ram made Nishadraj, not only his bhakta but a friend too and proclaimed Sabri as having navda bhakti although a person even having one of the nine bhaktis, could get over the universe. Thereafter Udhava went to Badrikashram having attained Krishna's bhakti in fullest form.

As already indicated, Krishna had created Dwarka and his family for the purpose of annihilating the asuras. That job was now over and with the curse passed on them by brahmins, the offspring of Krishna was going to be finished. At that time Krishna, who may not have cared for his offspring but caring for the olds, ladies and children, as a matter of protocol, called them and warned them of the sinking of Dwarka in ocean. He ,therefore, directed them to go to Prabhas Kshetra. All obeyed Krishna and went there, and got absorbed in Bhagwad bhakti. His offspring got killed by fighting with each other. Krishna too one day sat below a tree and a hunter fired an arrow killing Krishna. Krishna, with his body, went to his abode. Similarly, Balram also killed himself by sitting in yoga at the beach of the ocean. Krishna told all those still left in Dwarka to leave Dwarka as it was likely to sink when he was no more.

As a matter of protocol, Brahma, Shiva, and other gods came to pay their respects to Krishna in his loka as Krishna had come incarnate of Vishnu in this universe to annihilate rakshasas and encourage sadhus at the request of these gods (including Brahma) only. So, as protocol required, they paid their respects and acknowledged the obligation on them by Vishnu.

Skandh – XII

This part deals with the post Duapur era. Krishna, at the time of sinking of Dwarka, annihilation of his offspring and while himself going to his loka, had indicated about the ensuing start of Kalyug. In Hindu mythology, at first Satya yug starts followed by Treta, Duapur and then Kalyug. Each of the yugas ended with the incarnation of God in one form or the other. Kalyug, after its duration would end with the incarnation of God as Kali Avtar, whenever the time is ripe for his incarnation. But our munis etc had been Trikaldarshi, (knowing all the three periods—past, present and future) could anticipate the arrival of Kalyug as also what would happen in Kalyug. This part explains the occurrences in Kalyug. Even Ramcharit Manas, although written in 16th Century A.D., when Kalyug was in existence, speaks of what has further to happen in Kalyug and that is coming out true after a period of over 400 years already passed.

Parikshit had asked Shukdeva about the advent of Kalyug and who would be the rulers during that yug. Shukdeva told that in Kalyug, the kingdom would revolve around Patliputra in Bihar and could shift from Hastinapur or Mathura. After Jarasandha's death by Krishna, his descendents would rule for about 300 years. Then would come the era of Shisunaga dynasty in which Mahapadam would be the greatest ruler, who would rule over entire universe. They would rule for almost 100 years. Then shall come Chanakya during Nand dynasty. Prior to Chanakya, we donot have much literature available but again we have from Nand dynasty. It is a historic fact, that Nand ruled from Patliputra. Chanakya (correctly forecast thousands of years before his advent) was responsible for the dethroning of that dynasty. Chanakya or Kautalya is known world-wide and his economic and political theories are adopted even to-day universally. He would establish Chandragupta Maurya as the ruler of India and in Maurya dynasty would there be Varisara (Bindusara) and then Bindusara followed by further rulers in that dynasty. They shall rule for137 years. Then would be Shunga dynasty, who shall rule for over a hundred years. Then would be Kanava rulers, four in number and shall rule for over 300 years. Then also many rulers have been mentioned but we donot have sufficient historical data pertaining to that period—all works having been destroyed by Mohammedans, when they came and ruled over India. We, therefore, only have to believe what is written in Bhagwat. Mauryas shall be followed by Kanava, then Kushan dynasty, then Abhir and then Yavana (Mohammedan) and Turks would rule India. This again is historically true.

ततोऽष्टौ यवना भाव्याश्चतुर्दश तुरुष्ककाः,

भूयो दश गुरुण्डाश्च मौना एकादशैव तु। (12-1-30)

The Yavanas and Turks shall rule in various kingdoms for several hundred years. They would be followed by smaller rulers in various states and no ruler over entire country. The varnashram institution will not exist during the period of Yavanas and thereafter and even during that period shudras shall rule some of the states. Then some foreigners shall come and rule over India, which shall by then be divided in many kingdoms. This is true of the English regime in India, when many states (about 300) had cropped up which ultimately were merged in Indian union. This is the calculation of our rishis in the past that has come true even after thousands of years.

(1) Further, with the advent of Kalyug, the religion, truth, purity, pardoning, mercy, force, memory etc. would get diminished.

(2) A man, rich in wealth, shall be considered of high family, and of high character.

(3) There will be love marriages, rather than on consideration of family and other merits of the boy and the girl.

(4) There will be the concept of 'might is right'.

(5) There will be no confidence amongst husband and wife.

(6) The brahmchari, sadhu, sanyasi etc. would be known by the clothes, they wear and not by the acts or knowledge.

(7) One will not be able to get justice from the courts without greasing palms.

(8) One, who is clever at talking, will be considered a learned person.

(9) People will consider even polluted ponds at distant places as places of pilgrimge and ignore Ganga, which may be flowing nearby.

(10) There will be no law and order and the ruler shall be in name only, who too shall be rude and crude and snatch the money and women from public.

(11) There will be no rain and there would be frequent famines.

(12) People will be suffering from hunger and other ailments.

(13) People will be of shorter life and there will be no following of varnashram institutions.

(14) People will live like animals.

After all these elements reach climax, Vishnu shall come incarnate in the house of a brahmin as Kali Avtar. Subsequently when God incarnate annihilates all bad elements and people will again resort to religion as per vedic tenets, then there will be the start of Satya yug again. The above forecast of what was to happen in Kalyug was pronounced thousands of years back and is all true now. Parikshit was told that all the kings would be assuming themselves as very great personalities and consider the vast kingdom as "theirs" only but neither they would remain any more there nor their kingdoms. They would be boasting that their grand fathers had been the rulers. Now they were the rulers and hereafter their offspring would rule the universe, but all in vain and without Bhagwad bhakti, they would all perish.

While Shukdeva had been narrating all this Bhagwat to Parikshit, his time of death was close by. Shukdeva, therefor, alerted him to think of God only diverting his attention from all worldly involvements as God then absorbs such a person within himself and he becomes the part of God only. Shukdeva also told that although Kalyug shall have all bad elements but it would be good in one sense that in Kalyug one would be able to attain salvation by remembering God and involving himself in his kirtan (कीर्तन). Such salvation could be attained in Satya yug by absorption in God; in Tretayug by performing yagyas etc. and in Duapur by worshipping the almighty, whereas in Kalyug, same attainment can be had by his kirtan only.

After having attained siksha (शिक्षा) from the guru (Shukdeva) the end of Parikshit had come. He expressed his thankfulness to the rishi for having enlightened him at that junction in a very short time. The discourse at that place could be of great use for the people at large and shall enable them to have a dip in the Bhagwad bhakti sarover and attain salvation. He then worshipped Shukdeva. Shukdeva too took leave of Parikshit and went to his place along with his other follower rishis etc. Parikshit got himself absorbed in the almighty God and left the universe. There was infact nothing left in him when Takshak snake came to bite him as a result of the curse passed on him by Sharingee Muni. Such a curse had infact become blessing for the raja as he could in this way listen to Bhagwat and get absorbed in God which may not have been possible otherwise.

Here the writer has mentioned another fact of life viz bribery. When Takshak snake was on way to bite Parikshit, he met Kashyap Brahmin, who was specialist in curing snake bite. This would indicate the specialisation in treatment of various diseases in those days. Takshak gave a lot of money to Kashyap for not proceeding to cure Raja Parikshit from bite as Takshak had to fulfil the curse passed by the rishi for causing death of the raja by snake bite. The snake then went in the garb of a brahmin to cause death of the raja by biting him. Infact the raja had already left the universe, having been absorbed in God almighty. By the poison of the snake, raja's body got burnt and became all ash. This would indicate that Kalyug had already set in when Parikshit died in as much as :

(1) The concept of bribery was in existence at that time. Even the animals did resort to bribing the human beings.

(2) Even the brahmins, who are considered to be above all worldly involvements and greed, were not above the crime of accepting bribery.

(3) Even a snake knew how to purchase a human being by bribing him. This would indicate bribery was prevailing in those days.

(4) Where did the snake bring money from to bribe the brahmin, is not clear. However, the snakes are said to be in possession of a jewel (मणी). The snake might have offered that jewel in bribery to the brahmin and seeing such a valuable jewel,the brahmin would have got tempted and accepting the jewel, diverted himself form proceeding to cure the raja of the snake bite.

(5) The curse passed by the muni was that the raja would be bitten by Takshak snake after seven days.

इति लंघित मर्यादं तक्षकः सप्तमेऽहनि,

दंक्षयति स्म कुलांगारं चोदितो मे ततद्रुहम्।

Therefore, the job of the snake was only to bite and whether the raja died or not was for the almighty to see. Then why did snake own it to himself to bite and kill the raja for which he had to resort to bribing the brahmin.

(6) After bribing and sending back the brahmin, the snake went in the guise of a brahmin to bite the raja. Why Takshak could not go as sanke?

(7) Possibly the sons of raja Parikshit would have been alert to see that their father did not die of snake

bite and they might have sent the brahmin to treat the raja but the brahmin, not even caring for the raja, went back accepting bribery. This is also confirmed by the fact that after bribing the brahmin, and sending him back, the snake went in the guise of a brahmin to bite the raja. Here too Takshak might be afraid of being killed by the sons of Parikshit and to fulfil the curse, Takshak had to proceed as brahmin so that he was not killed.

(8) The alertness of sons of Parikshit in saving their father from being killed by snake bite is also clear from subsequent events in which the sons of Parikshit having known that Takshak had bitten their father, got enraged and started killing snakes in agnikund.

Takshak seeing sankes being killed, went to Indra to take refuge. The brahmins having known that Indra had given refuge to Takshak, started mantras to kill Indra along with Takshak. Then Indra got afraid. This would indicate the power of the mantras in those days that even the head of gods could he killed by mantras. Brihaspati, the Guru of gods then came to his rescue and asked Parikshit's sons not to kill Takshak as it was not proper for them to kill all snakes, created by God. He also told the raja that killing of so many snakes was a sin as the birth and death of animals cannot be taken by human beings in their hands but should be left to the will of the almighty. Raja accepted Brihaspati's request. He stopped killing snakes further and worshipped him.

Parikshit putting a dead snake in the neck of the rishi out of rage; his son passing on curse on the raja; the rishi telling the raja about the curse having been passed on him that he would be bitten by Takshak after a week; raja leaving the universe; hearing the Bhagwat and getting absorbed in God; biting by Takshak after bribing the brahmin; Parikshit's death and consequently burning the snakes and then stopping that killing at the instance of Brihaspati was all ordained by God almighty. This is the spiritual protocol between the creator and the creature and is entirely monitored by God himself. This is how one creature annoys another and in the chain both suffer just because they are blind due to God's 'maya'. One, who sees God in everything, is absolved of his maya as such a person cannot annoy anyone and in turn none would annoy him and such a person is naturally absorbed in God. With this comes the end of Bhagwat.

नमो भगवते तस्मै कृष्णाया कुण्ठमेधसे,
यत्पादाम्बुरुहध्यानात् संहितामध्य गामिमाम्। (12-6-35)

Srimad Bhagwat Mahatmya

After writing a book, particularly a religious book, the writer has to indicate the afficacy of the particular God as propounded in the said book so that the readers are able to dedicate themselves in the contents. So, after having written twelve skandhas of Bhagwat, about the various incarnations (Avtar) of God, with emphasis on Krishna avtar, the writer, in conclusion, has indicated the greatness of the Lord. Here also the greatness has been made to be told by rishi sootji, who had, through the medium of Muni Shukdeva and Raja Parikshit, narrated the entire Bhagwat via same character Parikshit as protocol requires the conclusion to be illustrated through the main character of the book itself.

Yudhisthra had coronated Parikshit as the Raja of Hastinapur/Indraprastha and Vajranabha (great grand son of Krishna) as the raja of Mathura. All the sons, grand sons etc. of Krishna dynasty had perished fighting amongst themselves as a result of the curse of brahmins passed on them, except Vajranabha, who had gone to Indraprastha along with Arjun. Yudhisthra had established Vajranabha as Raja of Mathura and Krishna's thousands of queens had also been living in Mathura. After some time, Parikshit went to Mathura to meet Vajranabha with a view to extend all his help in the ruling of that state as Parikshit was elder; ruler of a bigger state and also relation and survivor of the Pandava dynasty and a great bhakta of Krishna and Vajranabha being the only survivor of the Yadava dynasty. When Vajranabha came to know of Parikshit coming, he, as a matter of protocal, went to receive him as any raja receives another raja outside the town; paid respects to him and brought him to his mahal; introduced him to Krishna's various queens, who too honoured him and blessed him. After settling in the mahal, Parikshit told Vajranabha that :

(1) They both were relations.

(2) Krishna, his great grand father had managed his survival before birth itself.

(3) He wished Vajranabha to rule comfortably.

(4) He should not worry from any shortage of money, army and foreign aggression and that Parikshit was available for all kinds of help required.

(5) Parikshit, however, requested him to take care of the queens of Krishna, as Krishna had entrusted them to Arjun for care and they were now with him after Arjun had left for vanprastha.

(6) Parikshit being the emperor of the area and Vajranabha, a small raja (like a vassal) had to be assured of all help by the emperor as such as also due to being his close relative.

Vajranabha felt assured and told Parikshit that he already had been depending on Indraprastha kingdom for his protection. He told that he was worried about non-existence of any subjects in Mathura, as all had been killed along with Kansa, being the asuras and without the subjects there was nothing to rule. Parikshit then sent some of his people of all Varnas—brahmins, kshatriyas, vaish and shudras to reside there as the residents of that area. Then Muni Shandilya was called and he narrated the importance of Brijbhoomi (Mathura). Vraj (व्रज) means 'pervaded' i.e. assimilated in entire area. This word denotes Krishna's presence every where in that area. The muni, therefore, told them to think of Krishna's lila in that place and they would feel the presence of Krishna. The two then searched all places and ultimately struck at Goverdhan, where they could have feeling of presence of Krishna and the gopis. The queens of Krishna were also taken there and they felt the eternal love between Krishna and the gopis, who dedicated their lives in love of Krishna only.

It is said that even today if one remembers Krishna there from his innerself, he does get the feeling of Krishna being there and his constant rememberance makes the person absorbed in Lord Krishna. Even if one reads a shloka of Bhagwat, everyday, he could have the kindness of Krishna. Such is the importance of Krishna bhakti in India.

भारते मानवं जन्म प्राप्य भागवतं न यैः,

श्रुतं पाप पराधीनैरात्मघातस्तु तैः कृतः। (मा.-3-14)

Krishna was born as incarnate of Vishnu with all the powers of rajoguna i.e. Brahma. tamoguna i.e. Shiva and satoguna i.e. Vishnu. All the three Gods had praised Krishna in Brij Bhoomi and had heard Bhagwat. Vishnu had even said that he would come incarnate in India, whenever, there would be loss of belief in dharma and would disappear after dharma had been established :

यदा यदैव कालेन धर्मग्लानिर्भविष्यति,

धर्म संस्थापयिष्यामि ह्यवतारैस्तदा तदा। (मा.-3-30)

The muni has made everyone eligible for listening and narrating Bhagwat but he must have belief in it. Vajranabha was so much impressed by the importance of Bhagwat that he handed over the rajya to his sons and himself, with mothers went and lived for the rest of his life near Govardhan and passed life listening to Krishna lilas and ultimately getting absorbed in Krishna. Bhagwat and Bhagwan are eternal and are in one form i.e. Satchidananda and has to be remembered as such only by the people of the universe.

श्रीमद् भागवत स्याथ श्रीमद्भगवतः सदा,

स्वरूपमेकमेवास्ति सच्चिदानन्द लक्षणम। (मा.-4-3)

Thus Bhagwat narrated by Shukdeva Muni to Parikshit is the only source of all pleasures and ultimate attainment of salvation in Kalyug :

कृष्ण प्राप्तिकरं शश्वत् प्रेमानन्दफलप्रदम्

श्रीमद्भागवतं शास्त्रं कलौ कीरेण भाषितम्। (मा.-4-48)

———×———

Index